GW01087144

FACTORY-ORIGINAL
TRIUMPH TWINS

FACTORY-ORIGINAL TRIUMPH TWINS

Speed Twin, Tiger, Thunderbird & Bonneville Models 1938-62

By
STEVE WILSON
Photography by
GARRY STUART

Herridge & Sons

Published in 2013 by
Herridge & Sons Ltd
Lower Forda, Shebbear
Beaworthy, Devon EX21 5SY

Photography by Garry Stuart
Designed by Ray Leaning, MUSE Fine Art & Design

ISBN 978-1-906133-50-4
Printed in Hong Kong

CONTENTS

FOREWORD & ACKNOWLEDGMENTS 6
HOW TO USE THIS BOOK 7
INTRODUCTION 8

CHAPTER 1: 5T SPEED TWIN 14

CHAPTER 2: T100 TIGER 500 48

CHAPTER 3: 6T THUNDERBIRD 650 88

CHAPTER 4: T110 TIGER 650 118

CHAPTER 5: T120 BONNEVILLE 650 148

APPENDIX A: COLOUR FINISHES 184
APPENDIX B: ENGINE AND FRAME NUMBERS 190

FOREWORD & ACKNOWLEDGMENTS

It has been a privilege to be part of the "Factory-Original" series of books, and a pleasure to have been working again with top photographer Garry Stuart, who has contributed so much to the finished article.

Grateful thanks are due to Tony East for making machines from his A.R.E. collection on the Isle of Man available to us, as well as his very comprehensive collection of original catalogues. Also to Cliff and Kevin Rushworth at Triumph parts suppliers and restorers Ace Classics (Tel: 0208 698 4273). The late Triumph guru, Meriden man and restorer Hughie Hancox once told me: "Today only cycle parts are hard to get, and now Ace Classics are getting to grips with that. I can get a rear mudguard off Cliff there, and I can guarantee that it will fit." Good enough! And thirdly, thanks to Barry Firth up in Yorkshire for letting us photograph his beautiful 1960 T120, arguably the pinnacle among pre-unit Triumphs.

To check the material, the UK's Vintage Motor Cycle Club (Tel: 01283 540557) kindly provided us with two contacts, marque experts Philip Pegg, and Jim Lee, an Ariel specialist but one who worked at Meriden for years and knew Edward Turner personally. They both proved valuable back-stops. The VMCC incidentally, among much else, run a transfer (decal) scheme, providing both information and accurate transfers for sale.

Finally, thanks to publishers Charles and Ed Herridge for their patience; and to my daughter Rosie for some nifty keyboard work when it was really needed.

Steve Wilson
Wantage, Oxfordshire,
1 July, 2013

HOW TO USE THIS BOOK

What this book includes

The subjects of this volume are the Triumph twin-cylinder roadsters known as "pre-unit"; that is, machines with the gearbox being a separate entity, made before a period when the engine and gearbox were built as one. The only pre-unit Triumph twin roadster not treated is the 1947-on 3T 350, with an engine which combined elements of the abortive military 3TU and of the post-war TRW. The 3T ceased production during 1951.

Also not included are the TRW, a military mount; the 1946-48 Grand Prix, a racing twin; and the pre-unit TR5 and TR6 Trophy models, which were aimed specifically at dual on/off road functions, as indicated by their usually high-level exhaust systems, and often, Trials tyres. All the above would, in the author's view, if treated in the necessary detail, expand the contents of this volume well beyond its allocated space.

Model Years

Motorcycle production generally shifted to new models after a factory's two-week summer break in August. A new or modified machine would usually appear at the November Cycle and Motor Cycle Show at Earls Court, London, in say, 1952, but we follow the maker's intentions and refer to these machines as "1953 models", with the model year customarily ending in late July/early August. With Triumph there were variations to that pattern, however, as a model year could start in late July, or September, or even later. The best checks on a particular machine's year of manufacture (not of sale, which could be, as with some US 1959 T120s, in the following model year), are the engine/frame numbers provided in Appendix B.

Model Year organisation in this book

Each year for the different models is treated to its own section, beginning, for years of significant change, with an introductory paragraph or two, providing context and highlighting points to recognise. Then comes:

Engine and gearbox
This includes consideration of the carburettor(s), air filter, the throttle twistgrip and the speedometer.

Frame and suspension
Details of chassis, front forks, and rear suspension where present.

Cycle parts
This includes the "tinware", mudguards, petrol and oil tank, etc., as well as the exhaust system, wheels and brakes.

Electrical equipment
Ignition and lighting systems.

Optional equipment
Every option available from the factory for every year could not be included; instead, significant ones are mentioned for the year when they were introduced, or altered.

Additional points

• The default position for the roadsters detailed in this volume is the Home and General Export specification, though where possible with mention of significant differences for US Export variants.
• Unless otherwise stated, fuel and oil capacities are recorded in Imperial (Imp) gallons and pints, an Imperial gallon equalling 1.2 US gallons.
• Machine weights quoted are "dry", i.e. without fuel or oil, which customarily add about 20lb to create "kerbside" weight.

INTRODUCTION

Edward Turner and the Triumph Twins

The first Triumph parallel twins of Edward Turner were announced in July 1937, just 18 months after Turner, aged 35, had taken the helm of the Coventry company recently bought out by businessman Jack Sangster. Turner wanted something that would give the reborn outfit, the Triumph Engineering Company, a distinct identity, and it was widely expected that his new model would be a "multi", an engine with more than the then-normal single cylinder. Turner had, after all, designed the Ariel Square Four. And Triumph was already producing a parallel twin, though in very limited numbers. This was designer Val Page's 1934 650cc Model 6/1, a tall, heavy, unit-construction machine, intended for sidecar duties.

Turner, who exercised personal control over every aspect of the new company, from design and styling to buying and marketing, had his own ideas. They were summed up in his new model's name (after a brief period as "the Model T") – Speed Twin. His machine was to be fast, and light – his Square Four engine had been forced into heavy cycle parts by Ariel's management, and he believed had suffered fatally from that. These qualities, however, he wanted allied to smooth running and a quiet engine, in a package that would be affordable enough to sell to the mass market.

To achieve the latter, he had to use several aspects of what Triumph was already making. These were handsome sporting examples of the universally accepted single-cylinder machines, ably designed by Val Page, and then given must-have styling touches by Turner, things such as chromed tanks, high-level exhausts and a blue-lined silver sheen finish, together with a new name: Tiger.

With these singles established favourably in the motorcycling public's consciousness, by adapting their cycle parts and, for 1939, the Tiger name for his sporting twins, at one stroke Turner both overcame the well-known conservatism of riders, and kept his new models' costs down, so that at £75 in 1938, the Speed Twin was only £5 more than the top 500cc Tiger 90 single.

He could use the single's chassis because his new twin engine was actually slightly narrower than the Tiger 90's, which permitted an identical chain-line, as well as avoiding intimidating bulk and weight; the new 500 twin was only 4lb heavier than the 500 single. The Speed Twin, with plenty of chrome, looked reassuringly familiar to its potential buyers, even down to its twin exhausts, as twin-port cylinder heads with two silencers were not uncommon on the big singles of the day. Yet its separate identity was ensured by purple-tinged scarlet "Amaranth Red" paintwork, which strikingly extended to the frame and forks. Sales success and celebrity endorsements came quickly; Land Speed record-holder Sir Malcolm Campbell wrote that "in my opinion the Speed Twin has no equal." Another coup was the selection of the model by the Metropolitan Police, soon to be followed by many other Forces at home and abroad.

Turner's genius may have lain, as Dave Minton wrote, "not in origination but in exploitation." That was, exploitation of Triumph's existing production systems, as well as the exploitation of "a single-accustomed public's desire for the impossible – a cheap 'multi'." (The car world's equivalent was William Lyons at Jaguar.) The key to the design's success was its simplicity; two 360 degree big end journals flange-bolted to a central flywheel, all spinning on a pair of ball-journal bearings. But as Turner's collaborator/foil Bert Hopwood pointed out when Turner threatened to sue him over the crankshaft design of Hopwood's Norton Dominator parallel twin, "neither his claim nor mine would hold water, for I knew that Vauxhall motors had used a very similar principle, with central flywheel and all, for their 3 litre racing engine of 1922." However, Turner's use of RR56 Hiduminium aircraft quality alloy for the con rods with their white metal big ends, was an innovation, for motorcycles if not cars, and played to the first half of Triumph's tongue-in-cheek formula for success – "add lightness, and simplicate."

Turner's most well-known debt was to the British inter-war automotive genii, Riley, particularly in respect of the hemispherical cylinder head with valves set at 90 degrees. But as Minton has pointed out, that partly had come about indirectly. It was Val Page who had been in personal contact with Percy Riley in 1932. Shortly afterwards Page designed his 250 single, later the Tiger 70, complete with hemispherical combustion chambers and valves at 90 degrees to one

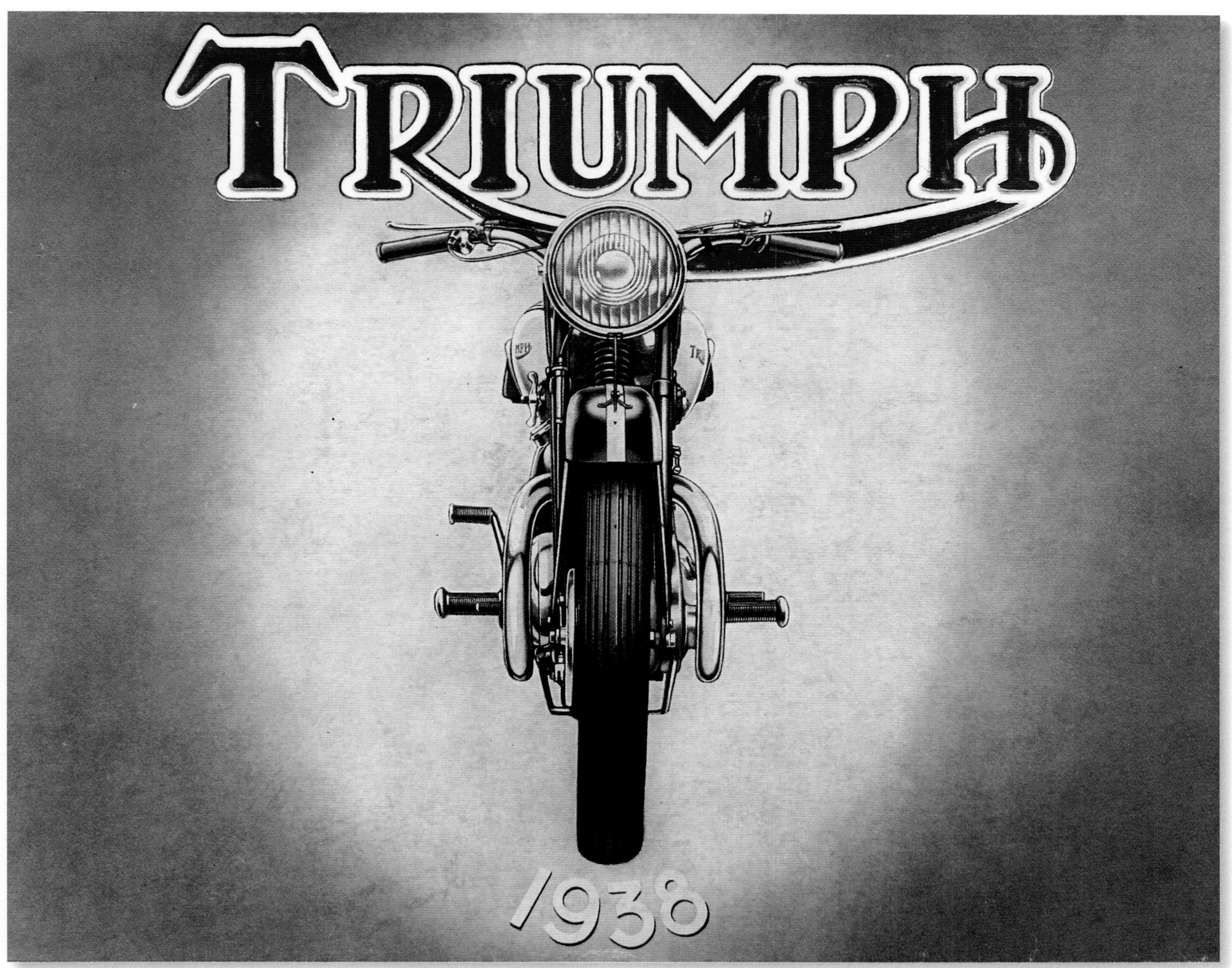

another, which Turner then co-opted for the Twin. Turner too borrowed from Riley, with a similar layout of the rocker gear as well as its positive lubrication by external pipes; and in the use, for maximum timing accuracy, of gears to turn the two camshafts, though he could not afford Riley's helical-cut timing gears, and his straight-cut ones gave the Triumph twin engine its characteristic whir.

It was Turner, however, who pulled all these disparate engineering strands together and made them into a supremely satisfying motorcycle. In a sense he had already invented the twin, during the three years he had spent Ariel developing the Square Four, which could be viewed as two twins coupled together. It was he who recognized and cultivated the twin's smoother torque, better low speed pulling, exciting acceleration, the pleasure it was to ride and the way it was easier to silence. Hopwood and Val Page had

The early Fifties Triumph twin range (left to right) – 5T, T100, 6T

been with him in the Square Four days, and being technically accomplished, their subsequent twins, for Norton and Ariel respectively, were in some respects better engineered than the Triumph. But because Turner had grasped to the depths of his motorcyclist's being what would be a delight to ride, his twin was the classic.

It was not long before positive reasons to buy a Speed Twin became common knowledge. Triumph's publicity man Ivor Davies recalled that, with twin-cylinder torque, "acceleration was incredible after a single," in part thanks to the lighter moving parts in a twin's engine. Fast singles had been high-geared, noisy, and concussively vibratory, as well as often requiring both a knack and muscular effort to kick-start. The Speed Twin purred along by comparison, with a quiet, whirring engine, easy starting and smooth running – ironic in view of the parallel twin's later reputation for vibration.

Partly this smoothness was down to modest power outputs, partly to the retrospectively-named "pre-unit" configuration, with its separate gearbox evidently providing less abrupt power transmission and "a lot more give – and indeed, forgiveness," as Triumph guru the late Hughie Hancox put it. Every pre-unit Triumph twin I have been lucky enough to ride has surprised me with its exceptional smoothness, including 650 sports models.

The Speed Twin had been joined for the following year, 1939, by the Tiger 100, its name echoing the chrome-and-silver-sheen finish it shared with the Tiger singles. The "100" indicated the model's potential top speed, and this was achievable – though only if the end-caps of its "cocktail shaker" silencers were removed. With its big 8-inch chromed headlamp and 4-gallon petrol tank, this was a sensationally good-looking motorcycle, and despite some handling problems at speed, an ideal ambassador to what later would be the Triumph Engineering Company's major market, the USA. As war descended on Europe, it was largely there that the 1940 T100s were sold.

Turner himself established sales links in America early on, and had it written into his contract that he should spend six months a year in the States. The story of the Triumph twin became inextricably linked with the USA. The first 650 took its Thunderbird name from Native American mythology (though via Turner having spotted a motel called that in South Carolina); and the exuberant '57-on chromed "mouth organ" tank-badges had been inspired by the grilles of Fifties' Buicks. More fundamentally, if the Triumph twins were fast, it was the Americans who pressed continually for them to be faster.

Even the war was kind to Triumph, though this had not been immediately apparent when their Coventry works had been blitzed in 1940. But the result had been the move to a new green-field factory at Meriden outside the city by the end of 1942, the modern premises giving them a further lead post-war over their competitors. When peace came, at a time when others were content to sell off recycled military singles, Turner took the bold step of turning over all Meriden's production to twins. And he was right; from then on, demand for Triumph twins would always exceed supply. Meriden Experimental Shop man and record-breaking sprinter Norman Hyde has written, "There was never a build-up of stock – bikes like [the 1959 TR6 650] went down [the line] and every frame had a label on it to say who had ordered it." By the end, in 1983, over three-quarters of a million Meriden twins had been built, with their nearest British rival, BSA, who offered a more varied range, managing about a fifth of that twin-cylinder output.

One reason demand exceeded supply was that the all-controlling Turner on his watch kept production limited to no more than, and often less than, a maximum of around 20,000 twins a year, supplemented from 1953 onwards by up to 10,000 lightweight Terriers and Tiger Cubs. There were good commercial reasons for this: at first the limited supplies of raw material available post-war; and then the UK's stop-go economy, where fluctuating Hire Purchase rates created uncertainty about demand. Another was that Edward Turner aimed at, and in those days largely achieved, a standard of reliability which would ensure that his Triumphs could complete 20,000 miles without major mechanical attention – which meant not only a good reputation, but fewer expensive warranty claims. Standards were higher and pride in work at Meriden more widespread in the Forties and Fifties than would be the case later – another point in favour of the pre-unit twins which were made then.

The same reasoning, the avoidance of unnecessary expense, applied to the paradox that while Triumph were making some of the world's fastest production machines, Turner actively discouraged any factory involvement in road-racing. Off-road sports (beyond the scope of this volume) were grudgingly undertaken, but winning races and breaking records were left to privateers – and to the Americans.

In 1950 the American operation had been split into two, based on the West and East coasts respectively (the two organizations were to be fierce rivals from then on). From the first, both were concerned with the competition potential of the twins, for unlike in Europe, motorcycles as everyday transport had died in the face of the cheaper-to-buy (four-wheeled) Ford Model T. US motorcycle historian Richard Renstrom wrote of the 1950s that "anything British then was a 'racer'", and "Win On Sunday, Sell On Monday" was the US dealers' slogan of choice. Tuning goodies proliferated, especially for the 500 class to which the imports were confined in many race classes, as the sport's US governing body was controlled by the native industry.

More power was demanded anyway by American road riders, and also by a home market where one out of three large capacity motorcycles were hitched to sidecars. Turner responded late in 1949 with the 6T Thunderbird 650, launched spectacularly with a trio of T-Birds at Montlhéry, France, which successfully averaged 90mph for 500 miles. The 34bhp 650 was economic to produce, basically involving, as Ivor Davies put it, "just bigger holes in the cases and barrels," and it ushered in even better looks, as 1949 had already begun a re-vamp of the Triumph twins' appearance. It had seen the introduction of the wonderfully smooth fork-top component, the nacelle, a word with enviably modern aircraft associations, a styling touch much imitated but never equalled for graceful proportion. Pull-back handlebars accentuated the nacelle's streamlining.

The 1949 model year had also brought as an option, for that year only, the chromed tank-top parcel grid, which filled the space where the previous instrument panel had been; 1950 saw it as standard equipment, together with the four-bar-and-badge tank embellishment. Both distracted from the permanent demise, following one too many labour disputes with the chromers, of chromed petrol tanks. "We shall design a motif to provide the glitter," Turner told his draughtsman Jack Wickes – and it worked. Turner, with his intent focus on every aspect of his design, had already supervised detailing as small as the 1946 clip to hold the ht plug leads neatly to the inlet manifold before they came out between the rocker boxes, and the slender 1948 bridge to the rear light/number plate which doubled up as a lifting handle. In practice it was Wickes who often drew out the final form of designs such as the elegant front number plate, and that rear light bridge, but they were Turner's ideas and "from his office", an inner sanctum where never more than five draughtsmen, including Wickes, operated in complete secrecy.

The 6T Thunderbird got it pretty much right first time.

Marlon "Wild One" Brando with 1950 6T.

There were a few early crank breakages, principally in the USA, but that was never an epidemic, and would be cured by 1954's "big bearing" motor. Over the years the 6T was to be the preferred model of seasoned riders like Ivor Davies and VMCC founder Titch Allen, as well as, under Neale Shilton's direction, becoming the basis of the well-regarded Police 650, The Saint. They knew that the softer-tuned, single-carb big twins were easier to live with and better all-rounders than their nervier though still tractable T110 and then T120 cousins.

BSA's pre-unit A7/A10 twins, despite lacking the Triumph sparkle, were formidably durable opponents – even though, from March 1951, Triumph had become part of the BSA Group. Though unhappy at the loss of the company's independence, Turner did well out of this sale by his "godfather" Jack Sangster. Turner reportedly profited to the tune of nearly a quarter of a million pounds from the additional sale to BSA of his E.T. Developments, home of his own patented designs such as the Spring Wheel and the Slickshift. In practice Triumph would remain Turner's independent fief until Sangster stood down in 1961, with ET following early in 1964.

BSA's twins were excellent, but as mentioned, made in smaller numbers, and the same applied even more to twins from the other British manufacturers. BSA's pre-unit twins were more solidly built than their Triumph equivalents, but consequently 30lb heavier. And while the ride-to-work, primary-transport, reliable two-wheeler was still the norm in Europe for most of the Fifties, riding a motorbike, especially as a young man, can be an ephemeral experience, where sensations of speed and freedom outweigh practical considerations. Triumph twins exemplified this, particularly in America where already motorcycles were all about recreation, sport and fun – as well as increasingly about expressing a rebel streak. This went public with Marlon Brando's character Johnny on his 1950 Thunderbird in the 1953 movie *The Wild One*. Followed by countless others including James Dean, Bob Dylan, Steve McQueen and Bruce Springsteen, the notion that "only rebels ride Triumphs" might initially have alarmed Bill Johnson of West Coast importers JoMo so much that he tried to have *The Wild One*'s production halted, but in the end it was to do Triumph sales no harm at all.

Even if the twins were doing something they had not been designed for, it had been largely American competition needs which produced the next stage, 1954's T110 650. Turner in austerity Britain concentrated on petrol economy, adopting the SU carburettor for the 6T to help achieve it, and pursued production economy with the less happy adoption of alternator, distributor-controlled ignition and electrics for the 5T and 6T in '53 and '54 respectively. Meanwhile it had been the American importers who had been quietly passing back to interested parties at Meriden components and information on gas-flowed and re-ported big valve cylinder heads, stronger valve springs, high-lift camshafts, roller cam followers and higher compression; US gasoline in the early Fifties was 87 octane, compared to the UK's 72 octane "Pool" fuel.

The 1954 T110 incorporated much of this, and also coincided, not before time, with a new rear-sprung frame, though its unsupported swinging-arm would maintain the Triumph tradition of "interesting" high-speed handling. The T110 also introduced a stronger crankshaft and the "big-bearing" motor. It was a big step forward for the twins, but in a rather different direction than Turner ("smooth running and a quiet engine") had envisaged originally.

For five years the "Ton-Ten" ruled the roost, while Turner, who had long been interested in an "Everyman" motorcycle, concentrated on trying to counter, or cash in on, the current European scooter boom – in the UK they were outselling motorbikes – by crafting a machine that would be something like a bigger-capacity scooter. He opted for a bike with smaller wheels for a non-threatening, unisex height, a rear end enclosed by easier-to-clean "bath-tub" panelling which could also display bright two-tone colours, and a smaller, more compact twin engine, built in unit with the gearbox. The chosen capacity was 350.

There had been a pre-unit 350, the 3T, which had been found underpowered and marginally less reliable and appealing than the Speed Twin, while being nearly as expensive to build; it had been dropped in 1951, and for reasons of space is not included in this book. For 1957 (the 21st anniversary of the Triumph Engineering Company), the 3TA/Twenty-One would be much more successful, and the economies of unit construction made it the coming thing. But the rear panelling would prove a blind alley, especially unpopular in America where it was well understood that a motorcycle might be many things, but it wasn't a scooter.

In 1956 one of the top American tuners, Big D's Jack Wilson down in Dallas, Texas, had built a twin-carb 650 engine for Johnny Allen's streamliner, and taken the World Land Speed record for two-wheelers with it at 214mph on the salt flats at Bonneville, Utah. This was disputed by the FIM but accepted by everyone else. The US pressure for a twin-carb production model became irresistible, boosted by the increasing UK popularity of Production racing and of the coffee-bar Rocker culture. Late in 1958 – too late to appear in the Triumph catalogue – Turner consented to the ultimate pre-unit, the twin-carb T120 which would take its name from the world record venue – Bonneville.

With all the tuning expertise incorporated, and at its heart a still stronger one-piece forged crankshaft, the very first Bonneville only fell down, for America, in the styling department, as it retained the nacelle and valanced mudguards, plus a two-tone Pearl Grey and Tangerine colour scheme that did not appeal to most tastes. All this was soon remedied by 1960, and in addition there came a new twin front downtube frame to try and address the handling of the 117mph production rip-snorter, which nevertheless had retained its user-friendly flexibility. (Ironically the rare early 1959 "Tangerine Dream" T120s are now among the most sought after.)

The UK home market from 1960 on was in the process of falling off a cliff, and from now on the pre-unit twin would be increasingly US-oriented. In the States in December 1960 Edward Turner watched the Triumph-dominated Big Bear Run enduro, and saw a rider thrown and killed when his twin downtube frame fractured below the steering head lug. He immediately authorized a test programme at MIRA to identify the problem, which was then rapidly remedied. The 1961 Sky Blue and Silver Sheen Bonnie was arguably a peak, combining stunning looks and raw, searing acceleration. The frame cure might have involved increased vibration for the machine if not the rider, but the episode demonstrated how Turner took an interest in his flagship 650s to the end.

That end approached in 1962, the pre-unit's final year. The 5T had gone the unit way after 1958, the T100 followed a year later, and the T110, already relegated to a sports tourer and swaddled with Turner's "Bath-tub" rear enclosure, had been dropped after 1961. Turner himself was mostly engaged with an actual scooter, his 100cc automatic Tina, a real achievement which anticipated today's twist-'n-go models by 40 years, but fell down fatally on reliability. However, he and his collaborator/antagonist Bert Hopwood, newly returned from Norton and shortly joined by genius developer Doug Hele and Brian Jones, oversaw the unitising of the 650 engine, with Jones revising the frame to dramatically improve handling. The big change to unit 650 construction took place successfully for 1963.

The twins' creator, 63 years old and suffering from diabetes, stepped down the following year. There was serendipity to this, as the pre-units had been his core business and finest achievement, and under his (usually) benevolent dictatorship, if the design decisions had sometimes been less than perfect, his presence and involvement, as well as his policy of holding down production, had meant that at Meriden pride and production standards had stayed high. This was probably the last era when one man could impose his imprint on a volume produced design, and to me it is this discernible personal touch which makes the pre-units such a rewarding subject. That, and from an age where elsewhere form followed function, their invariably graceful design, and, yes, truly classic nature.

1955 Triumph twin range

5T SPEED TWIN 500

The Speed Twin, announced in July 1937 with production commencing in November, possessed both historical significance, as the machine that set the course for the British industry's majority products over the following four decades, and immediate popular appeal. Edward Turner, as Cyril Ayton observed, "knew...what motorcyclists wanted before they knew it themselves" – something fast and light at an affordable price, and something with style.

The 27bhp 5T's relatively modest performance, while startling in its day, meant that the imperfections of its handling, then and later, were less prominent; and the less stressed engines, properly cared for, could be very durable. Police forces both in the UK and abroad, as well as for a time the AA, adopted the 5T, keeping Triumph's profile high (though Meriden's accountant Charles Parker would assert that "we never made a penny profit out of police business," due to the differences in specification for electrics, suspension, etc., compared to the civilian model, as well as between the various Forces. On these machines mileages of nearly 100,000 were commonplace, and 150,000 not unknown.

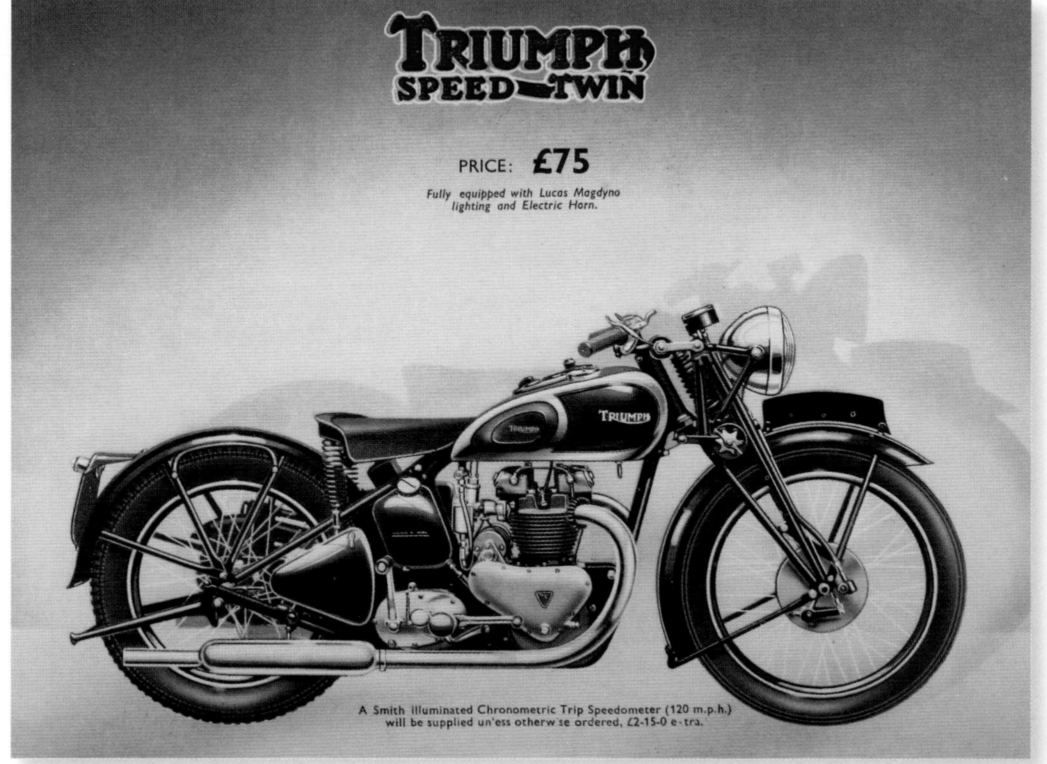

1938 5T

1938

Engine and Gearbox

The cylinder block was of cast iron. The 5T engine's 63 x 80 cylinder dimensions were those of the existing 250 Tiger 70 single. The engine featured a bolted-up crankshaft, with the left and right crank-webs fastened by six high tensile bolts to a central flywheel. The crankshaft was supported on two ball races. Compression was 7.0:1, and the pistons rose and fell together, on H-section connecting rods forged in aircraft-quality RR56 light alloy Hiduminium. These featured a bronze bush in the small end, and, unusually, plain white metal big ends; the lower steel end-cap had the white metal fused to it, while the upper half of the bearing was machined directly onto the alloy con rod.

The inlet camshaft sat across the rear of the engine, the exhaust one across the front, both high-mounted, with the fore-and-aft pushrods contained in chromium plated tubes lying between the cast iron cylinders. The cylinder block was attached to the vertically split aluminium alloy crankcase by six fixing studs. The cylinder head with its Riley-type hemispherical combustion chambers was also of cast iron, with two bolted-on polished alloy rocker boxes. These housed the short rockers and their spindles. They were lubricated by a small-bore metal pipe from the timing cover, which also operated the oil pressure gauge in the tank-top instrument panel. Lubrication for the dry sump system was from a twin-piston plunger oil pump, with the pressure controlled by a ball-type release valve.

The engine was fed by an Amal $\frac{15}{16}$in Type 276 carburettor, with its float chamber mounted on the right (off) side, to clear the rear-mounted magdyno. An air filter was an optional extra. The choke was operated by a cable mounted on the right side of the handlebars. Triumph's own patented twistgrip featured a ratchet friction device so that it would stay where it had been set even with the rider's hand removed from the throttle.

The Triumph gearbox in its separate alloy casing featured four speeds and a positive-stop foot control on the right side. The layshaft ran on both cast iron and phosphor-bronze bushes, while the mainshaft and high gear were supported on ball journal races. Primary transmission was by a single row ½in-pitch chain, housed in an alloy oil bath chaincase. The engine sprocket/mainshaft assembly incorporated a spring-loaded face cam shock absorber. The clutch was multi-plate with four pressure springs, and alternate steel and corked plates. It was operated via a rod through the mainshaft to a lever on the gearbox's right side, which attached to the clutch cable. A thoughtful detail was the rubber cover over the cable end at the gearbox.

Frame and Suspension

The frame was a single-downtube, brazed-lug one adopted for the Mk V Tiger singles, with main tank and seat tubes and a tapering front downtube. It was of full cradle type, featuring forged lugs with tubes pinned and brazed into them. The engine/gearbox were cradled by two tubes running underneath them. These converged at the rear spindle with the pair of tubes from the saddle nose, the rear frame being bolted up to the front section.

The frame rested on a rear stand which pivoted below the rear wheel spindle, supplemented by the front mudguard's hinged lower rear stay, which doubled as a front stand.

The heavyweight Webb girder front forks were constructed of tapering tubes. They featured a single central compression spring, and lower links with hand-controlled friction dampers, which could be adjusted from the saddle. A large Bakelite knob above the forks controlled the steering damper.

Cycle Parts

The welded steel fuel tank held 3¼ gallons (Imperial). Its top was recessed to take the illuminated instrument panel, chromed for that year only, with oil pressure gauge, light switch, the ammeter, and an inspection lamp with extension lead, which when switched on and left in position, lit the instruments from underneath. The tank's filler cap was hinged, and retained by a "butterfly" cross lever. The flexible fuel lines were of braided metal. The oil tank, also welded steel, had a screw-on filler cap and contained 6 pints. A steel triangular toolbox, hinged on the lower edge, was fitted on the right, between the rear chainstays, and held closed with a lever screw. These early examples featured a rubber sealing band for the lid. The De Luxe saddle, either Lycett or Terry, was hinged at the nose, and had long parallel springs which could be adjusted for height.

The handlebars, with an unusually large 1in diameter, were mounted on big rubber bushes. The bars carried solid forged clutch and brake levers. A manual ignition control lever went on the left, the air lever on the right, with the ignition cut-out

1938 T100 engine was a development of the 5T's

Below: 1938 5T engine specs

SPECIFICATION

"SPEED TWIN" MODEL

ENGINE: Entirely new design. Bore 63 m.m. Stroke 80 m.m. 497 c.c. O.H.V. double high camshaft, vertical Twin. Crankshaft mounted on massive ball bearings with central flywheel. Forced feed lubrication to big ends and valve gear. Oil gauge in instrument panel. All-gear drive to camshafts and magdyno. Totally enclosed valves with accessible tappet adjustment. This engine is designed to give sustained high power output, with even slow speed torque and mechanical silence.

CRANKCASE: High tensile aluminium alloy, heavily webbed and of great rigidity.

CRANKSHAFT: Built up construction with centrally disposed flywheel.

CONNECTING RODS: 'H' section in R.R.56 Hiduminium alloy. Split big end bearings with steel caps lined with white metal

VALVE SPRINGS: Duplex Aero quality.

CARBURETTER: Large bore Amal. Latest Triumph Special quick action twist grip control (patent applied for).

PETROL TANK: All-steel welded, combining shapely streamline contour with large capacity. All-metal permanant Triumph Badge. Flush rubber mounted illuminated instrument panel carrying oil gauge, ammeter, switch and dash lamp. Quick-opening filler cap. Capacity: 3¼ galls.

OIL TANK: All-steel welded with accessible filters, drain plug and separate vent: capacity ¾ gall.

FRAME: Brazed full cradle type, from tubes of finest alloy steel combining immense strength with lightness and correct weight distribution. Large diameter tapered front down tube. A comfortable riding position with the highest possible standard of road holding at speed is secured.

FRONT FORKS: Taper tube girder incorporating dampers with finger adjustment on the lower bridge.

GEARBOX: Four-speed all-Triumph design and manufacture. Gears and shafts of nickel-chrome steel of Triumph accuracy and precision. Large multi-plate clutch, patented positive stop foot change.

TRANSMISSION: Primary chain running in polished cast aluminium oil bath of streamline design. Rear chain adequately protected.

BRAKES: Triumph 7" diameter brakes with special alloy detachable ribbed drums and extra wide shoes. Powerful and smooth braking with long life. Finger adjustment. Front brake adjustment accessible from saddle.

SADDLE: De luxe soft top type, adjustable for height.

HANDLEBAR: Triumph, resiliently mounted, eliminating fatigue and shocks, full range of adjustment provided. Control levers grouped and adjustable to suit individual requirements. T.T. type brake and clutch levers.

MUDGUARDS: Of adequate width with streamline section stays. Detachable tail piece to facilitate rear wheel removal.

WHEELS & TYRES: Latest Triumph wheels with spokes of approximately equal length taking braking and transmission stresses. Dunlop tyres, front 26" x 3" ribbed, rear 26" x 3.50 Universal.

TOOLBOX: Large capacity and water-tight. All steel construction; rubber sealed. Complete set of good quality tools, grease gun and instruction booklets.

FINISH & EQUIPMENT: Entirely finished in Amaranth (dark) Red. Petrol tank finished in chromium plate with Amaranth panels lined out in gold. Spokes and rims chromium plated, rim centres Amaranth, lined out in gold. Specially shaped knee grips for comfort and security at high speeds. Lucas 6-volt Magdyno lighting with voltage control, 8" diameter chromium plated, anti-glare head lamp. Altette horn. Chromium plated down-swept exhaust pipes. All aluminium parts smooth and highly polished and both chromium plate and enamel of the highest quality. All nuts Cadmium plated.

Where it all began. The seminal 1938 5T Speed Twin got it very nearly right from the start. The all-Amaranth Red and chrome finish had immediate "eye-appeal", and for a public used to single-cylinder machines, the unthreatening lack of either width or bulk to the engine is evident. Speedometer, pillion footrests and sprung pillion pad were all extras. This 1938 example wears the chrome front number plate trim introduced the following year, something which could easily have been retro-fitted by an original owner. Petrol taps and pipes are from a later model, a feature on several Triumphs from Tony East's "A.R.E." collection, deliberately done by Tony to help prevent flammable leaks in a crowded showroom.

button and dipper switch on the left and the horn button on the right. The handlebar diameter was swaged down on the right end to take the patent twist grip with its internal ratchet.

The twin exhaust pipes were of large (1¾in) diameter, leading to tubular silencers with tail-pipes. The mudguards were steel, with a raised centre band. The front guard had three stays and carried Triumph's shapely "bacon-slicer" front number plate. The rear guard was two-piece, the back section being detachable from just behind the top of the rear number plate. Two fixed loop stays supported the main section, while another was bolted to the detachable section. A pair of curved lifting handles were attached to the two main stays.

The wheels used WM2-20 front and WM2-19 rear rims, both chromed, with lined and painted centres. They featured a hub design of fabricated steel, and equal length spokes, also chromed. A 3.00 x 20 ribbed front tyre, and 3.50 x 19 Dunlop Universal rear tyre, were fitted. 7in brakes were fitted front and rear, with steel drums, the front one circumferentially ribbed. The cast alloy front anchor plate was polished, the rear one was of pressed steel. The rear brake was rod-operated, the front by both a cable and a rod. The cast iron rear hub featured a separate bolted-on drive

1938 5T. Pre-war twins featured a Magdyno behind the cylinders. Note the external pipe lubricating the rockers. The original saddle springs would have been parallel; barrel-shaped ones were introduced for 1950.

1938 5T. The optional extra sprung pillion pad.

1938 5T. Triumph patented gearbox, complete with neat rubber cover for the end of the clutch cable and the operating arm.

1938 5T. Timing case, with oil feed pipe to the rocker boxes.

1938 5T. The engine and gearbox were cradled by twin tubes running beneath them.

sprocket. The rear chainguard came with a lower and a top portion, with pegs on the top part to hold the tyre pump.

Electrical Equipment

The 6 volt negative earth electrical system and its components were Lucas, including the MN2 RO3 anti-clockwise magdyno, mounted on a platform behind the cylinder block, with the E3 HM dynamo on top of the magneto. It was gear-driven off the inlet camshaft and the train of gears in the timing case gave the engine noise a distinctive Triumph whir. The magneto featured manually-controlled advance/retard.

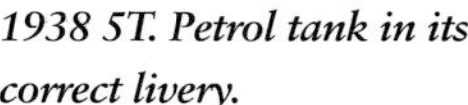

1938 5T. Petrol tank in its correct livery.

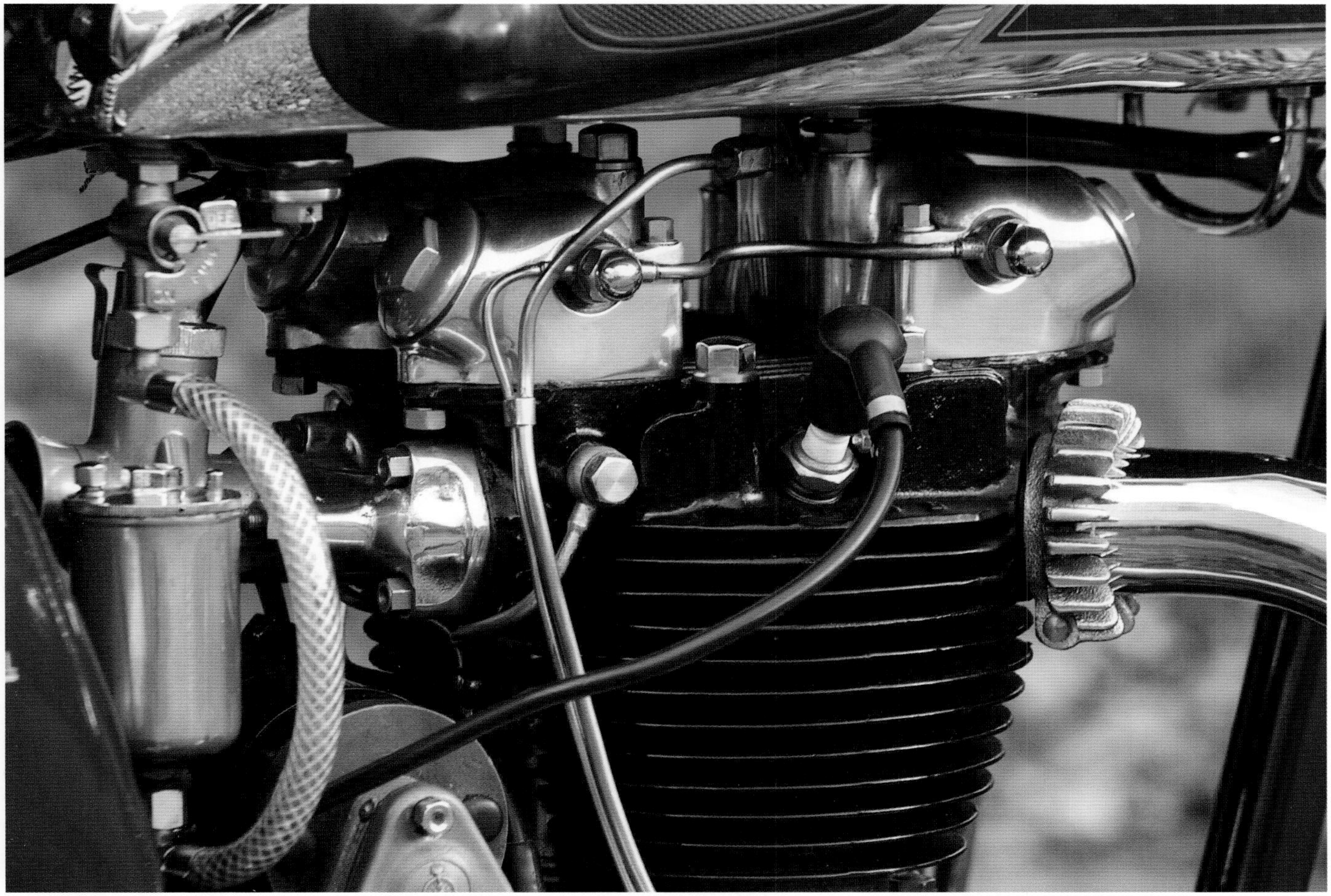

1938 5T. Cast iron cylinder block and head, polished alloy rocker boxes. Note the metal tube at front connecting the fuel in the two halves of the petrol tank.

1938 5T. Correct Lucas MT110 rear light unit. The rear number plate's top "bridge" would be re-shaped post-war in 1948, to double as a lifting handle.

Dynamo output was controlled via an MCR 14 automatic compensated box, and charged the Lucas 6 volt PUW 7E-4 battery.

The D142F headlamp with fluted domed glass was of 8in diameter and had a chromed shell. The rear lamp was a Lucas MT110 unit. The horn was a Lucas Altette with a chrome outer ring, mounted on the nearside saddle pillar, on the outside of the rear chainguard.

Optional Equipment

The Chronometric 120mph Smiths speedometer was fixed to the top of the front forks and operated via cable to an angled box, screwed into a threaded hole on the front brake plate, and driven by an internal-toothed ring fitted to the wheel hub.

A sprung pillion seat, together with pillion footrests, was an extra.

An air filter, a quickly detachable (QD) rear wheel, a rear carrier, valanced front and rear mudguards, and a prop stand, were further available options at extra cost.

1938 5T. Rear stand in operation, with its spring painted the machine colour; the catalogued colour was black.

1938 5T. The Amal 276 carburettor with separate float chamber on right, and bell-mouth. Note three of the six cylinder base studs, increased to eight for the following year.

1938 5T. The upright tube was a period proprietary accessory, the "Stand-Easy", a prop-stand ingeniously retracted by pulling in the clutch lever. Note position of the standard issue tyre inflator, and of the Lucas "Altette" horn.

1938 5T. Front brake, with speedo drive.

1938 5T. Tank-top instrument panel, chromed for 1938 only, with, clockwise from top, inspection lamp, oil pressure gauge, light switch and ammeter.

1938 5T. Left bar carried ignition advance/retard, dipper switch and ignition cut-out button; right bar had choke control and horn button.

1938 5T. Big 8in chromed headlamp and chromed tank were eye-catchers. Webb-type girder forks were among the best available. Speedo, where fitted, was driven from the front wheel.

1938 5T. Toolbox and oil tank.

1938 5T. Smiths "Rev-o-lator" speedo face indicated rpm in each gear as well as speed, but was not offered until the following year.

1939 5T

1939

Remarkably, very little was wrong with the 5T as originally conceived. One area of weakness has been the cylinder block to crankcase fixing, and this was revised, with eight fixing studs replacing the previous six. Otherwise changes were to detail, as for that year the new Tiger 100 moved into pole position.

Engine and Gearbox

The new 8-fixing stud arrangement involved small changes to the cylinder block, crankcase and timing cover.

There were also revisions to the lubrication system, with the primary chaincase modified to give extra rear chain lubrication. A coil spring retained a tapering screw which allowed oil from the case through it onto a small trough, and from there onto the rear chain. Further up, oil feed to the rockers was reduced by a restrictor, a coarse-threaded stud screwed into a threaded tube.

The valve timing was slightly changed, and the engine shaft shock absorber's cam contour was altered for added smoothness.

Frame and Suspension

Note that the 5T's frame differed from the T100's due to the latter's altered steering head angle, and that the fork lower links were shorter.

Cycle Parts

The handlebars became less wide and with a sweptback angle to the rear, which from then on would be very characteristically Triumph. The shapely front number plate gained a detachable chrome die-cast bead around its outside. The petrol tank badges, previously embossed, became die-cast in relief, with a red background. The tank-top instrument panel became of moulded Bakelite.

The front 3.25 x 20 tyre became a Dunlop ribbed pattern one.

Electrical Equipment

The 8in headlamp's glass changed from domed to flat and fluted.

Optional Equipment

The 120mph speedometer had its face altered to show the rpm in each gear by concentric bands, in addition to mph. It was also available alternatively with a strikingly large 5in dial.

1940

Despite Britain having been at war since September 1939, and factory efforts concentrating on the military singles and the ill-fated 3T WD light 350 twin, a limited number of 5T and T100 machines were produced, some pressed into Service use and some for US export, before the Coventry factory was blitzed on 14 November 1940. After that only 3H W singles were made, and with the move from May 1942 to a new factory, the greenfield Meriden site four miles outside Coventry, the only twin-cylinder engines made were auxiliary generator motors for the Army and RAF.

Engine and Gearbox

Compression was lowered to 6.0:1. To improve sealing under pressure, the oil feed to the crankshaft was redesigned to incorporate a bronze piston with a tubular extension located in the end of the crankshaft; this was an oil release valve, replacing the previous ball release valve. The big ends were also given greater clearances to provide increased oil flow through the crankshaft, and to lubricate the pistons and cylinder walls better.

With petrol rationed, to improve fuel economy, gearing was raised by changing the 22-tooth engine sprocket to a 23-tooth one.

Frame and Suspension

The 5T adopted the T100's increased head angle to increase trail. The front forks were given a lighter main spring, with on either side of it small check springs to help cope with fork movement. Some late 5Ts may have the T100's longer bottom fork links fitted.

Cycle Parts

The fuel tank became the T100's 4-gallon one, complete with its larger screw-on knee grips, with the tank's rear recessed so that its overall width was kept the same. The instrument panel changed from Bakelite to pressed steel, with a crystalline black crackle finish. For machines fitted with speedometers, the cable became a slimmer one.

1945/1946

Apart from some civilianized military 3H W singles made just after the war, from November 1945 Triumph turned over their entire production to twin-cylinder motorcycles, and that was how things stayed till the advent of the 150cc Terrier single for 1953. Since demand for the twins would always exceed supply, this was a good decision.

The post-war twins differed principally in sporting Meriden's own one-way damped telescopic front forks in place of girders. Though simple and attractively slim, the long forks were overstressed, and would contribute to Triumphs' problematic handling at speed, as well as being prone to leak oil from their seals. The slimness had been achieved by putting the springs inside the forks' inner tubes. These "inside spring" forks could literally bend under stress, and suffered by comparison with those from other manufacturers; but they would be modified over the years, and as with the handling generally, riders accepted flaws which could be lived with because of the overall satisfaction delivered by the Triumph package.

The mildly restyled and tidied up 500 twins were scheduled to be joined by a 350 variant, the 3T, though in fact it did not enter production until 1947, and space does not allow consideration of this long-stroke machine, which would be dropped after 1951.

Engine and Gearbox

Compression was reduced from 1939's 7.0:1 to 6.5:1, due to the low-octane Pool petrol that supplied Britain's pumps.

The crankcase was redesigned to accommodate a dynamo, which was now front-mounted, sticking through into the extended primary chaincase, where it was driven by the exhaust cam gear, and a rear flange-fitting magneto.

The inlet and exhaust valves were modified. The oil feed to the rockers was redesigned to be taken from the return pipe at a T-junction by the oil tank. The external drain pipes for the rocker lubricating oil were deleted, replaced by internal vertical drillings through the cylinder head gasket and cylinder barrel, to the top of the pushrod tubes. Care had to be taken if rebuilding to use the correct gaskets. The engine breather was revised, becoming a timed rotary valve driven by the inlet camshaft, and venting via a flexible pipe on the near (left) side.

The gear camplate spring became tighter wound. From eng. no. 74760, there was a redesign of the dogs of mainshaft 2nd gear to mainshaft 4th gear, for easier engagement.

FEATURES

FRONT FORKS.
This new Triumph fork has been developed to provide maximum riding comfort, perfect steering and a high standard of road holding. The design provides plenty of movement and incorporates hydraulic damping and automatic lubrication. The elimination of adjustments is an important feature.

VERTICAL TWIN ENGINE.
A power unit with a proved reputation for high performance, even torque, impressive low-engine-speed output and easy starting. Modifications and improvements include magneto and dynamo as separate components, the latter being mounted in front of the engine. Accessibility and efficiency are thereby greatly improved.

GEARBOX.
Universally acclaimed as the most efficient modern motor cycle gearbox. Compact layout with high load carrying capacity and easy accessibility to patented all-enclosed foot-change and gear operating mechanism. First class design, workmanship and materials ensure a high standard of silence and oil-tightness.

BRAKES.
Front and rear brakes are designed for maximum efficiency, and the adjustment necessary over a prolonged period is reduced to a minimum by the use of the finest brake lining material on wide shoes. Special front brake operating gear to suit new telescopic fork.

All Goods are sold subject to the Guarantee, a copy of which is supplied to Triumph Dealers and will be published in the post-war catalogue, together with the Company's terms of business

Printed in England by EDWARDS THE PRINTERS LTD.

1946 Telescopic forks, engine, gearbox

The Amal 276 carburettor's choke lost its cable and was now operated by a spring-loaded plunger on top of the mixing chamber. The float chamber changed from the 64/192 to the 1AT.

Frame and Suspension

There were new telescopic "inside spring" forks, with one-way hydraulic damping, hydraulic locks at both ends of travel to prevent clashing, and 6½in of movement, though the rear end was still rigid. The front frame was modified to suit.

Cycle Parts

A new handlebar, still sweptback, was fitted to suit the new forks. The front wheel went from 20 to 19 inches, and its tyre, previously 20 x 3.25, became 19 x 3.25, with a Dunlop Universal replacing the previous ribbed tyre.

A clip was fitted to hold the ht plug leads to the inlet manifold.

The oil tank increased to 8-pint capacity and its hinged filler cap became of 2in diameter, as on the T100. Mid-season the 5T's oil tank reverted to the pre-war 6-pint tank with screw-on cap.

The speedometer drive was now taken from a drive box on the rear wheel.

The throttle cable now featured a 90-degree chromed metal elbow guiding the cable out of the twistgrip.

The foot change lever lost its rubber.

Electrical Equipment

Both Lucas K2 F-RO and BTH KC2 magnetos were fitted, the majority being BTH until 1952/53, and both types featuring automatic advance/retard.

The Lucas D42 CPR headlamp size reduced from 8in to 6½in diameter, though this was catalogued as 7in.

Optional Equipment

Alternative sidecar-strength fork springs were offered.

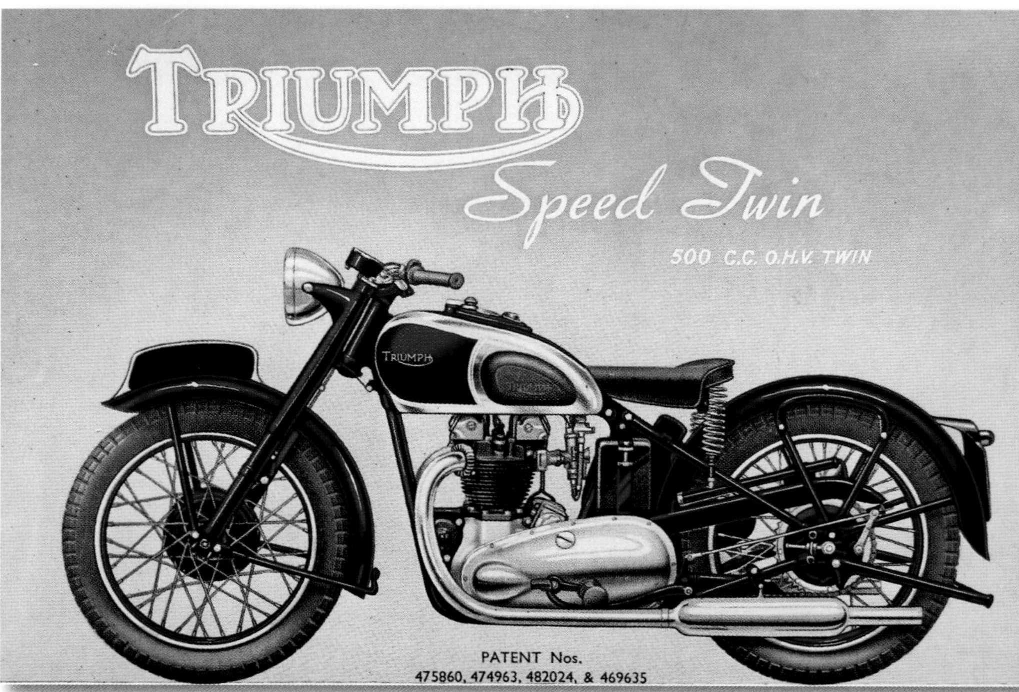

1946 5T

1947 brochure cover, 5T

1947

Engine and Gearbox

The carburettor float chamber was changed from the right to the left side, which meant a carburettor with the throttle stop screw and pilot mixture screw now on the right. This was designated Amal 276 BN/1AT, with mixing chamber 76/132M.

Cycle Parts

The chromed headlamp shell became painted Amaranth Red with a chromed rim, with the headlamp becoming the Lucas M42 CPR

Optional Equipment

A new-type prop stand was offered, this one bolted on under the primary chaincase, as the pre-war stand's mounting place had been taken by the position of the post-war dynamo.

1948

This model year brought the Mk 1 Spring Wheel also known as the Sprung Hub. It may be noted this could retro-fitted to machines back to 1938.

Engine and Gearbox

With the introduction of the optional Spring Wheel (see below) from frame no. TF19577, the rear wheel speedometer drive box was replaced by an alternative drive box at the rear of the gearbox, driven from the back of the final drive sprocket, with a shorter cable.

From eng. no. TF23324 (August 1947) the carburettor's throttle valve changed from 6/3 to 6/3 1/2.

1947 brochure cover: Police 5Ts at WW2 Victory Parade, London June 8 1946.

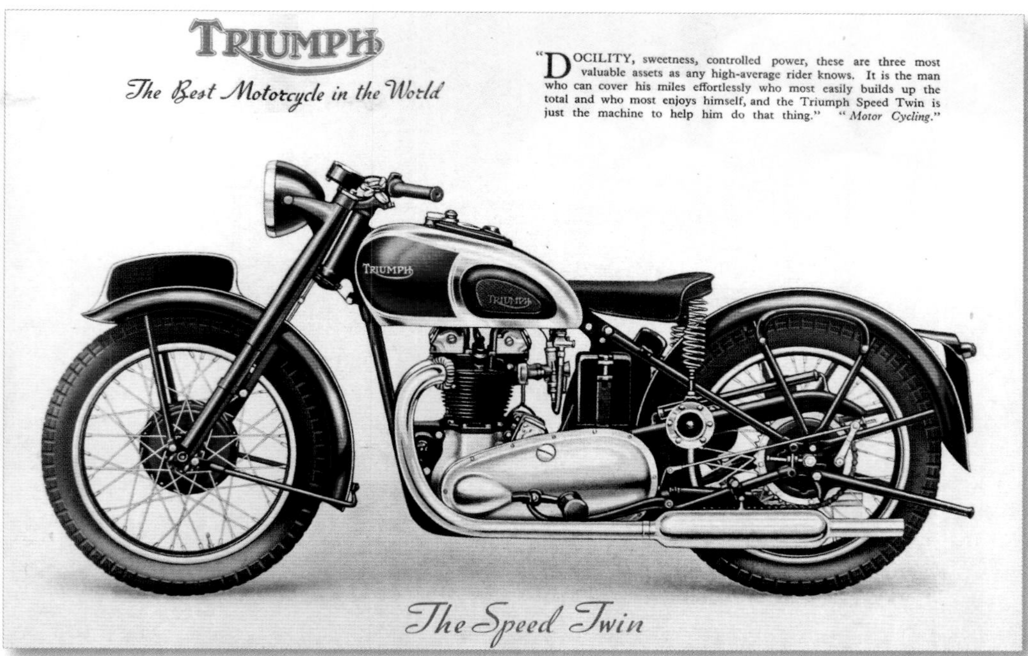

1947 5T

Frame and Suspension

Due to a new rear mudguard (see below), the rear frame from eng. no. TF17790 was modified to suit.

Cycle Parts

From frame no. TF16277 (November 1947) a new front mudguard, with two detachable front stays and a raised front edge for more effective protection, was fitted. From TF17790 (1 January 1948), a new, wider, one-piece rear mudguard with only two fixing stays, and fully detachable from a junction under the saddle, was adopted.

The front number plate's chrome styling beading was now cast onto the plate itself. The rear number plate's top "bridge" portion was narrowed and re-shaped to double up as a lifting handle to help haul the machine onto its rear stand, since the previous rear mudguard's two side handles had been deleted.

The steering damper became of smaller diameter, made of alloy in place of Ebonite, and embossed with the Triumph logo.

The footchange lever regained its rubber.

Electrical equipment

The headlamp was fitted with domed glass. From eng. no. TF17790 (1 January 1948), the Lucas MCR-1 voltage control gained a new fitting, a nut and bolt across the rear sub-frame, to two small welded brackets.

Spark plug caps became a standard fitment, in place of the previous leads held on by the spark plug's threaded top cap.

Optional Equipment

Edward Turner's patented Spring Wheel was offered, in the form known retrospectively as the Mk 1. This was a large diameter rear hub which fitted into the existing Triumph frame, and provided around two inches of movement by means of two compression and one rebound springs, contained in spring-boxes within the hub; it ran on cup and cone bearings. The first was fitted to frame no. TF15069 (mid-September 1947). The brake size with any Spring Wheel increased from 7 to 8 inches.

Cover of main 1948 brochure, 5T

1949

A big change year in style terms, with the introduction of the headlamp nacelle and deletion of the tank-top instrument panel.

1949 was also the first year for another 500 pre-unit, the TR5 Trophy, which as a dual-purpose machine is beyond the scope of this work, but which would contribute developments to the 5T and particularly to the T100.

Engine and Gearbox

The 5T's compression was restored to 7.0:1.

With the tank-top oil pressure gauge gone, the oil pressure release valve was modified and fitted with an indicator button at the front of the timing cover on the right (off) side.

The engine breather discharge pipe was also re-sited, now pointing downward from a metal pipe in the crankcase, with a flexible rubber tube added.

The engine sprocket became heat-treated. On the carburettor, the spring-loaded choke plunger was replaced by cable operation, but with the black-painted choke lever positioned low down on the left side chainstay, beneath the saddle. For the first time, an air filter was specified as standard, and the battery carrier's back strap became stepped so that it would fit. The twistgrip's spring and plunger friction device was supplanted by one with a knurled adjustable knob and a friction spring.

Frame and Suspension

The upper part of the front forks was completely revised to incorporate the nacelle.

The front frame section was altered to fit a revised engine torque stay. The rear frame section included sidecar attachment points on both sides.

Cycle Parts

This first version of the nacelle housed the ammeter on the left and the light switch on the right, with an engine cut-out button between them, and the speedometer, which now became a standard fitting, between and ahead of them and the steering damper nearest the rider. The speedometer itself was as before, but with a new bezel to fit it in the nacelle, and with a trip-control protruding below the cover. The Lucas headlamp was the same 6½in diameter one, now with a chrome reducing or adaptor ring so that it fitted the nacelle. The nacelle itself consisted of upper and lower halves clamped together by the headlamp rim, with the join between them covered on each side by horizontal chromed flashes. Two small screws at the rear attached this assembly to the fork top covers. There were two more small screws on either side of the headlamp retaining ring, which could be turned to adjust the headlamp beam.

With the petrol tank's instrument panel deleted, the tank's top, when the optional-for-this-year parcel grid was not fitted, had the holes for it plugged with rubber grommets.

A new pullback handlebar was fitted to suit the nacelle, with a threaded hole on its left side to take the horn button.

The toolbox lid's fastener changed from a threaded knob to a twist-in Dzus fastener.

The rear brake pedal lost its previous rubber pad to become bare metal.

The oil tank was re-shaped to fit in with the new air filter.

Electrical Equipment

The horn was relocated inside the nacelle, with the latter's lower front portion slotted vertically to let the sound out. The horn push button was moved, now being screwed directly into a threaded hole on the left side of the new handlebar. The dip-switch was now fitted to the front brake lever's clamp bracket, with a chrome surround.

At frame no. TF29130 (early April 1949), the dynamo was uprated from the previous 40 watts to the Lucas E3L-LI-0, 60 watt, "long" type. This required a new type Lucas MCR-2-L regulator box.

The rear light cable became armoured, and now ran inside the rear mudguard down its centre channel, and packed tight up into the rear number-plate's bridge section, emerging to the lamp through grommets.

Optional Equipment

A 5-bar petrol tank top parcel grid was offered.

The Mk I Spring Wheel now fitted hardened slipper pads and shims in its alloy hub, and the brake drum gained a water deflector shield.

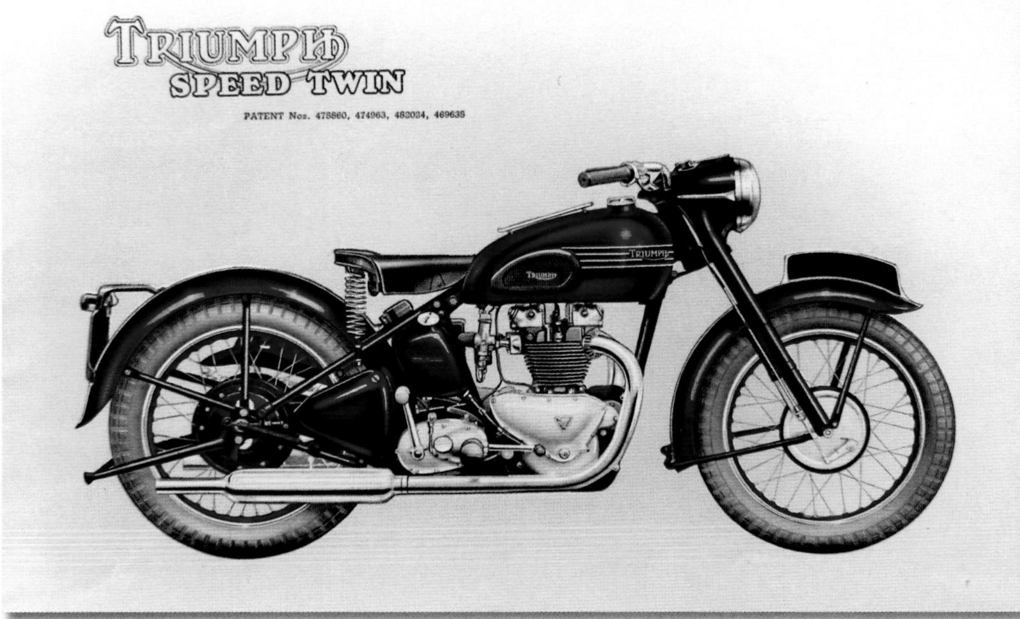

1949 5T. The artist appears to have anticipated the introduction of the four chromed tank bands in 1950.

1950

Several changes occurred due to the introduction of the new 6T 650, including a new gearbox.

Engine and Gearbox

The method of crankshaft manufacture changed, with the crankshaft becoming fully machined and with more material left on the crank cheeks and less in the flywheel. The 5T's cylinder block since 1945/46 had included extra holes to drain lubricant from the rocker boxes; external drain pipes, made necessary by the 6T's wider bores, were now reintroduced. A 1938-type pushrod cover was fitted, with reduced diameter for much of its length, and a drainpipe boss low down on the larger part.

The valve guides were altered to suit. Camshafts with a breather valve slot were now used for both inlet and exhaust. For increased oil flow, the diameter of the oil pump feed plunger, and thus the oil pump body, increased from 5/16in diameter to 3/8in diameter. The spring for the engine shaft shock absorber became the one from the TR5 Trophy, as did the clutch pressure plate.

The previous alloy con rods had featured separate bolts with their heads fitted under the rod cap, and the cap formed with integral fixed fixing studs secured by nuts and split pins. Early in the model year, from eng. no. 713N, they were changed, with the inverted bolts going in from the rod side, and nuts holding the cap in place; self-locking nuts were adopted, and the split pins deleted. The end caps were still lined with Babbitt white metal. For this year only, the 5T rods differed from the 6T's.

The redesigned and strengthened gearbox had both its layshaft and its gears altered, the latter giving it different internal ratios. The previous separate floating layshaft was replaced by a driven layshaft with integral high gear pinion, a much stronger arrangement. The speedometer drive was now taken from the right-hand end of the gearbox, with a 10-tooth pinned-on pinion driving a 16-tooth gear coupled to the speedometer cable. It emerged via a right-angle drive, from the front of the gearbox inner cover.

None of the shafts and gears were interchangeable with those from the previous box. The sleeve gear now featured an oil seal, and a full garter oil seal was incorporated on the final drive sprocket. There was a modified mainshaft selector fork, and a new layshaft one. The clutch chainwheel now fitted a pressed-in hardened bearing outer race.

Frame and Suspension

The frame's rear petrol tank support was modified to accommodate an altered fixing bolt size. The rear frame was given a prop-stand lug.

1950 brochure cover, 5T

Cycle parts

Petrol tanks were no longer chrome-plated, but fully painted. New four-bar chromed metal styling bands were fitted, running from the front of the knee-grips to the front of the tank. Two small chromed Triumph name badges with raised painted backgrounds were held on by the same screws as the bands. The previous hinged petrol cap was replaced by a standard push-and-twist bayonet one. The parcel grid became a standard fitment.

The saddle's springs became barrel-shaped.

Electrical Equipment

The horn became the Lucas HF1441.

Optional Equipment

A Twinseat became optional for the first time.

Wide, standard and close ratio gear sets were offered, with the wide ratio one differing from the previous wide ratio set and becoming as on the 6T.

From eng. no. 7439N the Spring Wheel was now in Mk II form, with its previous cup and cone bearings replaced by large diameter (3½in) journal ball races, and identifiable externally by its new circumferentially ribbed end plate.

1951

This year saw the 5T fitting the timing-side roller bearing which the T100 had adopted for 1949, and the 6T fitted on its appearance for 1950.

Engine and Gearbox

The timing-side main bearing became a single-lipped roller, with a fixed chip shield. The camwheel pinions changed to the T100's, which incorporated three keyways to give vernier adjustment for the cam timing. The cam followers became Stellite-tipped. The con rods became stronger, as on the 6T and T100. Piston rings of taper-faced section were fitted.

1951 brochure, 5T

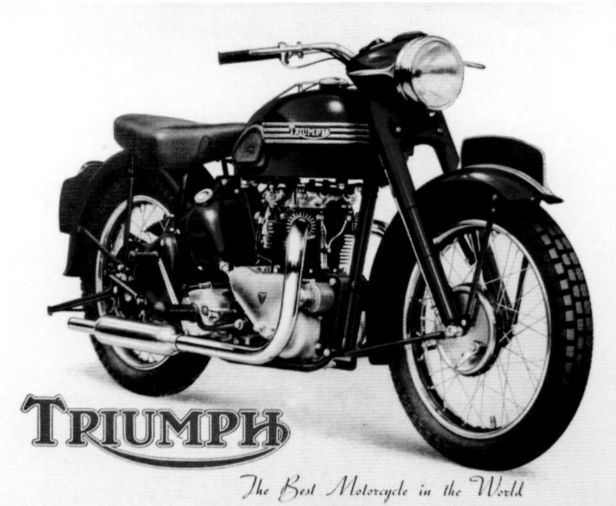

Cycle Parts

The front brake replaced its previous composite pressed steel pattern drum with a stiffer Mehanite cast iron drum. The oil tank filler cap became more angled, and changed to a plain screw-on cap without the previous "butterfly"cross-bar.

Electrical Equipment

A Lucas 53216A tail lamp was fitted giving a larger reflecting area, and room inside it for a brake light.

Optional Equipment

The "Rev-o-lator" Chronometric S467/19 speedometer, whose needle indicating 0mph had previously been at 1 o'clock, changed to the S467/99/L, with the needle being at the bottom at 7 o'clock" for 0mph, so that the 30-70mph segment was higher up and more readable.

Valanced mudguards were offered.

The parcel grid was now a standard fitting, but the plugs for its mounting holes were still available for those who wished to remove the grid.

1951 5T

1952

A revised frame with a hole through the seat tube was adopted. The electrical system changed from negative to positive earth.

Engine and Gearbox

The primary chaincase's oil retainer plate lost its central boss and became a simple disk. The retaining plug holding the oil pump plunger springs was altered to a castellated one. The previous bolts for the sump plate and its filter were changed to studs and nuts.

In the gearbox, layshaft 2nd and 4th gears and their mating dogs were altered.

Frame and Suspension

A new frame featured a lug with a large hole through it set in the seat tube, to permit connection of the carburettor to a new Vokes D-shaped air filter.

With a new, enlarged and re-styled nacelle, the 20in fork springs were shortened by ¾in on visual grounds, to stop the fork seal holder being visible and breaking up the painted section of the fork.

Cycle Parts

The nacelle became larger in diameter. At its front beneath the headlamp, the previous slots were replaced by an underslung pilot lamp.

The oil tank eliminated a pommel in its back and replaced it with a welded-on strap-fixing to the rear mudguard. It also had its vent pipe moved from the previous position down the seat tube and venting to atmosphere, so that it now vented into the rear of the primary chaincase via two small rubber pipes joined by a steel one. The battery carrier, to accommodate the new centrally-located air filter, changed from one with a cranked dog-leg back bracket to a straight back, as fitted in 1938.

The petrol tank became of a new-type construction with a visible central welded top seam. The previous bridge pipe connecting the two halves was eliminated, and a single petrol tap was again fitted, with the previous tap's right side threaded tap boss blanked off by a plug , and the left side tap changing to include both main and reserve facilities. The petrol pipes changed from braided steel to clear plastic.

The rear brake pedal now had a narrower, more squared-off foot-pad, with a pinnacle finish. On the rear wheel, the previous bolted-on sprocket and separate brake drum were replaced by an integral drum and sprocket.

Nickel shortages due to the Korean War meant that from August 1951, or possibly a little earlier, previously chromed parts had different finishes. Handlebars were painted in the machine colour, wheel rims painted silver and centre-lined as previously, while the kickstart lever, foot change lever, clutch operating arm, pushrod tubes, rocker feed spindle dome nuts, and exhaust pipes finned clips, were cadmium-plated. This continued until just before, or at, the start of the 1953 model year.

1952 brochure cover – 5T, 6T.

1952 brochure – 5T.

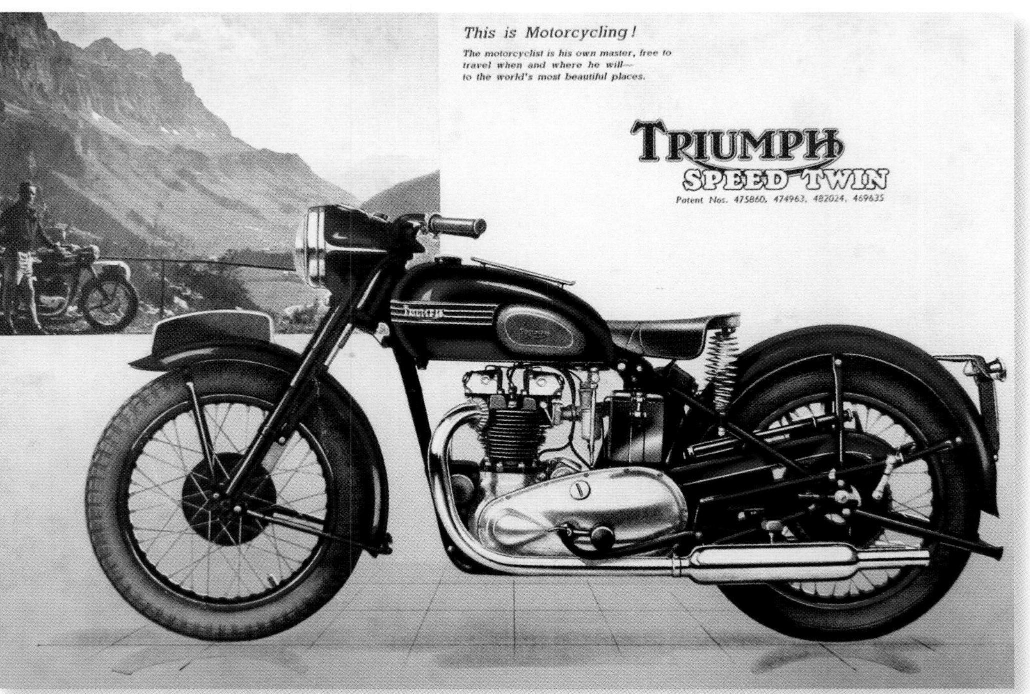

1951 was an excellent "middle period" year for the Speed Twin. This example displays the slimness of the "inside spring" telescopic forks, the stylishness of the headlamp nacelle and sweptback handlebars, the way that the petrol tank styling bands and parcel grid, in a sober post-war era, provided the right amount of glitter to replace chromed tanks, and the unobtrusive (if not particularly effective) rear suspension supplied by the patented Spring Wheel, by now in Mk II form. Minor deviations from standard on this example include the coloured, not black, HT leads, and the chromed, not painted, rear stand spring.

Electrical Equipment

Within the new nacelle the Lucas MCF700 7in headlamp became a sealed-beam pre-focus type, with Lucas 517 underslung pilot light. Early in the model year, at eng. no. 19706NA, the electrical system changed from negative to positive earth, to harmonise with the car industry.

It appears that the changeover to the exclusive use of Lucas magnetos, rather than a mixture with BTH ones, had been completed by the end of this model year.

A multi-coloured Lucas wiring harness was adopted.

1951 5T. The single "push-pull" petrol tap giving a reserve facility is correct for the year.

1951 5T. A Lucas 53216A tail lamp was now fitted.

1951 5T. Mk II Spring Wheel, introduced during the 1950 model year, is identifiable by its circumferentially-ribbed end plate

1951 5T. The tyre inflator is clipped to the chainguard.

1951 5T. The Amal 276's float chamber had changed to the left side of the instrument for 1947. Its choke lever, here chromed, should be black-painted.

1951 5T. Nacelle fitted with, clockwise from top, Smiths Chronometric speedo with needle re-positioned that year to 7 o'clock at zero; light switch; steering damper; ammeter; and in the middle, kill button for the magneto. Note the D-shaped grommeted holes for the 1in handlebars and for cables.

1951 5T. Slim "inside spring" telescopic forks looked better than they worked. Painted and lined wheel centres, polished alloy brake plate on 7in drum, and graceful chrome-surrounded front number plate, were all touches of Triumph style.

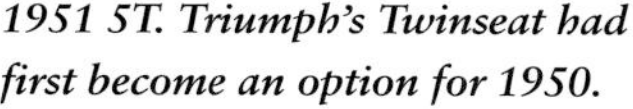

1951 5T. Triumph's Twinseat had first become an option for 1950.

1951 5T. Post-war and pre-alternator, the magneto stayed behind the cylinder, while the dynamo went in front.

1951 5T. A view of the sweptback handlebars.

1953

A significant change occurred, as the 5T adopted coil ignition with a distributor, and a crankshaft-mounted alternator behind a revised primary chaincase, with the nacelle modified to suit.

1953 5T

Engine and Gearbox

The crankshaft had a $\frac{7}{16}$in x 26in tpi stud screwed into the lengthened drive mainshaft end, to hold the alternator rotor and the engine sprocket in place. This drive-side crankshaft portion was of parallel section. The dynamo drive was eliminated and the crankcases modified to suit, as were the front engine plates.

New inner and outer primary chaincases featured, to accommodate the alternator, the outer one losing its shapely "teardrop" protuberance, and now with a circular portion for mounting the alternator stator. The timing cover was also modified. From eng. no. 33868 (mid-October 1952), the engine shock absorber moved from the engine sprocket to the clutch, with the clutch hub nut and washer modified to suit. The new shock absorber had a four-paddle vane working in eight rubber blocks.

From eng. no. 37560 (mid-February 1953), new camshafts incorporating quietening ramps were introduced; although with them the valve timing remained the same, tappet clearance changed from 0.020 to 0.010. To indicate their presence, alongside the engine number a small "spoked wheel" logo was stamped in.

The rocker spindles were fitted with O-rings.

In May 1953 a steel gear selection camplate replaced the previous alloy one.

Frame and Suspension

The frame's rear petrol tank support was again modified to accommodate an altered bolt size.

Cycle parts

The left (near) side exhaust pipe gained a kink to give clearance round the new alternator primary chaincase.

The toolbox deleted its top P-clip fitting, now bolting directly to the front section of the rear mudguard.

The rear number plate was altered to fit a new rectangular stop/tail light. The rear brake rod operated a stop-switch for it, which was fixed to a plate fastened on the pillion footrest bolt.

The nacelle was modified to feature, for this year only, two switches, one on the right for the lights and one on the left for ignition, with a removable key.

Electrical Equipment

The Lucas RM12 alternator was fitted, along with a new wiring harness and a Lucas DKX2A distributor, mounted horizontally behind the cylinders in the previous magneto position, with a Lucas 6VQ6 coil mounted above it. The distributor drive shaft projected into the timing chest and was driven by a pinion in the same location as the one for the previous magneto. No voltage control was now fitted, the output being "switch-controlled" i.e. with the lighting switch used to bring into circuit four out of the six stator windings

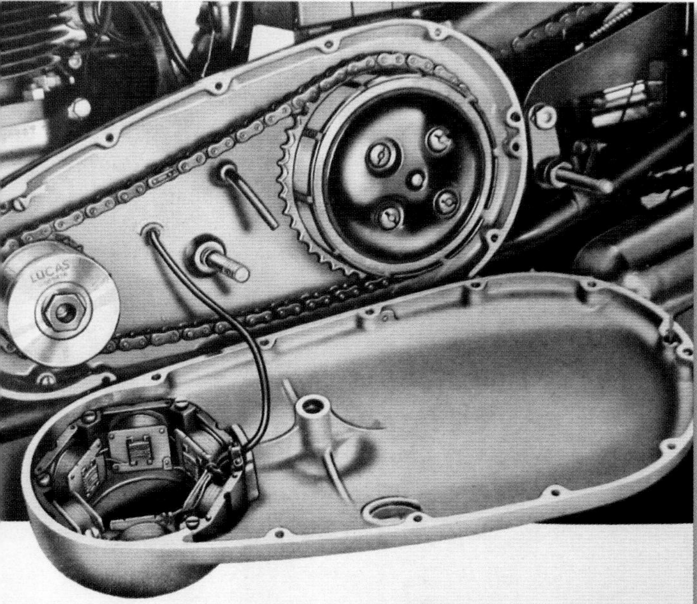

THE TRIUMPH A.C. LIGHTING-IGNITION UNIT

The introduction of this new lighting and ignition system on the Triumph Speed Twin marks a further step forward in progressive motorcycle design. The normal separate gear driven magneto and dynamo are replaced by a single alternator mounted on the crankshaft and enclosed in the primary chain case. This means a minimum loss of power in driving it, and generator bearings are eliminated altogether. A distributor and coil are fitted behind the engine and a rectifier is mounted above the air-cleaner. Lighting and Ignition switches are on the nacelle top. **Battery failure cannot affect engine starting as an "Emergency Start" position on the ignition switch diverts all the current produced by the alternator direct to the ignition circuit.** This new system offers simplicity with remarkable efficiency.

[PAGE TWO

1953 alternator, 5T

so that the alternator output was stepped up. There was provision for emergency start with a flat battery; turning the ignition key to the left put the majority of the alternator's output through the ignition system.

The system was modified twice during the model year. Initially System A featured four leads from the alternator stator and a Westinghouse double rectifier housed under the seat, replacing the previous Lucas MCR2 regulator. System B from eng. no. 35317 (mid-December 1952) featured simplified wiring and a single bank rectifier. System C from eng. no. 40294 (early May 1953) added a resistance unit and featured 6 leads from the alternator stator.

The stop-tail lamp became the squarer Lucas Diacon Type 525 unit.

Plug caps with suppressors were fitted now that the magneto was gone.

Optional Equipment

The prop-stand's footpiece was enlarged, to clear the kink in the left exhaust pipe.

1954

Engine and Gearbox

In mid-year from eng. no. 54946 the timing side main bearing switched from a roller bearing to a larger MS11 ball journal. From eng. no. 54986 the bearing reverted to the previous smaller roller bearing.

Cycle Parts

The silencers became "barrel-shaped", with the body tapering down slightly from front to rear, and a less pronounced shoulder where the body of the silencer met the tail pipe.

The nacelle was modified to suit a new combined lights/ignition switch. This was mounted to the right, in a 2in diameter hole, while the ammeter, which had sat between and to the rear of 1953's twin switches, moved to a 2in diameter hole on the left.

Rear wheels on rigid models had their spoke angles modified, and were fitted with non-adjustable bearings.

Electrical Equipment

The alternator became a 3-wire Lucas type RM14.

A Lucas PRS8 dual lights/ignition switch was adopted.

The rectifier, still mounted beneath the saddle, became a round 4-plate 4½in diameter Lucas Sentercel unit.

The spring set in the distributor was revised.

Optional Equipment

The close ratio gearbox option had its mainshaft and 3rd gear altered.

1955

The pre-unit 5T's final major change year, with the adoption of the swinging-arm frame introduced for the previous year's big twins and T100. The 5T's engine became stronger, but the 500's weight increased by at least 25lb to 386lb.

Though officially the rigid/Spring Wheel 5T was no more, in fact the last orders, mostly for Police machines, continued to be met during the 1955 model year, with the final earlier model being eng. no. 68296 (6 June 1955).

Engine and Gearbox

The previous year's crankshaft for the other twins, with increased crankpin shaft diameters and a larger drive side main bearing, was fitted. The bearing was an MS11 ball-race with a clamping washer between the race and the timing gear. The flywheel was revised as on the 1954 T100 (see below). Early on, from eng. no. 56811 (24 August 1954), a sludge trap was fitted to the crankshaft.

The larger shaft diameters meant revised con rods, with the big end diameter increased to 1.6250/1.6255in (1⅝in).

1954 5T

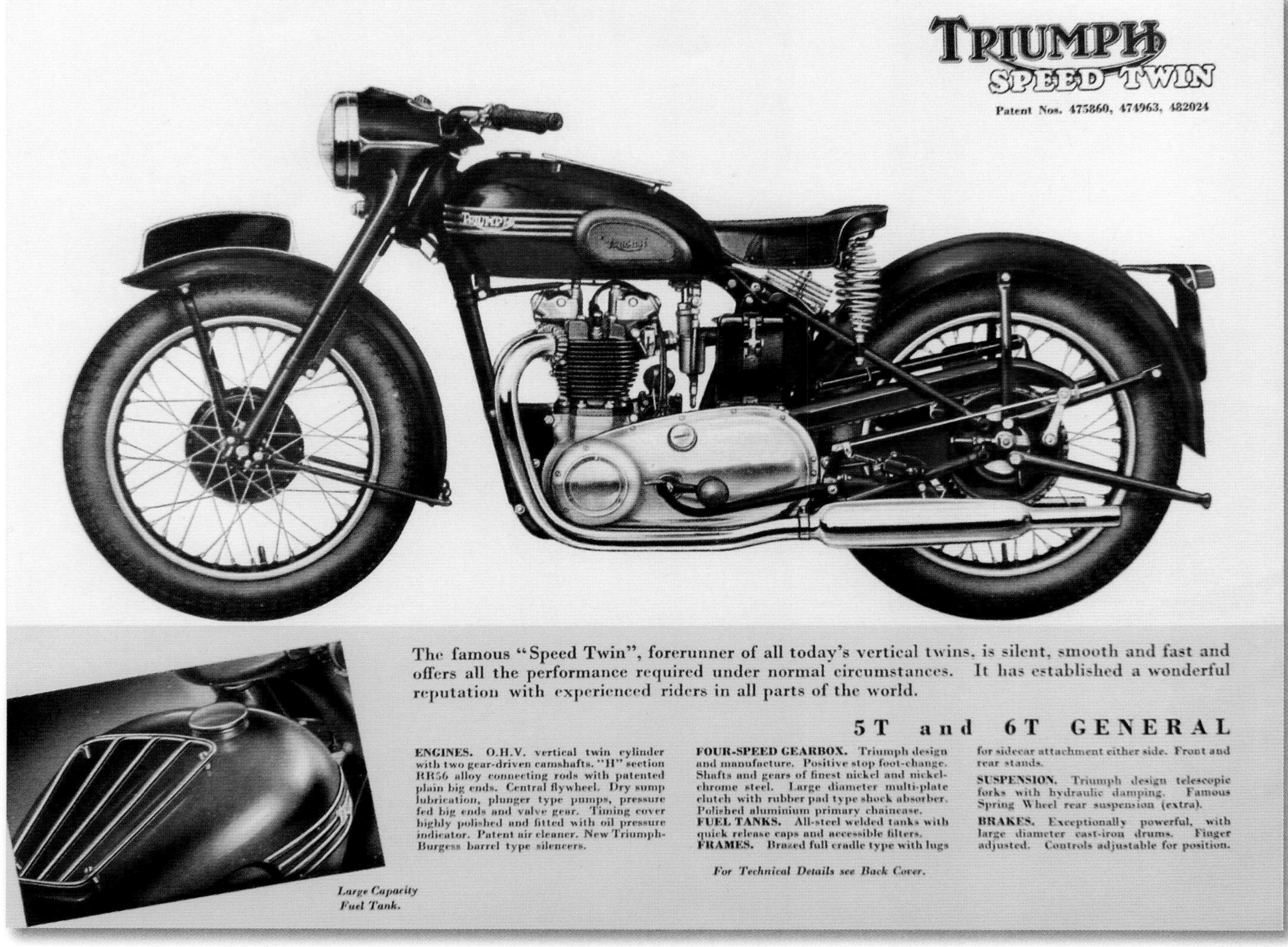

All this meant new crankcases to suit, which also had to be shorter to fit in the swinging-arm frame; so the primary chain shortened from 78 to 70 links, while the rear chain length increased from 93 to 100 links. The primary chaincase deleted the circular section and now featured a larger version of the previous "horizontal teardrop" bulge, which now carried the cast-in Triumph and Speed Twin names.

The fastening screws for the engine and gearbox covers changed from the slotted cheesehead type to Philips crossheads.

The gearbox also moved closer to the crankcase. Its main casing now had a top pivot fixing as well as a bottom one, to suit the swinging-arm frame. The gearbox inner cover was also changed to provide an angled cable adjuster which would not foul the box's mounting plates. The previous gear indicator and pointer were dropped. The kickstart ratchet spring and sleeve were redesigned and their associated thrust washer deleted.

The 5T adopted the new Amal Monobloc carburettor, Type 376/25, with the choke reverting to a system involving a spring-loaded plunger within the carburettor.

Frame and Suspension

The swinging-arm frame was compact, with a 55¾in wheel-base being just under 2in longer than the rigid machine's. New rear chain plates, and the deletion of the previous lower chainguard, also contributed. The frame incorporated sidecar fixings. It was still a single front downtube frame, but with a swinging-arm fork pivoting on the saddle tube, on metal Oilite bushes. The bolt-on rear section supported the Girling units. The rear fork incorporated torque stay lugs, and a rear brake torque stay was fitted for the first time. The rear suspension was controlled by 12.9in long 3-position Girling units. The frame was the first Triumph one to feature a centre stand, and a new (still optional) prop-stand was fitted.

The rear wheels featured revised head angle spoking, and unlike those of the rigid models, which had run on taper rollers, they ran on ball races.

1955 5T

The "Speed Twin" originated the modern trend to the vertical twin and its effortless performance ensures its continued popularity. Over seventy police forces in all parts of the world ride Triumph "Speed Twins"—sure proof of fine quality.

SPECIFICATION

WHEELS. Triumph design, with heavy duty dull-plated spokes and chromium-plated rims. Dunlop tyres.
ELECTRICAL EQUIPMENT. Triumph pioneered A.C. Lighting-Ignition unit with emergency start circuit. Wide angle rear/stop light. Powerful Lucas 7-in. built-in headlamp with combined reflector/front lens assembly, "pre-focus" bulb and adjustable rim. Separate parking light.
TOOLBOX. Combined with the oil tank, air cleaner and battery container in a streamlined "one piece" unit. Complete set of good quality tools and grease gun.
MUDGUARDS. Efficient "D" shaped guards with central rib. Rear guard heavily valanced.
NACELLE (patented). Neat streamline shell integral with top of forks, enclosing headlamp, instruments and switchgear. All instruments rubber mounted and internally illuminated.
SPEEDOMETER. Smiths 120 m.p.h. (or 180 km.p.h.) chronometric type with r.p.m. scale, internal illumination and trip recorder.
OTHER DETAILS. Finish: 5T Amaranth Red; 6T Polychromatic Blue; quick-action adjustable twist grip; integral horn push; rubber knee grips; tank parcel grid.

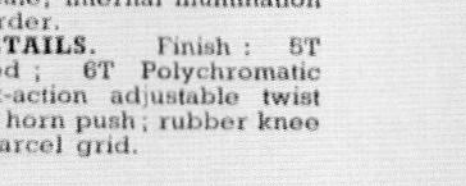

PAGE FIVE

Police riders in Australia —all Triumph mounted.

Cycle Parts

The oil tank was reduced from a catalogued 6 to 5 pint capacity, and was amalgamated in one unit with the D-shaped air cleaner, the battery case and the toolbox, with the latter now fastened by a long slotted screw.

A Twinseat now became standard: not the previous optional flat one, but two-level as on the other roadsters and with white piping around the top.

The rear mudguard changed to a new one with pressed steel valances spot-welded to its sides.

The rear brake pedal became a single forging for the pedal arm, pivot bush and rod arm, with the rod end no longer forked but bent and secured by a split pin.

The front fork springs became 20in long again, and the fork's rigidity was aided by replacing the previous 5⁄16in stanchion pinch bolts with 3⁄8in diameter ones.

The silencer clip was now linked to the frame on each side by a simple strip stay; at eng. no. 64324 the strip was strengthened.

Electrical Equipment

The alternator layout changed, with the stator thinner and now mounted on the primary chaincase inner cover, rather than its outer case as before, and this arrangement's increased rigidity allowed the air gap between stator and rotor to be reduced to 0.008in.

A smaller, 2¾in diameter, Lucas Type SFX 150 1AS Sentercel rectifier replaced the previous one.

The stop/tail light became the Lucas Type 564 with integral rear reflector and a Lucas 22B stop-lamp switch.

Optional Equipment

The QD rear wheel, still 19in diameter, now ran on special thin taper rollers.

The valanced front mudguard now featured stays formed in one and riveted to the guard.

This is a nice example of "late period" pre-unit Speed Twin, now with full swinging-arm rear suspension, alternator electrics, "big bearing" engine and the 6T's crankcases. The oil tank/air filter/battery box were all in one neat unit, and the petrol tank was the two-piece construction type, so with a chrome central styling strip and 4-bar parcel grid. Still a handsome motorcycle but at 386lb definitely one with some weight gain and looking it, with the solid mid-section larger Twinseat and valanced rear mudguard. On this example, an incorrect petrol tap has been fitted. The wheel rims were plain chrome as standard that year, but one source says that painted centres, as seen here, were still an option until the following year.

1956 5T

1956

Engine and Gearbox

The crankcases of the 6T were adopted, with a new 5T cylinder barrel to match them. This change had begun in fact at the very end of the 1955 model year, at eng. no. 70076 (20 July 1955). With the 650's cylinder flange and crankcase joint employed, the centres of the outer cylinder fixing holes became 2¼in apart rather than 2in. This new barrel would not fit earlier cases. The inlet manifold was also altered, and gained an 'O' ring at the carburettor flange joint.

The con rods, previously with white metal big ends, now had Vandervell VP3 shell bearings, with the con rod eye enlarged to take them, and balance weights adjusted to retain the previous balance factor.

From eng. no. 72028 (23 September 1955) the inlet camshaft was redesigned with only one breather hole, to reduce oil being vented through the pipe.

On the gearbox, the shell and inner cover became that of the 1954 T100. The previously phosphor bronze layshaft bushes were now of sintered bronze. The clutch shock

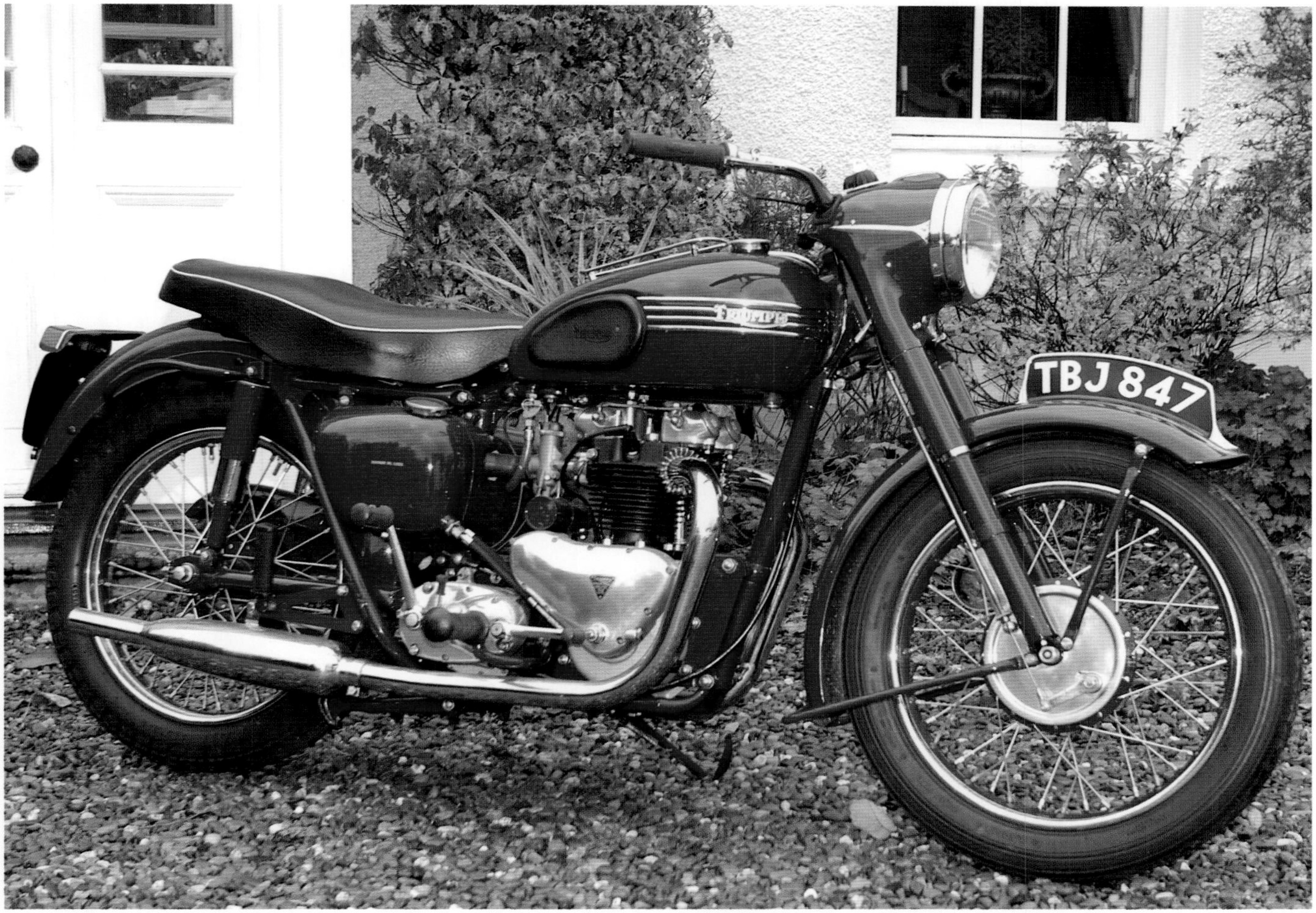

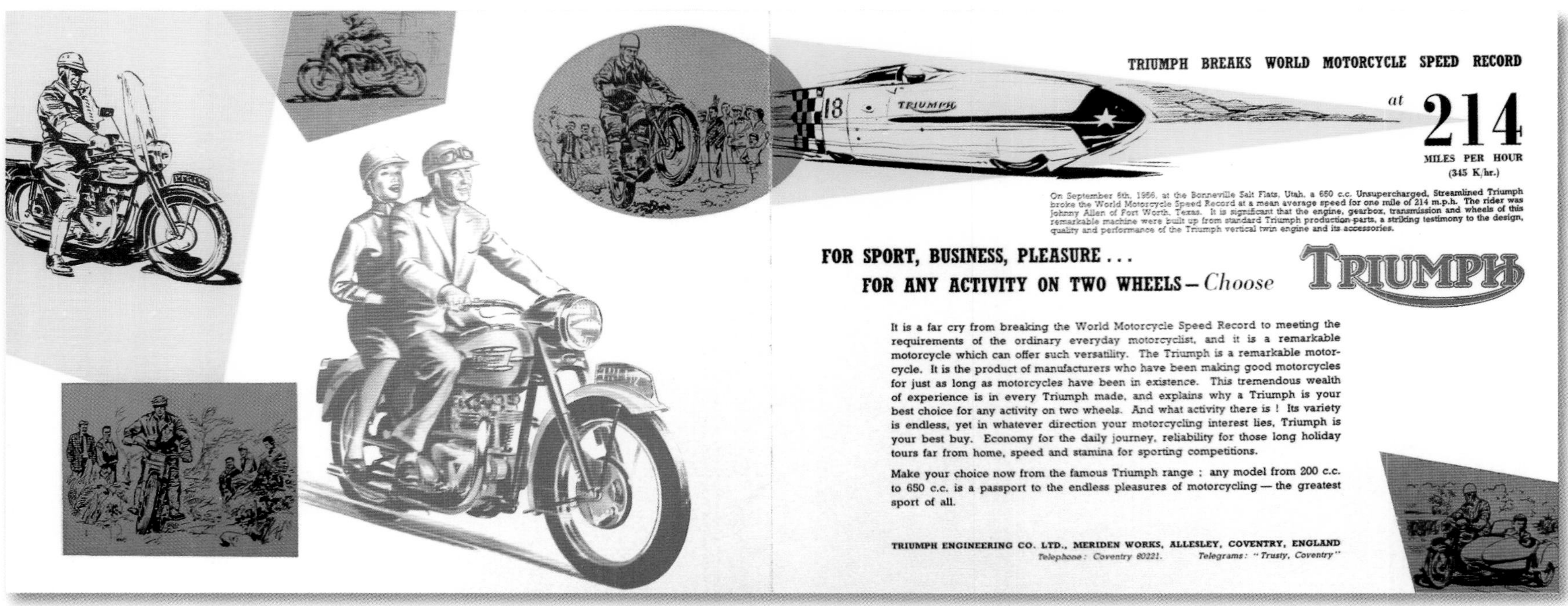

This 1956 brochure promoted all sorts of Triumph motorcycling including the World Land Speed record at Bonneville.

1956 5T. The Spring Wheel is history, replaced by full swinging-arm rear suspension.

1956 5T. Small rear reflectors were a Triumph accessory. The tail-light, with its own internal reflector, is the correct Lucas Type 564 adopted for 1955 on.

absorber rubbers were altered in composition. Clutch plates were modified, the driven ones becoming solid not pierced, and the drive plates now fitted with bonded Neolangite segments.

Frame and Suspension

The 5T's frame now incorporated an additional sidecar lug at the bottom of the seat tube. It also had a new headstock lug. The lower cup of the headrace cup-and-cone became in common with the top cup, and a new top cone was fitted. The ball bearings of the upper and lower headraces became common, both the same as the previous lower balls. The steering lock stops became adjustable.

Inside the front forks there were now modified hydraulic bump stops to help prevent bottoming out. The front brake cable adjuster and abutment was moved to a brazed lug on the right-hand fork slider. The rear units had softer 100lb springs and their bleed and bump stops were revised.

1956 5T. An oval chrome grille beneath the nacelle occupied the space filled by the separate pilot light until this year.

1956 5T. This was the final year with the classic 4-band tank decoration; the following year Bling would be back with the "mouth-organ" tank badge. The key in the combined lights/ignition switch indicates alternator electrics.

Cycle Parts

The petrol tank now featured rubber bushes for its revised rear mounting. Its central seam was covered with a chromed strip, and as a result the parcel grid lost its fifth, central bar, to become the 4-bar type.

On the handlebars, the previous integral threaded horn-push was deleted.

The centre stand was modified to give greater ground clearance. The top fork shrouds had now lost the pilot light, which was replaced by an oval-shaped chromed grille.

The wheels no longer had painted centres, becoming plain chrome, though according to marque specialist and ex-Meriden man Jim Lee, they could still be had to special order until the end of this model year.

Electrical Equipment

The pilot light was moved into the headlight. A new type of wiring harness was fitted, enclosed in a 1mm thick pvc sheath rather than the previous woven cloth. A new combined horn/dipswitch was mounted on the handlebar clutch lever bracket clamp.

1956 5T. Sleek "tear-drop" silencers derived from the Tiger Cub.

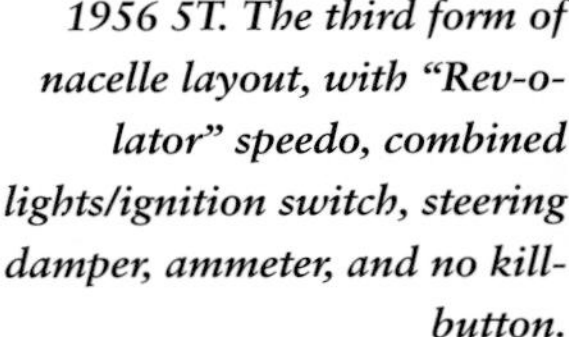

1956 5T. The third form of nacelle layout, with "Rev-o-lator" speedo, combined lights/ignition switch, steering damper, ammeter, and no kill-button.

1956 5T. With nacelle models, the mileometer's trip control protruded on a stalk beneath.

1956 5T. The two-level Twinseat adopted as standard with the swinging-arm frame, broader and more comfortable than the previous optional one

1956 5T. Amal Monobloc carburettor would stay on Triumph twins (bar the '52-'58 6T) until 1967. Rubber tube passed through eye in frame, to air cleaner. Note the ignition coil horizontally mounted in a pressed steel can, "piggy-back" above distributor.

1956 5T. Speedo drive cable emerges from gearbox and passes up the frame to the nacelle.

1956 5T. Front brake cable adjuster was at brake end.

1956 5T. A good view of the tank with its centre joint and the decorative strip to hide it, which was why the parcel grid had gone to the 4-bar type. Note also the knurled knob for the friction device below the twist-grip, and the metal tube "arm" guiding and protecting the throttle cable.

1957

The main changes were cosmetic: a full-width front brake hub, and the "mouth organ" tank badges.

Engine and Gearbox

The 5T's camshaft reverted to the type with a single keyway.

In the gearbox, to counter oil leaks which often ended up on the rear tyre, new sleeve gears with bushes to suit were fitted, with the mainshaft high gear sleeve bush extended through the primary chaincase oil retainer plate into the primary chaincase to divert the oil into there. The chaincase oil retainer disk plate was now of a larger bore to suit. Also

1957 5T

in the chaincase, a garter-type oil seal was fitted, with the engine sprocket boss machined to accommodate it.

On the clutch's vane-type shock absorber, more oil-proof and resilient rubbers were used. The kickstart cotter pin was modified.

Frame and Suspension

The front fork ends and wheel spindle were changed, with the previous threaded hole in the right leg end and split hole on the left changed to bolted-on split ends on both legs, with a new spindle.

The swinging-arm was modified to suit a revised rear chainguard.

At eng. no. 08563, the Girling units were fitted with 110lb springs, marginally harder than the previous ones but providing 3 inches of movement. Also, where their top and bottom eyes had been fitted with rubber bushes and sleeves, they now changed to Metalastic-type bushes.

Cycle Parts

The front brake hub became full-width, though inside it the 7in brake and its shoes were unchanged. A full-width cast iron drum fitted in a finned pressed steel hub, with a slightly larger alloy anchor plate retaining the brake shoes, and a chrome styling plate with decorative radial rings on the near (left) side. The front wheel spokes became straight and butted, while the spokes on the rear wheel, to counter fractures, replaced the previous 9 gauge with heavier 8/10 G gauge ones. The brake anchor plate mounting brackets became induction-brazed. The bottom members of the front mudguard's middle stays gained brazed-on lugs, with the previous loose clips being deleted. Stronger section silencer clip-stays, plus added brackets, and strengthened exhaust pipe brackets, also featured.

The centre stand now had a longer foot peg.

The rear chainguard gained greater enclosure at the back and a deeper flange. It was hinged on a new bracket at the front, and was bolted up independently at the rear, no longer to the suspension unit's clamp bolt.

The fuel tank was new, to suit its new decoration. The badges were chromed, and there were two chromed median strips (which facilitated the use of two-tone colour schemes on other models). The tank's screw pommels were modified to suit. The tank's rear mounting pads were extended sideways to the tank edge.

Electrical Equipment

The coil, though still above the distributor, was re-positioned.

Optional Equipment

An "Easy-lift" centre stand, developed for Police models, was offered.

The previous full valanced front mudguard was no longer available.

1958

The pre-unit 5T's last year was marked by the adoption of the Turner-designed Slickshift in the gearbox, to permit gear changes without pulling in the clutch lever, though an overriding mechanism meant that the clutch could still be operated normally. The rider's foot touching the gear pedal operated the clutch automatically, so that the handlebar clutch lever could be seen working independently! Denoted by a small oval chromed cap on the gearbox cover, the device was unpopular with riders, who often disconnected it by removing the roller thrust pin fixed to the clutch operating arm.

Engine and Gearbox

A sealing rubber sleeve was fitted onto the kickstart spindle outside the cover. On the Slickshift gearbox, the vertical outer clutch lever was modified to a horizontal cable arm on top of the gearbox with a vertical pivot shaft, the clutch cable stop being transferred from the top of the inner cover to the primary chain adjuster drawbolt. The mechanism's previous rubber cap was deleted, along with the cable adjuster at the gearbox. The gearbox inner cover deleted the cable lug in the top of the casting. It adopted a filler hole in its top face, in place of the previous hexagonal-headed filler on the outer cover, whose space was now occupied by the oval chromed inspection cap.

Internally, the Slickshift worked by a foot-change quadrant ramp operating on a roller thrust pin fixed to the clutch operating arm. The clutch lever mechanism had been swung round so that its pivot shaft was now vertical. The roller imparted the gear pedal movement to the clutch, and this required a shorter clutch pushrod with a chamfered end.

Frame and Suspension

The steering stem and head lug were modified to accept an optional anti-theft steering lock.

The front fork legs were modified to take a single, rear-mounted mudguard stay, with a brazed-on boss on the inside of the legs replacing the previous clip supporting the central mudguard bridge, both for a new valanced mudguard. The front brake cable stop moved to the bottom of the right-hand fork leg and deleted its previous adjuster there, as well as deleting the previous steel tube over the cable's lower run.

Cycle Parts

The exhaust pipes' diameter changed from 1¾in to 1½in.

New deeper-valanced mudguards front and rear provided a half-way house to the enclosed, more fully covered styling of the coming unit 500 5TA. They were deep pressings, rather than having the valances spot-welded on as previously.

The silencers for that year only became unbaffled.

The front brake's chrome styling plate became radially fluted.

The centre stand's foot extension acquired a rubber.

The oil tank filler cap moved closer to the tank's centre, to prevent fouling the rider's leg during kickstarting.

The nacelle gained a larger hole for the steering damper, and two new small holes where the clutch and front brake cables now passed though it, protected by small grommets. The right nacelle leg was modified.

The control cables (clutch and brake) now featured detachable nipples at the lever end, secured by a split pin, and their handlebar levers now featured inbuilt cable adjusters.

Optional Equipment

A steering-head lock was offered, located to the right of the headstock lug, with a slot cut in the steering stem, and the Neiman-type lock and key fitted in a tube in the head lug.

1956 5T. This view emphasises the slimness of the bike, despite the parallel-twin engine across the frame.

T100 TIGER 500

1939

The Tiger 100 was Triumph's cutting-edge model until the coming of the 650 for 1950. Even then, alloy-engined from 1951, the T100 effectively continued as such at least until the tuned T110 650s came in 1954.

The Tiger 100's launch for 1939 conformed to a Triumph, and indeed industry, pattern: test the water (and hopefully iron out the problems) with a cooking roadster, and then follow that with a sports model. The Tiger 100 certainly looked the part with its big 4-gallon chromed tank and blue-lined frosted silver panels, and its eye-catching 8in chrome headlamp. At £80 the Tiger cost just £5 more than the 5T on its launch in November 1938.

The model number was intended to indicate this Tiger's top speed; in fact it was around 96mph, unless the silencer end-caps with their baffles were removed, or optional straight-through pipes were fitted. But it was still extremely vfast for any motorcycle then, and though handling at top speeds was prone to "tank-slapper" wobbles and to weave, off the boil the motor remained delightfully flexible and tractable. The twin's tuning potential had been obvious following Ivan Wicksteed's supercharged 5T taking the 500cc Brooklands lap record in October 1938 at over 118mph, while reliability was emphasised by the 1939 Maudes Trophy going to a 5T and a T100, selected at random from dealers in March of that year and covering 1800 frequently snow-covered road miles in a week, topped with another non-stop 450-plus miles in 6 hours at Brooklands, averaging over 75mph.

1939 T100

Cleverly, in production terms the T100 basically resembled the 5T closely, so for greater details, see also the 5T section, 1938-40.

Engine and Gearbox

The all-iron engine was as described for the 1938 5T, with the following exceptions. The T100's crankshaft and con rods were lightly strengthened, with the flywheel differing in detail from the 5T's. The compression was raised from the 5T's 7.0:1 to 7.8:1 by the use of forged aluminium alloy slipper-type pistons. Claimed output for the T100 was 34bhp at 7000rpm, against the 5T's 27bhp at 6,000rpm. The 5T's former 6 cylinder base holding-down studs were increased for both 1939 5T and T100 engines to 8. The T100's cylinder head ports and passages were polished, as was the outer alloy primary chaincase.

The T100's carburettor was a 1in Amal Type 76, against the 5T's 15⁄16in, and was fitted with a bell mouth.

Frame and Suspension

The T100's front full cradle frame differed from the 5T's, with a different steering head angle, increased to 60¾ degrees to provide greater trail; though the bolted-up separate rigid rear section was the same. The T100's forks too differed, with longer (100mm) bottom links, though both featured a central compression spring and dampers with finger adjustment on the lower bridge.

Having stunned the motorcycling world with the Speed Twin in 1938, Edward Turner made it a one-two the following year with the sports version, the Tiger 100. Both the name and the finish were reassuringly familiar from Triumph's sporting Tiger singles, but this was something else. Its magnificent chromed 4-gallon tank, and "cocktail shaker" silencers with detachable end caps and baffles, effectively masked the basic similarity to the Speed Twin. There were differences, an altered steering head angle, modified forks and a different flywheel, but beneath the skin there was much in common. This fine example amply demonstrates the T100's instant appeal. Minor deviations from originality include barrel-shaped, not parallel, saddle springs, and as mentioned re the 5T, the fitting of later petrol taps as found on many of the A.R.E. collection, on safety grounds.

Cycle Parts

The T100's big, eye-catching chrome and frosted silver fuel tank held 4 Imp. gallons, and was recessed at its slimmed-down rear to take big knee-grip rubbers. As on the '39 5T, it featured a rubber-mounted Bakelite instrument panel. The oil tank was also bigger, with a hinged quick-opening "butterfly" cap and an 8-pint capacity against the 5T's 5 pints.

The T100 was catalogued with markedly bigger wheels than the 5T's, with 26 x 3.00 front and 26 x 3.50 rear, on WM2 rims, though in fact the same 20 x 3.00 front and 19 x 3.50 rear appear to have been fitted. The T100's 7in front brake was of ribbed cast iron for better cooling, whereas the 5T's was of plain dished iron.

The T100 "cocktail-shaker" silencers were also distinctive, with detachable end-caps fastened to the silencer body by three screws (the late Hughie Hancox believed that a few of the first T100s were sold with silencers of that shape but without the detachable end-caps). Removing the ends, and the baffles attached to them, left open megaphone exhausts. Where the unusually large Triumph 1¾in diameter exhaust pipes met the head, they were held in place by finned clamps, which were chrome-plated.

On the T100 the rubber-mounted 1in diameter handlebars were narrow for 1939, and fitted with chrome-plated TT-type brake and clutch levers, as well as the click-action friction-damped twistgrip.

A detachable chrome surround for the front number plate was fitted, as on the 5T for that year.

Electrical Equipment

As 1938/39 5T (see page 18).

Optional Equipment

The Smiths Chronometric speedometer with its additional concentric bands showing rpm in each gear, known as the "Rev-o-lator", was listed as an extra at £2.15s but was fitted (and charged for) as standard, unless the truly optional version with the big 5in dial, or the export alternative km-per-hour variant, were fitted.

A "bronze-skull" competition cylinder head was a highly desirable extra for the improved cooling it provided at high rpm, though its valves seated directly on the bronze, without cast-in iron valve seats.

1939 T100. The lower run of the rear chainguard was a neat touch.

1939 T100. Chrome-plated TT-type handlebar levers were special to the T100. The chromed surround for the front number plate was new for 1939.

1939 T100. The engine had higher compression than the 1938 5T at 7.8:1, and gave 34bhp at 7000rpm against the 5T's 27bhp at 6000rpm.

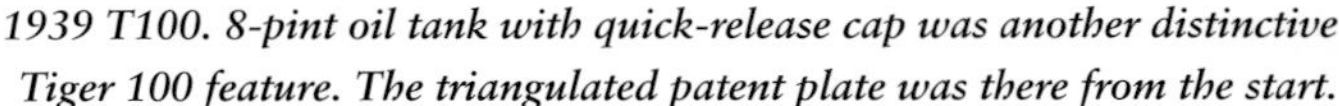

1939 T100. 8-pint oil tank with quick-release cap was another distinctive Tiger 100 feature. The triangulated patent plate was there from the start.

1939 T100. Note two of the three retaining screws for the end cap and baffles on the "cocktail-shaker" silencers. Remove them to turn the Tiger loose! The stand spring should be black painted.

1939 T100. The speedo, an extra but fitted and charged for unless otherwise specified, was driven from the front wheel. Cable became thinner the following year.

1939 T100. The period pocket watch and its clips are a nice touch. Turner wanted the "Triumph" logo as well known as the London Underground's. Clever grips with a logo facing either way could be used on either end of the handlebars.

1939 T100. The unsprung pillion pad lacked that touch of luxury.

1939 T100. The design of the finish on the tank was superb.

1939 T100. The tank-top instrument panel was made of Bakelite for 1939 only. So was the steering damper; From 1948 it would be painted metal.
The Tiger 100's 1-inch diameter handlebars were narrow by 1930s standards.

1940

With war declared in September 1939, the 1940 programme was truncated, before being terminated by the blitzing of the Coventry works on 4 November 1940. However, some T100s were built either for US export ("we shall," Turner wrote in an advert, "be permitted to send to the USA and Canada supplies of our twin cylinder types which have made so many friends amongst sporting American riders.") Others were pressed into service; in London, for instance, the Admiralty's WRNS female despatch riders, serving, among others, Winston Churchill and James Bond's creator Commander Ian Fleming, were T100- mounted.

Engine and Gearbox

The previous slipper-type pistons were replaced by full skirted ones, with compression reduced to 6.0:1. The lubrication system was modified – for details see 1940 5T. The previous ball release oil pressure relief valve was replaced by a piston-type. As with the 5T, the 22-tooth engine sprocket gained a tooth, to raise gearing and improve miles-per-gallon.

Frame and Suspension As 1940 5T (see page 24)

Cycle Parts As 1940 5T (see page 24)

Optional Equipment

Fully valanced mudguards, front and rear, were now offered.

1946 catalogue cover showing post-war T100.

1946 T100

1946

The T100 returned as Triumph's flagship, produced in numbers limited by the availability of raw material. The main change was the adoption of telescopic forks. Some of the pre-war swagger – the big headlamp, those silencers – was gone, but this was still a good-looking, fast and very desirable motorcycle.

Engine and Gearbox

For this year only, all T100 engines were now claimed to be bench-tested, stripped, reassembled, and only then built into motorcycles, each of which was supplied with a certified test card. Compression was again catalogued at 7.8:1.

Otherwise as 1945/1946 5T, with front-mounted dynamo and rear-mounted magneto, and crankcases modified to suit. See 1945/46 5T (page 25) for more details.

Frame and Suspension As 1945/46 5T (see page 25).

Cycle parts

The 4-gallon petrol tank remained as pre-war, but the headlamp was now down to 6½in diameter, and its shell was painted black, not chromed, though with a chromed front ring.

The T100's handlebar controls now featured simple long clutch and front brake levers.

The wheels and tyres were again 3.25 x 19 front and 3.50x 19 rear, as on the 5T, and both wheels were shod with Dunlop Universal tyres.

The T100 silencers on their 1¾in exhaust pipes became of parallel cylindrical shape with long fixed tail-pipes, as on the 5T.

Otherwise as 1945/46 5T (see page 26).

Electrical Equipment As 1945/46 5T (see page 26).

1947

There were few changes as, with demand strongly outstripping supply, production got into its swing.

1948

The main new feature this year was the patented Spring Wheel at the rear. It incorporated an 8in single leading shoe brake, compared with the standard 7in one, and provided 2 inches of suspension movement.

Engine and Gearbox

From eng. no. 19576, the speedometer drive changed from the previous drive gearbox on the rear wheel to a gearbox-driven type, to suit the newly-arrived Spring Wheel. The T100's speedometer was now officially a standard fitting.

Cycle Parts

As 1948 5T, with a new front mudguard, the front number plate's styling beading now cast onto the plate, and a new one-piece rear mudguard with the previous side-handles deleted, and the rear frame modified to suit. The rear number plate mounting's top was narrowed so that it could double as a lifting hand-hold.

On the T100's front wheel the previous 3.25 x 19 Dunlop Universal tyre was replaced by a 3.25 x 19 ribbed one.

Electrical Equipment As 1948 5T (see page 27).

Optional Equipment

From eng. no. TF15069 (September 1947), the Spring Wheel, in the form known retrospectively as the Mk 1, became available as an option. See 1948 5T (page 27) for details.

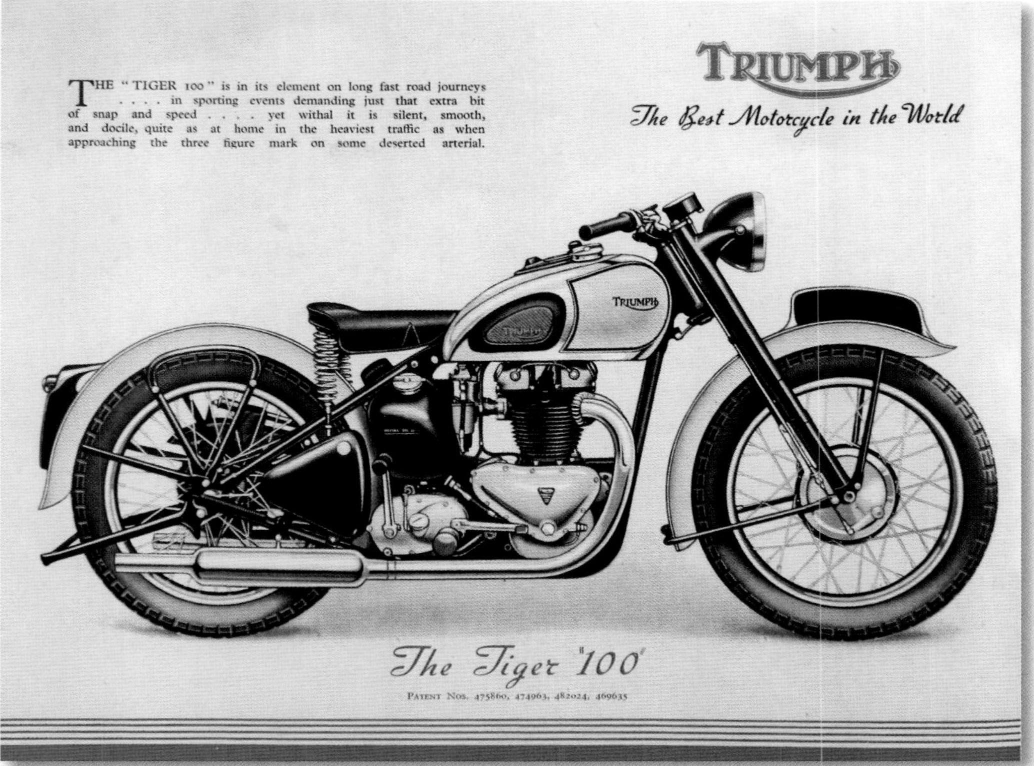

1947 T100

1948 T100

1949

A major change in appearance came with the first headlamp nacelle and the end of the tank-top instrument panel. There was also for this year a new timing-side main bearing.

Engine and Gearbox

On T100 engine the timing-side main bearing was replaced with a single lipped roller, later with a fixed chip shield; the 5T would not adopt this until 1951. The timing case oil pressure relief valve with tell-tale button was adopted. For details and further changes, see 1949 5T (page 28).

Frame and Suspension As 1949 5T (see page 28).

Cycle Parts

The T100 oil tank's capacity was reduced from 8 to a catalogued 6 pints. Its previous chromed, hinged filler cap was replaced by a polished aluminium threaded one, and the oil tank was reshaped to fit in with the new air filter, all as on the 5T. Otherwise as 1949 5T (see page 28).

Electrical Equipment As 1949 5T (see page 28).

1949 brochure cover, T100

1949 Detachable rear mudguard and Mk I Spring Wheel

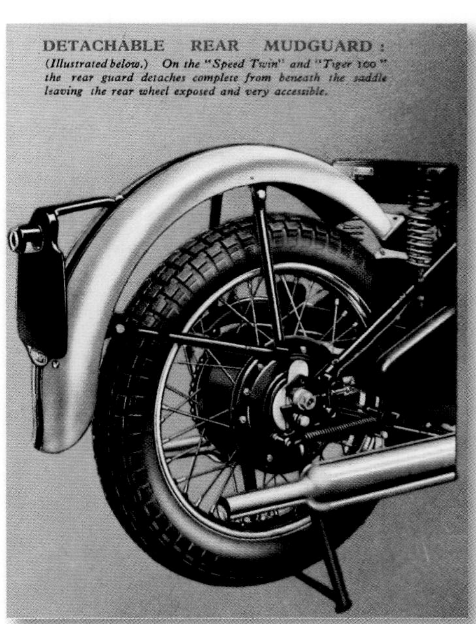

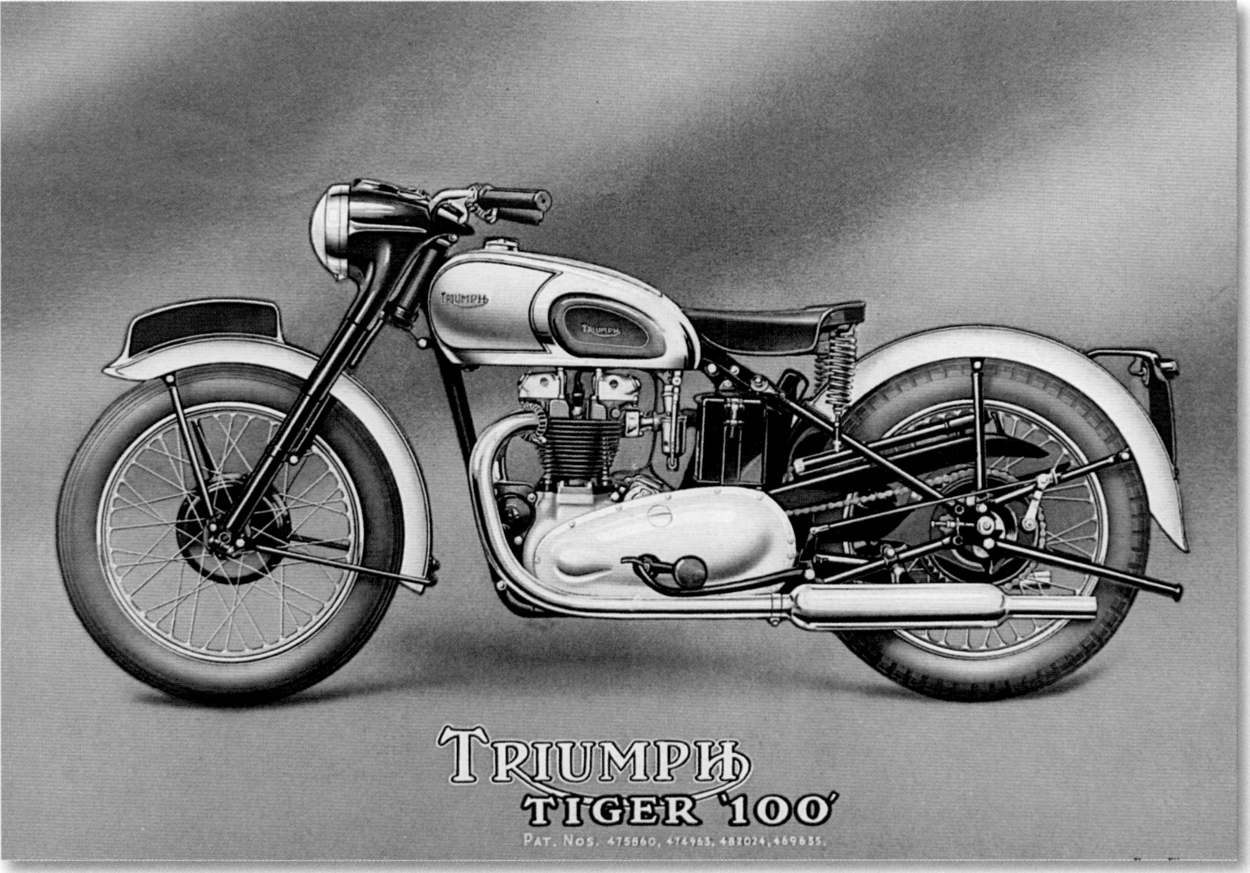

TRIUMPH FEATURES

The famous TRIUMPH
SPRING WHEEL
(Patent No. 524885)

This remarkable springing system has achieved great popularity in all parts of the world. It is essentially simple, efficient and reliable. The massive aluminium alloy hub shell totally encloses all the moving parts and attached to this is a powerful eight-inch brake. The Spring Wheel is mounted in the frame in exactly the same way as a normal wheel and adds a mere three per cent to the total weight of the machine.

HOW IT OPERATES. The spindle remains stationary bolted into the frame as usual while the wheel and hub move on a curved path taken from the centre of the gearbox sprocket which ensures that chain tension remains constant at all times. This movement is controlled by springs, two below the spindle and one above. Lubrication is by a single grease nipple.

PARCEL GRID (above).

A useful tank-top fitting available as an extra on all models. Chromium plated grid to which small parcels may be attached—particularly valuable to the long distance solo rider.

OTHER TRIUMPH FEATURES

The detachable rear mudguard fitted to the "Tiger 100" and "Speed Twin" is illustrated and described on Page Four. The Triumph instrument "Nacelle" is fully described and illustrated on Page Seven.

The Triumph TELESCOPIC FORK

With six inches of hydraulically damped movement these forks set a high standard of controllability and comfort. The sectioned drawing shows the internal arrangement. Note how long supple fork springs are enclosed inside the stanchions which enables these latter vital components to be of maximum possible diameter and strength. No adjustments of any kind have to be made by the rider and maintenance is reduced to checking the oil level every 10,000 miles.

PROP STAND (on left).

Available as an extra on all models. Attaches to the nearside cradle member of the frame. A spring retains the stand out as a prop or in the folded back position. Can be fitted to all Triumph models from 1937, state whether over or under 350 c.c. when ordering.

AIR CLEANER (on right).

Triumph design patented Vokes air cleaner. By means of a "transparent" oil tank the illustration shows how neatly this piece of equipment is fitted between the oil tank and battery. Very efficient oil-wetted muslin filament readily detachable for cleaning.

Page Eight

1949 details: Spring Wheel sectioned, tank grid, telescopic fork internals with '49-on nacelle, early air cleaner.

Optional Equipment

A 5-bar tank-top parcel grid became available. The Mk I Spring Wheel was modified. See 1949 5T (page 28) for details.

1950

With the coming of the Thunderbird 650, there were both styling and mechanical changes for the T100, with the petrol tank styling bands, plus the parcel grid as standard; and a new crankshaft assembly and gearbox.

Engine and Gearbox

The T100's flywheels were modified, as was its cylinder head, which had previously been in common with the 5T though with polished ports. For details of the other engine changes, and the new gearbox with its revised speedometer drive, see 1950 5T (page 29).

Frame and Suspension As 1950 5T (see page 29).

1950 T100

Cycle Parts As 1950 5T (see page 29).

Electrical Equipment As 1950 5T (see page 29).

Optional Equipment
The Mk II Spring Wheel was introduced; for details see 1950 5T (page 29). The flat, plain black Vynide-covered Twinseat was offered.

1951
This was the year when the T100's sporting potential truly began to blossom, with the adoption of a good-looking alloy cylinder head and barrel. An alloy top end had been used on Triumph's 1946-48 GP racer, only some 200 of which had been produced. They featured the modified wartime AAPP generator engine's alloy head and barrels, the latter still complete with their bosses on the right side of the cylinder block, originally for fastening a heat-guard on the generator. A version of this engine had then gone on the highly regarded dual-purpose 1949-on TR5 Trophy 500 twin. Now Triumph offered an all-new die-cast barrel and cylinder head – with splayed exhaust ports, and also distinguishable from the previous one by its less squared-off, closer-pitched fins, as well as by the lack of the bosses.

Even in standard form the new 32bhp alloy-engined T100 was good for 92mph on the poor fuel of the day, and there was now a further option, a £35 race kit to create what would be the twin-carb T100C (for "Convertible"). This transformed the T100 into a 40bhp 120mph racer, and one of them would win the 1952 Senior Clubman's TT, though both handling and the bottom end were stressed at the limit. Only for 1953 would Triumph offer the T100C as a complete motorcycle.

Until the 1954 coming of the 650 T110, this 500 was now Meriden's cutting edge, and much of the T110's engine technology would be pioneered by the T100.

1951 race-equipped T100

Engine and gearbox
The new cylinder head was of close-finned alloy, with splayed exhaust ports, larger inlet valves (going from $1\frac{5}{16}$in to $1\frac{7}{16}$in), cast-in Mehanite iron valve seats, and new steel screw-in exhaust pipe adaptors. The close-finned barrels originally came with cast-in steel liners, but very soon changed to centrifugally spun, replaceable liners of cast iron. For that year only, circular alloy tappet guide blocks were fitted, with valve clearances down to 2 and 4 thou. Pushrods became Duralumin to suit the alloy block's expansion rate. Also for 1951 only, the T100 had the TR5's pushrod tubes. A new type of tappet, interchangeable with the previous one, was fitted, with the foot induction-brazed on to reduce wear. The cam followers became Stellite-tipped.

The alloy pistons featured taper-faced second compression rings. Compression reduced slightly from 7.8:1 to 7.6:1. The flywheel and crankshaft assembly were now those of the 6T, as were the stronger connecting rods; the 5T had the same, but the T100's assembly and rods were claimed to be polished.

The T100's inlet manifold head studs adopted a new form, with the upper pair spread out further than the lower.

The T100's clutch also adopted the 6T's extra pair of plates to become 6-plate, with a deeper clutch centre and longer springs to match.

The "Rev-o-lator'"speedometer, as on the other nacelle models, changed the zero position of its needle from 1 o'clock to 7 o'clock, so that the 30-70mph segment would be easier to read.

Frame and Suspension
The front frame reverted to the 1948 type, identifiable by a top seat tube clip on the left; this allowed the fitting of a new additional front cylinder head steady. The rear frame was also modified to take stronger rear wheel and chain adjusters. There were additional lugs to take the T100C kit's higher level rearset footrests, and to accommodate the toolbox's new higher position, above the upper chainstay.

Cycle Parts
As on the 5T and 6T, a new welded oil tank with a more angled filler and a bayonet-type cap was fitted.

The T100's petrol tank for this year had twin larger-bore

petrol taps and, like the other models, a bayonet-type filler cap. The parcel grid was now fitted to all models as standard. The T100 adopted the Twinseat as standard, with its black Vynide cover.

The spoking on the front wheel was altered.

A new exhaust system was fitted to suit the T100's splayed heads and their steel screw-in adaptors, and welded-on tags were now incorporated below the front of the exhaust pipes, to marry with new chromed brackets attached to the engine front plate lower mounting stud.

The T100's toolbox, repositioned above the upper chainstay, gained a quick-release fastener for its lid.

The front brake, as on the 5T and 6T, gained a more rigid cast iron drum.

Electrical equipment

The T100 adopted manual advance/retard control for its magneto, via a lever on the left of the handlebars. (The instrument was catalogued as a BTH KC2, but Lucas K2F magnetos also appear to have been used at this time.)

Optional Equipment

The racing kit came in either CP 100 form, with 8.25:1 pistons, or CP 101 with 9.5:1 pistons for use with high octane gasoline or petrol/benzol mixture. The kit consisted of the pistons with rings, a pair of racing camshafts, racing valve springs, twin Amal Type 6 carburettors with a dual inlet manifold and a remote float chamber, dual throttle cables with a junction box, racing-type braided petrol pipes, a Smiths 8000rpm rev-counter driven by using the dynamo fitting and by gearing the right-angle box to the exhaust camshaft, an 8-pint oil tank, racing exhaust pipes with megaphones, a folding footrest, a dropped racing handlebar, a racing plate, a shortened rear brake rod, a folding-pedal kickstart, and a gasket set.

Close ratio gears, and a range of sprockets, were also available, as were alloy mudguards.

High-rise "Flanders" handlebars were introduced for US models.

1952

Engine and Gearbox

1951's alloy tappet block guide reverted to cast iron, and was used with the 1950-type pushrod cover tubes complete with bosses for the oil drain pipes.

For other changes see 1952 5T (page 31).

Frame and Suspension

The T100 frame was now standardised with the new one for the 5T, with a hole in the seat tube for the new air filter. For details on this and on changes to the nacelle, see 1952 5T (page 31).

1951 T100

Cycle Parts

For the T100 there was a change of section for the front portion of its rear mudguard. The T100's left footrest was modified. Otherwise, see 1952 5T (page 31).

Electrical Equipment

As 1952 5T, with from eng. no. 19706NA, the 6 volt system changing from negative to positive earth.

The Lucas K2F RO magneto with manually controlled

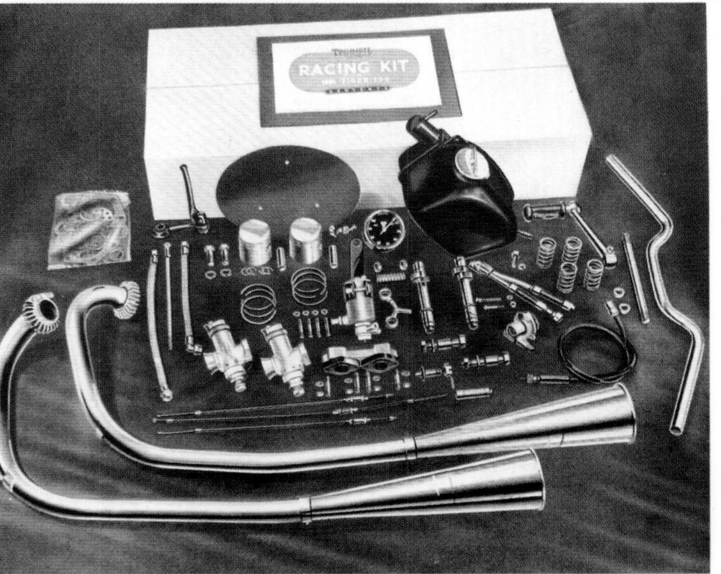

TIGER 100
RACING KIT

Comprises the following :—

(1) PISTONS. Complete with rings. Choice of Compression Ratios—see page 28.
(2) CAMSHAFTS. Two, racing lift type.
(3) VALVE SPRINGS. Four pairs racing type, inner and outer.
(4) CARBURETTERS. Two Amal Type 6 complete with special dual manifold and 'remote' float chamber.
(5) Dual THROTTLE CABLES with junction box.
(6) PETROL PIPES. Two racing type, flexible.
(7) TACHOMETER. Smiths 8000 R.P.M. with cable drive and gearbox.
(8) OIL TANK one gallon capacity with quick release filler cap.
(9) EXHAUST PIPES. Two small diameter with megaphones.
(10) FOOTREST. One folding pattern.
(11) HANDLEBAR. Racing type.
(12) NUMBER PLATE. One regulation oval pattern with brackets.
(13) BRAKE ROD. One short rear.
(14) KICKSTARTER with folding pedal.
(15) JOINTING WASHERS AND GASKETS. One complete set.

Note. All the above parts are available separately, if required, from the Service Department at usual list prices. Also available are Close Ratio Gears and Racing type alloy Mudguards.

4

Original race kit, first offered for 1951

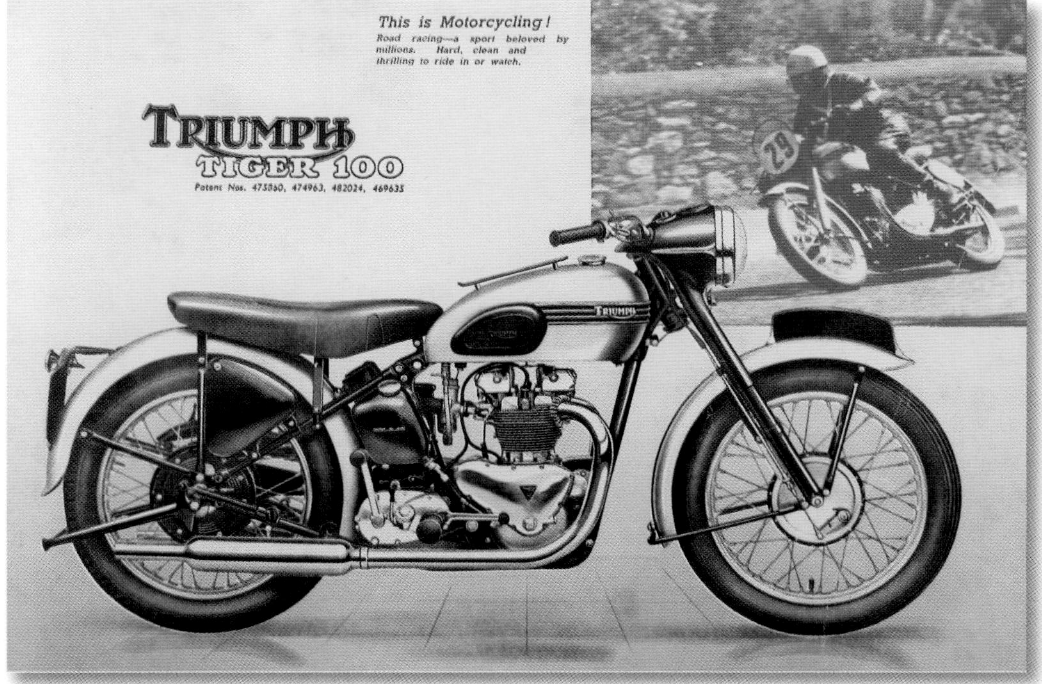

Neat and trim, the 1952 Tiger 100, with all-alloy engine since 1951, had evolved into a thoroughly modern sportster, poised-looking in no-nonsense black and silver. The black nacelle, this year with underslung pilot light, with its chrome flashes and pullback handlebars, actively enhanced the impression of speed. This fine example from the A.R.E. collection again features its twinned petrol taps sourced from a later period, and an incorrectly chromed, not painted, rear stand spring. As a 1952 model, originally some chromed parts might well have been painted or cadmium-plated (see Appendix A for details), due to nickel shortages from the Korean War – but very few twins were kept that way once the shortages had passed. A thoroughly desirable motorcycle, and Triumph's cutting edge at that time.

advance/retard appears to have completely replaced the BTH instrument by the end of this model year.

Optional Equipment

The CP 100 racing kit's pistons now gave 8.5:1 compression. Also a new cast iron cylinder barrel was available with 12:1 compression ratio pistons for use with alcohol fuel. 8.0:1 pistons were available on the standard roadster for US export.

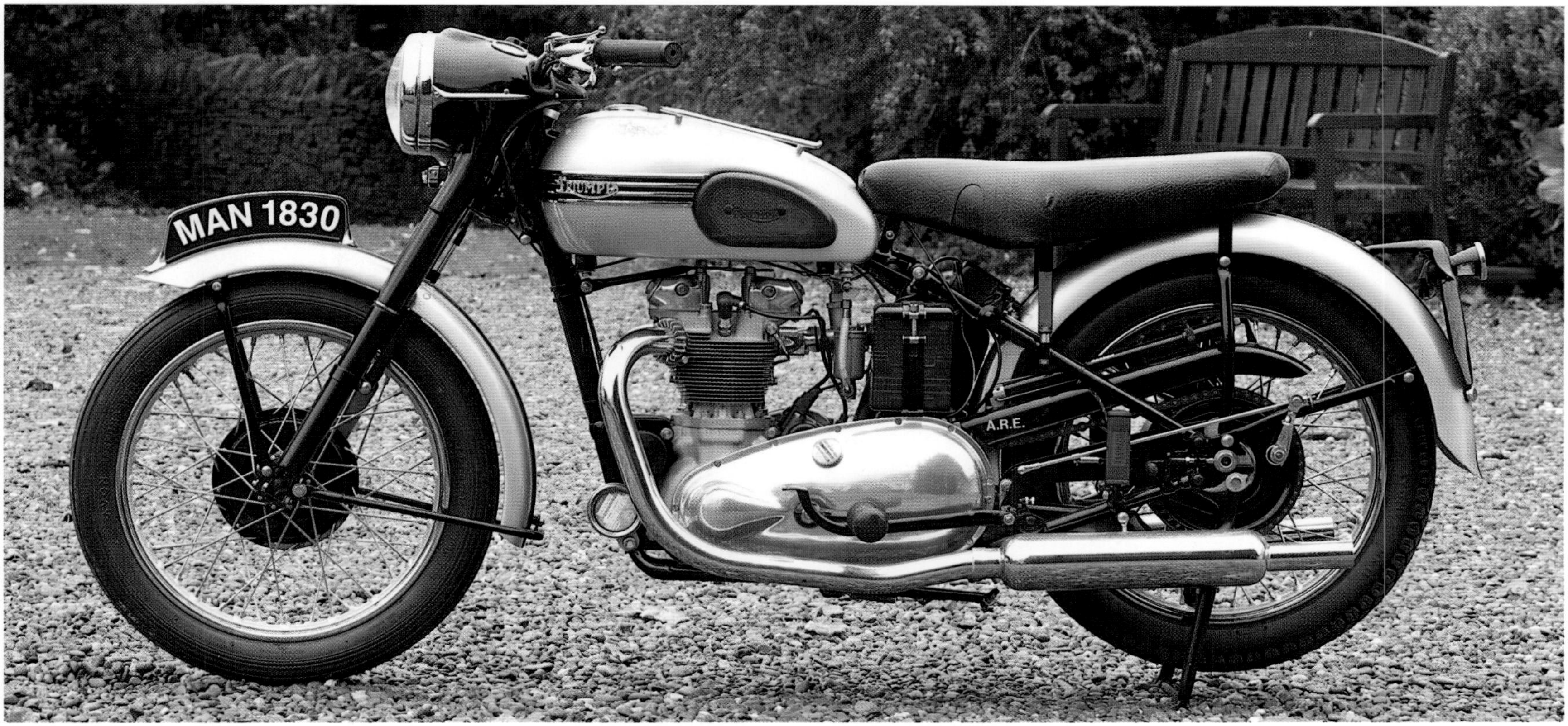
MAN 1830
A.R.E.

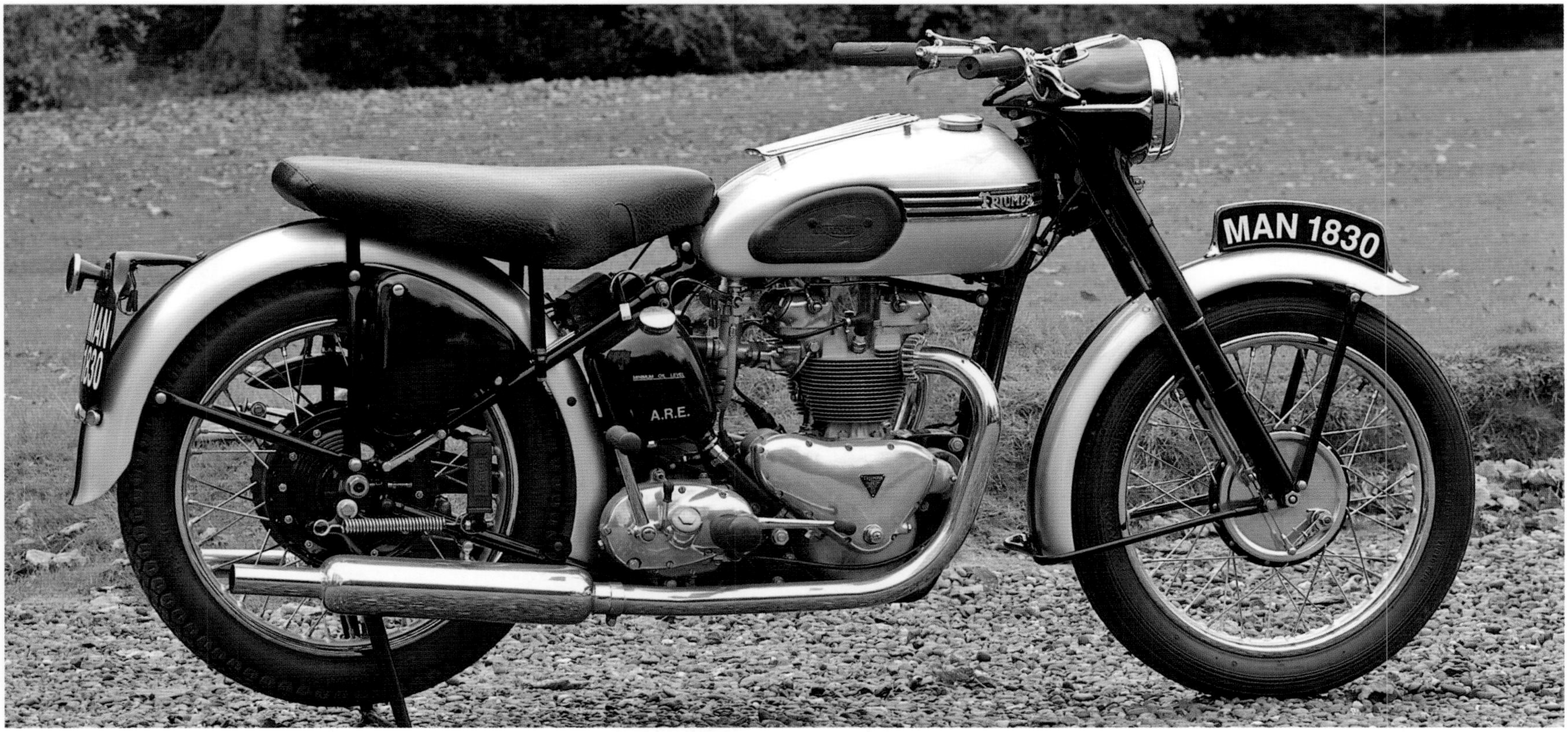
MAN 1830
MAN 1830
A.R.E.

1952 T100. Close-finned die-cast alloy barrel and head adopted for 1951, with splayed ports for the 1¾in exhausts, made for an exceptionally handsome engine.

1952 T100. The gearbox had been redesigned and strengthened internally for 1950 with the coming of the 650 6T.

1 FRONT BRAKE. Exceptionally powerful with new cast iron drum.

2 FRONT NUMBER PLATE. Unique Triumph design; no sharp edges.

3 TELESCOPIC FRONT FORK. For comfort and first class steering.

4 NACELLE. Streamlines lamp and instruments into easy-clean shell.

5 FRAME. Rigid cradle type for good handling at high and low speeds.

6 TIMING COVER. Highly polished, easy to clean, smart appearance.

10 PARCEL GRID. Unique Triumph feature. Ideal for light baggage.

11 TRIUMPH TWIN-SEAT. For solo and pillion riding. Luxurious latex foam.

12 TOOL BOX. Ample room for standard tool kit and extra items.

13 REAR MUDGUARD. Detaches in one piece from behind the saddle.

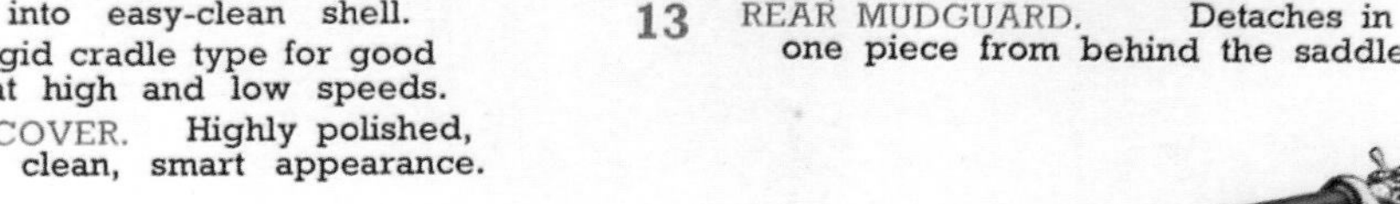

TRIUMPH FEATURES FOR BETTER RIDING

7 GEARBOX Designed for fast changing with a particularly sweet and light clutch.

8 AIR CLEANER. The answer to dust; neat and unobtrusive.

9 PETROL TANK. A smooth easily-cleaned tank of large capacity.

14 SPRING WHEEL. Comfortable ride at all speeds. Powerful 8″ brake.

15 SILENCERS. Reduce exhaust note with minimum of back pressure.

16 REAR NUMBER PLATE. Triumph design with lifting handle combined.

1952 T100

1952 T100. Amal 276 carburettor with separate float chamber on left.

1952 T100. Mk II Spring Wheel, which would fit in any rigid Triumph twin, and detail of barrel-shaped silencer. The spring should be black-painted.

1952 T100. Post-war pressed steel brake and clutch levers, but still chrome-plated for Tiger 100

1952 T100. This new old stock Smiths speedo still carries original sticker relating to US "break-in" (running-in) period.

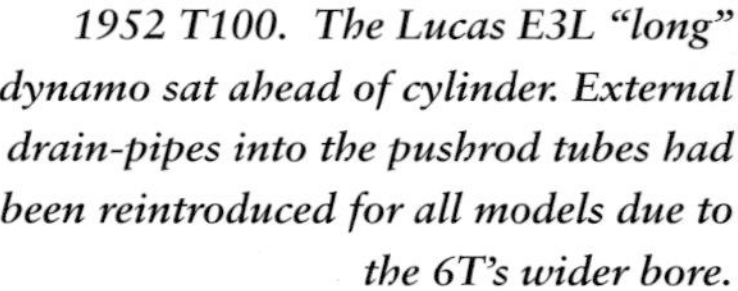

1952 T100. The Lucas E3L "long" dynamo sat ahead of cylinder. External drain-pipes into the pushrod tubes had been reintroduced for all models due to the 6T's wider bore.

1952 T100. The long lever on the left bar was for manually controlled advance/retard on the magneto ignition.

1952 T100. The underslung pilot light was introduced for 1952. Note also the neat tube guiding the cable for the 7in single leading shoe front brake along the off-side fork leg, with cable adjustment at its base

1952 T100. The Lucas MCF700 7in sealed beam headlight adopted for 1952, and another look at the underslung pilot light.

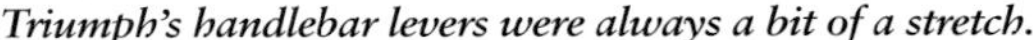

Triumph's handlebar levers were always a bit of a stretch.

Toolbox position had been raised for 1951. Blue lining of the central strips on wheels and mudguards was a faint echo of the original finish.

TRIUMPH
The Best Motorcycle in the World
well known in the Isle
other famous circuits.

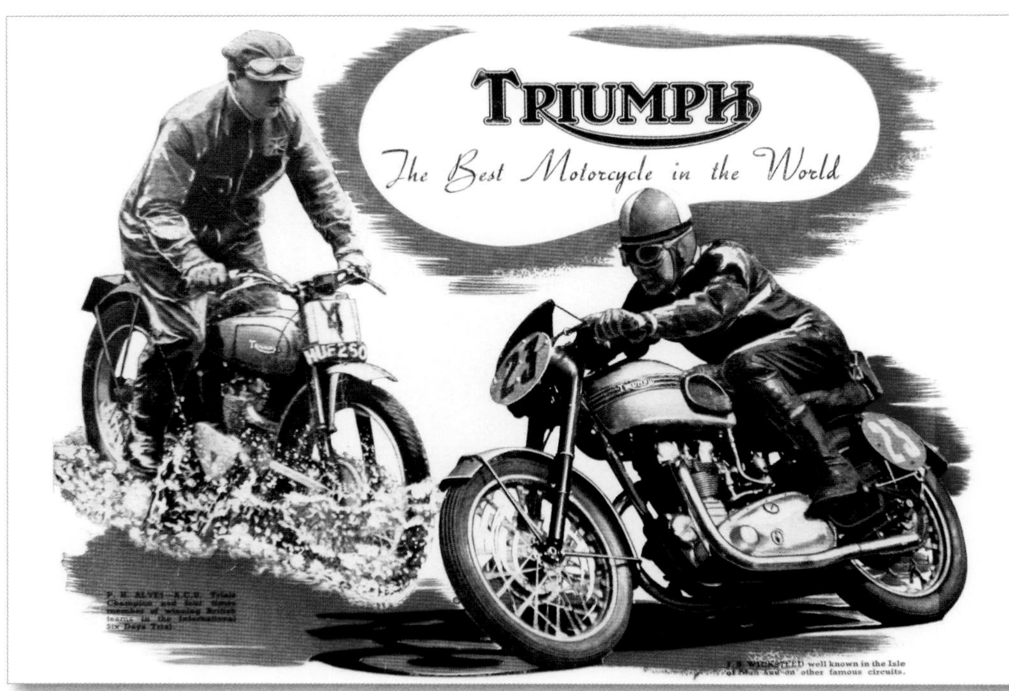

1953

The T100 became further removed from the cooking 5T with the latter's adoption, for this year onwards, of alternator electrics. Not only was the T100's self-contained magneto ignition system more reliable, but its dynamo could be removed while competing. This model's sporting character was emphasised by the offer, for that year only, of the T100C semi-racer variant. The latter came with twin carburettors, the legendary E3134 camshafts for both inlet and exhaust, and 8.0:1 compression pistons.

Engine and Gearbox

On the standard T100 as on the 5T, from eng. no. 37560 (16 February 1953), camshafts coded E3275 were fitted, featuring quietening ramps. Their presence was identified by a small "spoked wheel" logo stamped beside the engine number, and they required tappet clearances reduced from 0.020 to 0.010.

On the T100C, the twin carburettors had bell-mouths fitted, with no air filters.

For further engine changes, other than the crankshaft adaptation to an alternator, see 1953 5T (page 36). The T100's

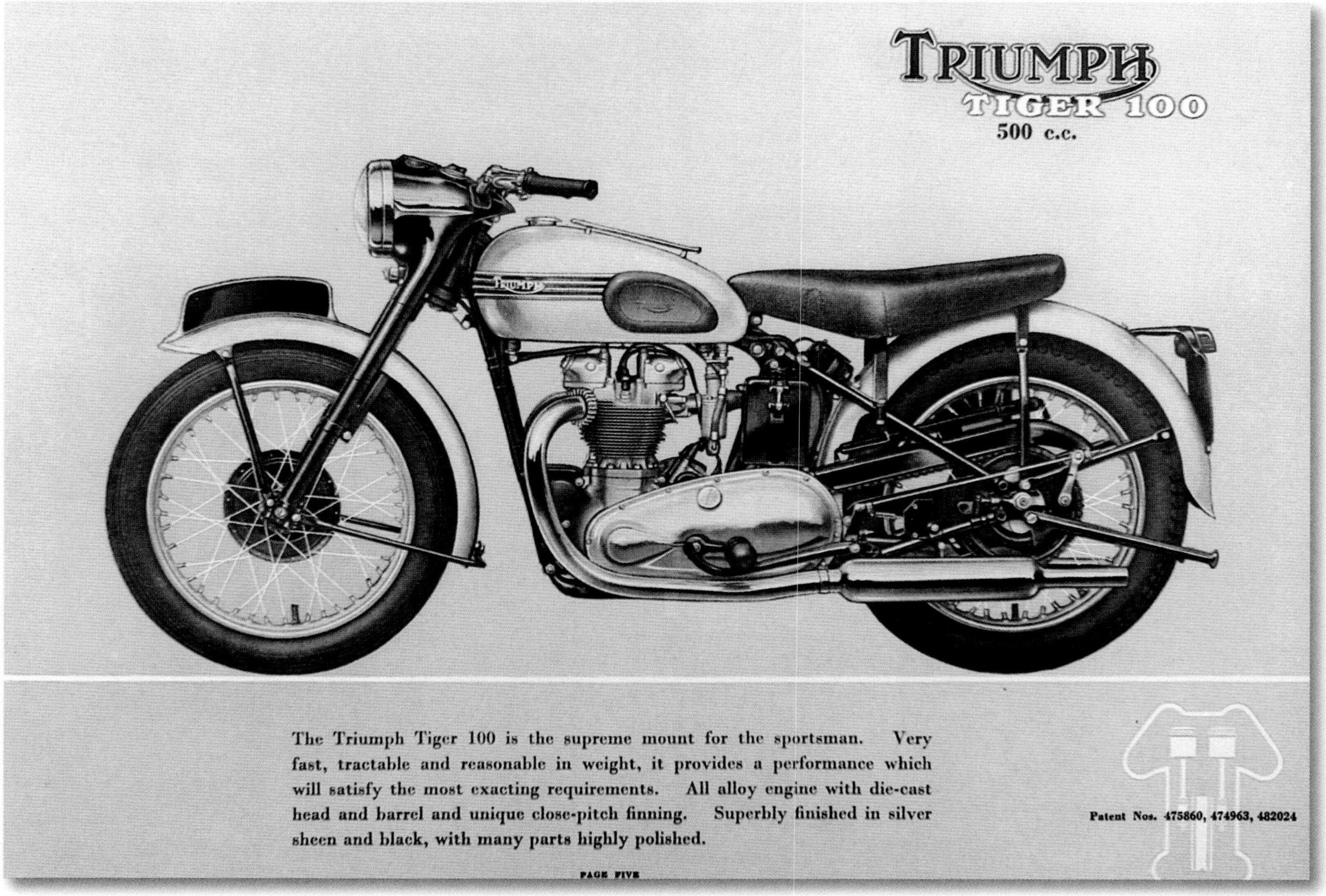
TRIUMPH
TIGER 100
500 c.c.
The Triumph Tiger 100 is the supreme mount for the sportsman. Very fast, tractable and reasonable in weight, it provides a performance which will satisfy the most exacting requirements. All alloy engine with die-cast head and barrel and unique close-pitch finning. Superbly finished in silver sheen and black, with many parts highly polished.
Patent Nos. 475860, 474963, 482024
PAGE FIVE

1953 T100

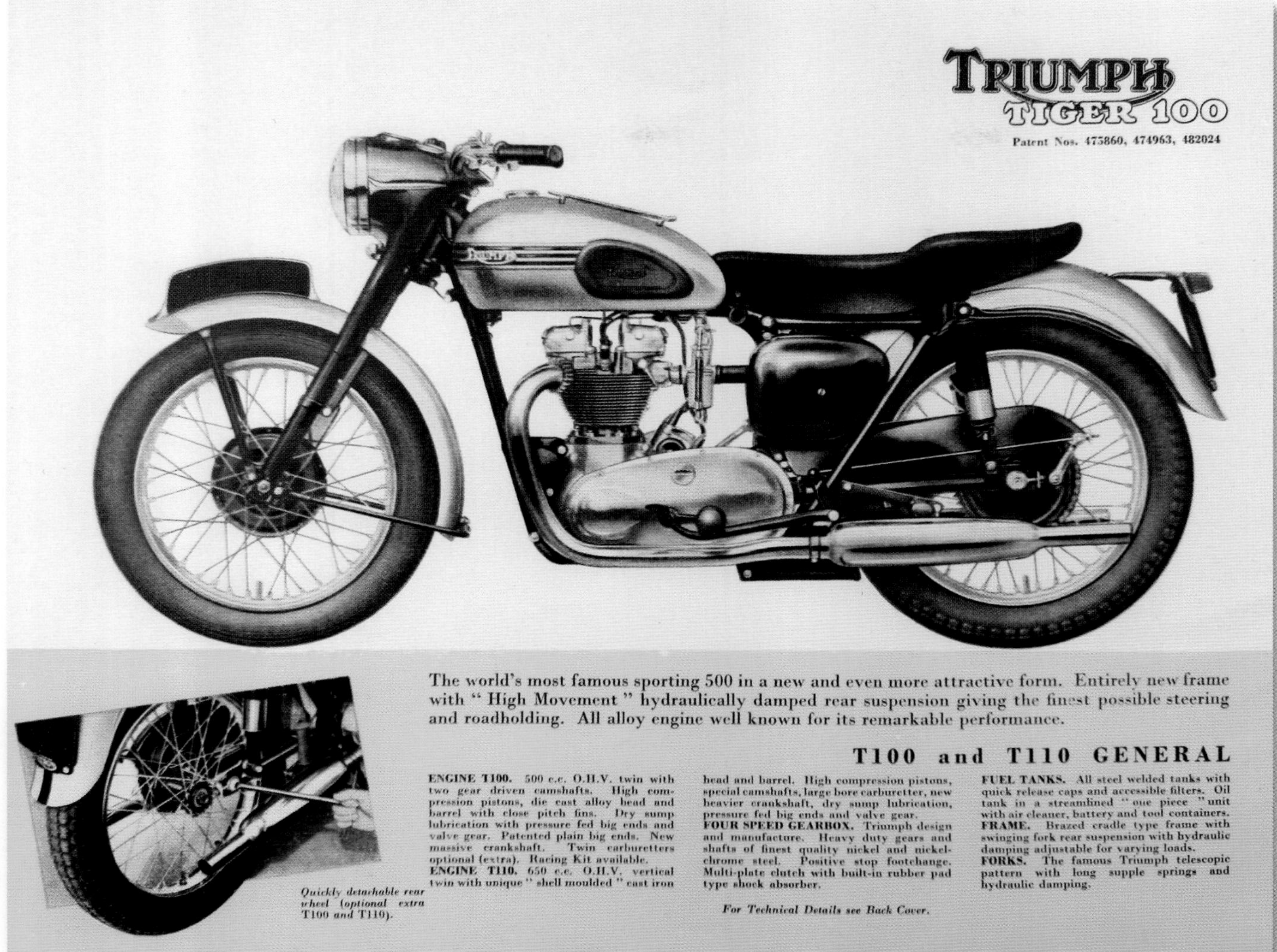

1954 T100

crankcases were not modified as the 5T's were for that year to suit the alternator, but it did adopt the new vane-type shock absorber on the clutch.

Frame and Suspension As 1953 5T (page 36).

Cycle Parts

The T100C was fitted with the 8-pint oil tank, which incorporated a quick-release "butterfly" filler cap, and an anti-froth tower.

The T100's rear number plate was altered to take the new tail light. The rear brake rod operated a stop-switch for it, which was fixed to a plate fastened on the nearside pillion footrest bolt.

Electrical Equipment

A new, rectangular Lucas 525 "Diacon" stop-tail light was fitted.

Optional Equipment

Close- and wide-ratio gear sets, and conversion kits for them, were offered. This was the last year that the full racing kits were available.

1954

This was a major change year for the T100, which the model celebrated by adopting a beautiful finish of Shell Blue Sheen. Triumph used the advent of the sports 650 T110 to introduce their swinging-arm frame, in conjunction with the "big bearing" motor. The T100 benefited from both, with its catalogued weight only going up from 365 to 375lb. Seat height did however rise from 27¾in to 30½in. The T100C had been discontinued, although twin-carb kits were still an option for the T100. The sprung frame was a big step forward, even if its unbraced swinging-arm could still cause alarming handling at speed.

Engine and Gearbox

On the pistons, chrome-faced second compression rings were fitted.

The new crankshaft and flywheel assembly from the T110 650 were fitted, with a stiffened-up crankshaft featuring increased shaft diameters; for the T100, however, the assembly was no longer polished. The crankshaft ran in a larger (1⅛in) SM11 ball journal on the timing side, with just a clamping washer between the race and the timing gear, thus dispensing with the previous circlip, inboard disk and chip shield. The con rod journals on the shaft were enlarged to 1⅝in to take the H-section alloy rods, which were polished; their bearings remained white metal-lined.

The need soon emerged to fit a sludge trap within the new crank journals. Early traps consisted of a simple vented tube within the central chambers. From eng. no. 56811 (24 August 1954) the new assembly gained a permanent sludge trap, pressed into, and located within, machined counter-bores within the cranks themselves.

Within a new primary chaincase, the inner case now carried a breather pipe boss forward of the nearside footrest hanger rod, and a modified cast guard around the gearbox shaft, so that the guard was no longer of a constant radius and semi-circular, but shaped a little.

The primary chain itself, within a shorter chaincase, was shortened to 70 pitches, as the gearbox had been brought closer to the crankcase to keep the swinging-arm twins' overall length down. That required new rear chain plates, and the previous lower chainguard was deleted, with the tyre inflator now fitted on pegs beneath the petrol tank. The gearbox shell was modified to suit, losing the previous gear indicator and gaining a new pedal, and its clamping screw and adjusting screw were made more accessible.

The carburettor choke was now controlled via a short cable by a lever mounted on the nearside rear frame top stay, beneath the Twinseat.

Frame and Suspension

The chassis, while all-new, nevertheless resembled the previous one in featuring a tapered single front downtube and a full cradle, but with a new brazed lug tubular rear frame, supporting 3-position Girling rear units. The springs in the latter were initially 110lb giving 4 inches of movement, but were stiffened in mid-year with 126lb springs giving 2½in of movement, with increased internal rebound damping and the use of bump stops.

The front fork springs became 20in long. The rear fork arms were Oilite-bushed at their far ends, and pivoted on a spindle pressed into a frame lug at the base of the saddle tube, with side play controlled by shims on the right side, and lubrication via an (inaccessible) grease nipple. This swinging-arm was, famously, unbraced.

Cycle Parts

A "Streamstyle" one-piece mid-frame unit now incorporated the toolbox, with Dzus fastener for its lid, the D-shaped Vokes air cleaner, the battery and a new oil tank catalogued at 6 pints but only holding 5.

The new frame was fitted with Triumph's first centre stand. The Twinseat was also revised, becoming a broader and a little longer two-level type, still black but with white piping around its top portion. The silencers changed to tapering "absorption" type, in a tear-drop style based on that of the lightweight 150cc Terriers. These were attached to the rear frame pillion footrest support bracket, and from frame no. 51200 this was modified on the nearside.

A new deeper-valanced one-piece rear mudguard was fitted.

At the front came an 8in single leading shoe brake with a cast iron drum, and a polished aluminium anchor plate with a chrome wire mesh-covered air scoop, plus a rear vent and for that year only, a scalloped, wavy drum side spoke flange. The rear wheel was offered in two guises. The standard one was as previously except that it now featured revised head angle spoking, and its former adjustable taper roller bearings were replaced by journal ball bearings. A previous-type anchor plate with its square peg sliding location within the left rear fork end was used, and the former rear brake anchor plate torque stay discarded. The QD (quickly detachable) wheel was optional.

The rear brake pedal lost its previous rubber pad, and became a single forging for the pedal arm, pivot bush and rod arm, with the rod end no longer forked, but bent and secured by a split pin. This assembly was modified at frame no. 51200.

Electrical Equipment

A Lucas RB107 cut-out voltage regulator was now fitted. The battery became a Lucus PU7E-9. The nacelle's light switch changed from Lucas 351584A to Lucas 31371B. At eng. no. 51200, the stop-light switch for the 525 Diacon rear light changed from Lucas 31437A to Lucas 31383. All magnetos were now Lucas K2F, and were modified within, adopting a brush located in the rear of the points plate.

Optional Equipment

Valanced front mudguards, with the stays formed in one and riveted to the guard, were offered.

A new QD rear wheel was introduced, with taper roller bearings within the hub. As on the standard wheel, it carried a pressed steel anchor plate with a squared peg sliding location within the swinging-arm's fork end.

Twin carburettors remained available, but not the racing kit or its other components.

1955 T100

*"Tiger 100" in action.
("Motor Cycling" Photo.)*

Famous for its performance in all fields of motorcycle activity, the Triumph "Tiger 100" has everything the enthusiast demands—speed, acceleration, brakes, suspension—plus the sleek good looks expected of a real thoroughbred.

T100 and T110 GENERAL

ENGINE T100. 500 c.c. O.H.V. twin with two gear-driven camshafts. High compression pistons, die-cast alloy head and barrel with close pitch fins. Dry sump lubrication with pressure-fed big ends and valve gear. Patented plain big ends. Twin carburetters optional (extra). Racing conversion parts available.

ENGINE T110. 650 c.c. O.H.V. vertical twin with cast iron head and barrel. High compression pistons, special camshafts, large bore carburetter, dry sump lubrication, pressure-fed big ends and valve gear.

FOUR-SPEED GEARBOX. Triumph design and manufacture. Heavy duty gears and shafts of finest quality nickel and nickel-chrome steel. Positive stop footchange. Multi-plate clutch with built-in rubber pad type shock absorber.

FUEL TANKS. All-steel welded tanks with quick release caps and accessible filters. Oil tank in a streamlined "one piece" unit with air cleaner, battery and tool containers.

FRAME. Brazed cradle type frame with swinging arm rear suspension with hydraulic damping adjustable for varying loads.

FORKS. The famous Triumph telescopic pattern with long supple springs and hydraulic damping.

PAGE EIGHT

1955

Engine and Gearbox

Compression for all T100s was raised from 7.6:1 to the American export machines' 8.0:1.

In the gearbox, due to locating problems, the pre-war camplate locating plunger was reintroduced. The kickstart quadrant was now made of nickel-steel chrome. The kickstart's ratchet spring and sleeve were changed, and their associated thrust washer deleted.

The single carburettor became the long-running Amal Type 376 Monobloc in 15/16in size (for the twin carbs, see Optional Equipment below). The choke reverted to a spring-loaded plunger within the carburettor itself. The existing D-shaped Vokes air filter was modified slightly to accommodate that year's revised oil tank.

Frame and suspension

The frame now had sidecar lugs. There were fittings for an optional new and more accessible prop-stand, and for a newly adopted rear brake plate torque arm's forward fixing point, on the swinging-arm.

The front fork stem was somewhat stiffened by fitting 3/8in clamp bolts in the lower fork crown, in place of the previous 5/16in.

Cycle Parts

The oil tank's internal construction was modified to overcome a cracking problem on its inner wall.

The nacelle was modified progressively during the year, now incorporating the pilot light, so that the deleted light beneath the nacelle was replaced by a small oval chromed grille.

The front brake's scalloped spoke flange became a plain constant diameter one, after fractures across the scalloped flanges had occurred. The rear wheel adopted a new, threaded, brake torque stay locating stud in its anchor plate, to take the rear end of the new stay, with the previous square

Though its flagship position had been taken over by the 1954-on T110 650, in 1956 the Tiger 100, unique with its optional twin carb set-up, was still an exciting motorcycle. And as this example demonstrates, a handsome one, with its Shell Blue Sheen and Black finish and shapely 8in front brake with air scoop. The high-speed handling from the spindly forks and unbraced swinging-arm may still have been hairy, but the engine's combination of thrilling urge and sweetness shone through.

1956 brochure cover: T100 surveying Coventry

peg in the anchor plate deleted.

The exhaust system now had chromed bracing stays on each side, from the base of the frame's seat tube bottom lug to each silencer entry clip. At eng. no. 64324, the stays were strengthened.

The toolbox lid was no longer secured by a Dzus fastener but by a screw-in one.

Marque expert and former Meriden man Jim Lee believes that this year painted wheel centres ceased to be the standard finish, but could still be had to special order until the end of 1956.

Electrical Equipment

A new Lucas 564 stop-tail lamp, incorporating reflectors, was adopted, along with a Lucas 22B stop-lamp switch.

Optional Equipment

A new, more accessible prop-stand was offered.

For US models, 3.6 US gallon (3 Imperial gallons) petrol tanks were available.

Twin carburettors were still an option, remaining Amal Type 6 with the remote float chamber.

1956

Engine and Gearbox

The previous white metal big end linings were replaced by Vandervell VP3 steel-backed shell bearing inserts. The big end eye was enlarged and the balance factor adjusted.

The depth of the T100's alloy cylinder barrel's liner spigot was reduced from $\frac{3}{16}$in to $\frac{1}{8}$in protrusion, with the spigot bore depth into the cylinder head reduced accordingly. This was to prevent the protruding ring of liner breaking off, and to improve the combustion chamber.

For gearbox and clutch changes, see 1956 5T (page 40).

Frame and Suspension As 1956 5T (see page 42).

Cycle Parts As 1956 5T (see page 43).

Electrical Equipment

As 1956 5T (see page 43).

Optional Equipment

The Lucas Type 42051 "Wader" magneto, or alternatively the Lucas K2FC sports "red label" magneto, were offered as options.

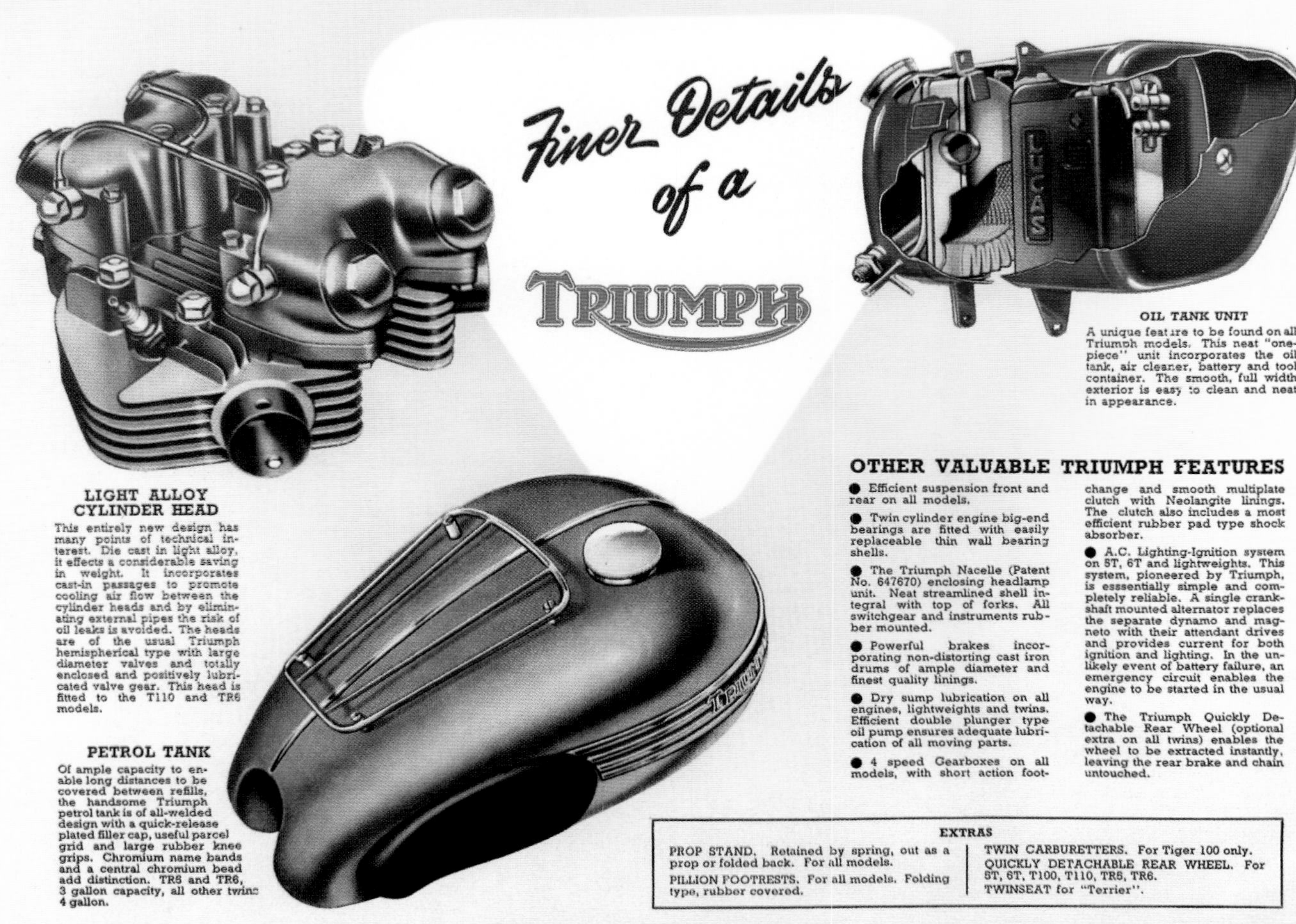

Finer Details of a TRIUMPH

LIGHT ALLOY CYLINDER HEAD

This entirely new design has many points of technical interest. Die cast in light alloy, it effects a considerable saving in weight. It incorporates cast-in passages to promote cooling air flow between the cylinder heads and by eliminating external pipes the risk of oil leaks is avoided. The heads are of the usual Triumph hemispherical type with large diameter valves and totally enclosed and positively lubricated valve gear. This head is fitted to the T110 and TR6 models.

PETROL TANK

Of ample capacity to enable long distances to be covered between refills, the handsome Triumph petrol tank is of all-welded design with a quick-release plated filler cap, useful parcel grid and large rubber knee grips. Chromium name bands and a central chromium bead add distinction. TR5 and TR6, 3 gallon capacity, all other twins 4 gallon.

OIL TANK UNIT

A unique feature to be found on all Triumph models. This neat "one-piece" unit incorporates the oil tank, air cleaner, battery and tool container. The smooth, full width exterior is easy to clean and neat in appearance.

OTHER VALUABLE TRIUMPH FEATURES

- Efficient suspension front and rear on all models.
- Twin cylinder engine big-end bearings are fitted with easily replaceable thin wall bearing shells.
- The Triumph Nacelle (Patent No. 647670) enclosing headlamp unit. Neat streamlined shell integral with top of forks. All switchgear and instruments rubber mounted.
- Powerful brakes incorporating non-distorting cast iron drums of ample diameter and finest quality linings.
- Dry sump lubrication on all engines, lightweights and twins. Efficient double plunger type oil pump ensures adequate lubrication of all moving parts.
- 4 speed Gearboxes on all models, with short action foot-change and smooth multiplate clutch with Neolangite linings. The clutch also includes a most efficient rubber pad type shock absorber.
- A.C. Lighting-Ignition system on 5T, 6T and lightweights. This system, pioneered by Triumph, is esssentially simple and completely reliable. A single crankshaft mounted alternator replaces the separate dynamo and magneto with their attendant drives and provides current for both ignition and lighting. In the unlikely event of battery failure, an emergency circuit enables the engine to be started in the usual way.
- The Triumph Quickly Detachable Rear Wheel (optional extra on all twins) enables the wheel to be extracted instantly, leaving the rear brake and chain untouched.

EXTRAS

PROP STAND. Retained by spring, out as a prop or folded back. For all models.

PILLION FOOTRESTS. For all models. Folding type, rubber covered.

TWIN CARBURETTERS. For Tiger 100 only.

QUICKLY DETACHABLE REAR WHEEL. For 5T, 6T, T100, T110, TR5, TR6.

TWINSEAT for "Terrier".

1956 details: T110 alloy cylinder head, 6T 1956 petrol tank and 4-bar grid, 5T central unit with battery/air cleaner.

1956 T100. Broader, more comfortable two-level Twinseat still looked good.

1956 T100. The headlamp and nacelle were revised for this year.

1956 T100 & T110

THE two Tiger models (500 c.c. T100 and 650 c.c. T110) offer the highest possible performance together with all the other features essential for fast and safe riding. First class suspension front and rear, immensely powerful brakes and outstanding ease of control make these models first choice of the sporting rider.

TRIUMPH TIGER 110

Patent Nos. 475860, 474963, 482024

The Little Mermaid watching over the shipping in busy Copenhagen Harbour, Denmark.

TRIUMPH TIGER 100

Patent Nos. 475860, 474963, 482024

TIGER 100 POWER CURVES

This graph shows the power available from the T100 engine in three conditions:— (a) Standard. (b) In racing trim with silencers, electrical equipment, etc. (c) Stripped with open pipes.

The "Motor Cycle"

T100 and T110 GENERAL SPECIFICATION

ENGINE T100. 500 c.c. O.H.V. twin with two gear-driven camshafts. High compression pistons, die-cast head and barrel with close pitch fins. Dry sump lubrication with pressure-fed big ends and valve gear. Patented plain big ends. Twin carburetters optional (extra). Racing conversion parts available.

ENGINE T110. 650 c.c. O.H.V. vertical twin with light alloy cylinder head of new and advanced design. Cast iron barrel. High compression pistons, special camshafts, large bore carburetter, dry sump lubrication, pressure-fed big ends and valve gear.

FOUR-SPEED GEARBOX. Triumph design and manufacture. Heavy duty gears and shafts of finest quality nickel and nickel-chrome steel. Positive stop footchange. Multi-plate clutch with Neolangite linings and built-in rubber pad type shock absorber.

FUEL TANKS. All-steel welded tanks with quick-release caps and accessible filters. Oil tank in a streamlined "one piece" unit with air cleaner, battery and tool containers.

FRAME. Brazed cradle type frame with swinging arm rear suspension with hydraulic damping instantly adjustable for varying loads.

FORKS. The famous Triumph telescopic pattern with long supple springs and hydraulic damping.

BRAKES. Cast iron drums, large diameter front brake with ventilating scoops and highly polished anchor plate.

WHEELS. Triumph design with chromium plated spokes and wheel rims. Dunlop tyres. Fully valanced rear mudguard with side lifting handles.

ELECTRICAL EQUIPMENT. Powerful Lucas 7-in. headlamp with combined reflector/front lens assembly, "pre-focus" bulb and adjustable rim. Lucas 6 volt 60 watt dynamo with full ball-bearing armature, automatic voltage control and 12 a.h. battery. Wide angle rear/stop light, and reflector. Gear-driven magneto.

NACELLE. Triumph Patent design. Imposing streamlined shell integral with top of forks, encloses headlamp, instruments and switch-gear. All instruments rubber-mounted and internally illuminated.

SPEEDOMETER. Smiths 120 m.p.h. (or 180 km.p.h.) chronometric type with r.p.m. scale, internal illumination and trip recorder.

OTHER DETAILS. Complete kit of good quality tools and grease-gun; Triumph "Two-level" Twinseat, latex foam covered black waterproof Vynide, white piping; tank top parcel grid; shell-blue sheen and black finish.

!956 T100. Ignition remained by Lucas K2F magneto, positioned as ever behind the handsome close-finned alloy barrels.

1956 T100. Alloy cylinder head's splayed exhausts, still large diameter.

1956 T100. Inside the 1956 gearbox, layshaft bushes, shock absorber rubbers and clutch plates were modified. Note the oil pressure "tell-tale" button on the timing side case below the patent plate.

1956 T100. Triumph primary chaincases were probably the handsomest in the business.

1956 T100. Amal Monobloc carb had arrived the previous year.

1956 T100. Central housing for the air filter/battery/oil tank, with the latter modified internally that year against cracking. Petrol taps are correct for year.

1956 T100. With the pilot light moved inside the headlamp, its previous position was now filled with a chromed grille.

1956 T100. Advance/retard lever, on left side of typically unclut-tered Triumph 1-inch handlebars.

1956 T100. Slinky tear-drop shape "resonator" silencers made beautiful music on song. The unbraced swinging-arm featured hard-to-lubricate bushes.

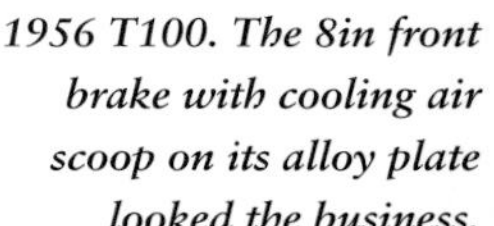

1956 T100. The 8in front brake with cooling air scoop on its alloy plate looked the business.

500 c.c. TWINS

TIGER 100

The 500 c.c. Tiger 100 has an engine specially designed for really high performance. The cylinder head and barrel are of aluminium alloy and with high compression pistons (8 to 1) 32 B.H.P. is produced. For those who require even higher performance than this, a new two-carburetter cylinder head is offered. The Tiger 100 in its immaculate silver grey and black finish, is the choice of the discriminating rider who demands the best in performance, suspension, braking and all the other attributes of the really classic sporting motorcycle.

1957 T100

1956 T100. The rear brake plate's torque arm had taken this form for 1955. Deeper rear chainguard would be redesigned the following year.

1957

Along with the "mouth-organ" tank badges, part of a modernising style effort, and a finish of Silver Grey, this year's most striking T100 development was an option: the twin-carburettor head became a version of the 1956 T110 650's alloy "Delta" cylinder head, with splayed inlet and exhaust ports and modified internals. A T100 thus equipped was tested at 105mph - and their existence helped create an irresistible demand for a twin-carb 650.

Engine and Gearbox

The pistons' chromed second ring was replaced by the previous tapered version. (This was the year that Meriden, having ceased to manufacture its own pistons, began buying them in from Hepolite.) Gearbox and clutch were as the 1957 5T (see page 45).

A whole new world for 1957. It was extraordinary the change that a few essentially styling touches by Edward Turner could make to the nature of a model. The "mouth-organ" tank badges and trim, and the two-tone paint schemes which they permitted, were completely in tune with the increasingly mid-Atlantic Zeitgeist of the "you never had it so good" late Fifties. The Silver Grey standard finish was still there for traditionalists, but two-tone was the way forward, rapidly taken up by Norton, AJS/Matchless and even Velocette. (Not to mention the car world, where, as with the British motorcycle industry, it was used as a stop-gap to defer expensive re-tooling for genuinely new models.) Arguably it would play better on Ventura Boulevard than the Balls Pond Road, but Blighty too had begun its California dreamin'. This example from Ace Classics is, as you would expect, pretty well dead original, though the nacelle appears to be from the following year or later.

Frame and Suspension

At eng. no. 08563, the Girling rear suspension units were fitted with 110lb springs, marginally softer than the previous ones and providing 3in of movement; and where the units' top and bottom eyes had been fitted with rubber bushes and sleeves, they now went to Metalastic-type bushes.

The swinging-arm was modified to accept a new rear chainguard.

The front fork ends, previously with a hole for the spindle in the right hand leg and a split hole on the left leg, now changed to more rigid bolt-up spindle clamps for both legs, with a new spindle to suit. The front brake cable abutment for finger adjustment of the cable at the lower end was transferred to a brazed lug on the right fork slider. A brazed lug also now anchored the brake backing plate.

Cycle Parts

The 8in front brake, though single-sided, and with the air scoop, gained a new drum and hub, plus a modified backplate to suit the new fork-end arrangement. For rigidity, the brake anchor plate mounting brackets became induction-brazed, as did the centre mudguard stay, which replaced the previous wrap-around clamps. Stronger-section silencer clip-stays and exhaust pipe brackets were fitted.

The front wheel spokes became straight and butted, and the fracture-prone rear spokes also became butted and of heavier 8/10G gauge than the previous 9 gauge. A Dunlop ribbed front tyre became standard.

For changes to the centre stand, rear chainguard and petrol tank, see 1957 5T (page 46).

Electrical Equipment

The Lucas E3L dynamo replaced its previous Bakelite end cap and band assembly with a one-piece metal end cover.

Optional Equipment

The new HDA "Delta" alloy twin-carburettor cylinder head (see 1956 T110 for further details) eliminated the single-carb head's external oil pipes, with valve chamber pockets draining oil directly into the pushrod cover tubes. Very much the heir of the T100C, this option had larger-diameter inlet valves, 9.0:1 compression pistons, the legendary E3134-profile camshafts and "R" cam followers, racing interference-fit valve spring inners and outers, and bronze valve guides. The twin carburettors, on their splayed inlet ports, were mounted on screwed-in steel adaptors locked with large nuts, and unlike the previous twin-carb options, were Amal 376 Monoblocs. They were connected by clear

1957 T100. Same nacelle, same alloy engine, but the optional Meriden Blue/Ivory changed everything.

1957 T100. Similar appearance, but the 4-gallon petrol tank was new, to suit its new jewellery.

1957 T100. The year brought Girling units with slightly softer (110lb) springs, and improved bushing; a revised, deeper rear chainguard with swinging-arm adapted to suit; and heavier gauge spokes for the fracture-prone rear wheel.

plastic tubing rather than the previous braided line, and again had no air filters, just small bell-mouths.

An "Easy-Lift" centre stand, developed for the Police, was offered.

The QD rear wheel still offered now featured the same heavy duty spokes as the standard wheel.

An example of the two-tone finishes made possible by the new tank, Ivory (tank top half, main mudguard colour) and Meriden Blue (tank bottom half) was an option for the UK (and a standard US finish).

The previous optional valanced front mudguard was no longer available.

The safety-strap on the Twinseat required by Californian legislation, which went out as a kit, became an option.

1957 T100. The nacelle's chrome flash was picked up by the one on the tank that helped permit the two-tone finish

1957 T100. Striped and gold-lined guards, uptilted silencers matching the uptilted seat tail, enough black to anchor the Ivory – nobody did this better.

1957 T100. Wonderful lines. The colour division was continued by a gold line tapering back from the knee rubbers. One penalty of sweptback bars was excessive reach to the control levers.

1957 T100. Many preferred the previous quainter-looking but more practical longer lever for magneto advance/retard control.

1957 T100. The number plate "bridge" could still double as a lifting handle, though handles were now fitted, and the "Easy-Lift" centre-stand, that year with an extended foot peg, was simpler to use than the old rear stand had been. Tail light is long-running Lucas 564.

1957 T100. Classic speedo/light switch/steering damper/ammeter nacelle layout, with central magneto kill button. But the small holes and their grommets for the clutch and front brake cables were for 1958.

1957 T100. Internally, the gearbox was modified for oil-tightness.

1957 T100. Petrol taps, pipes and fittings are correct for the year.

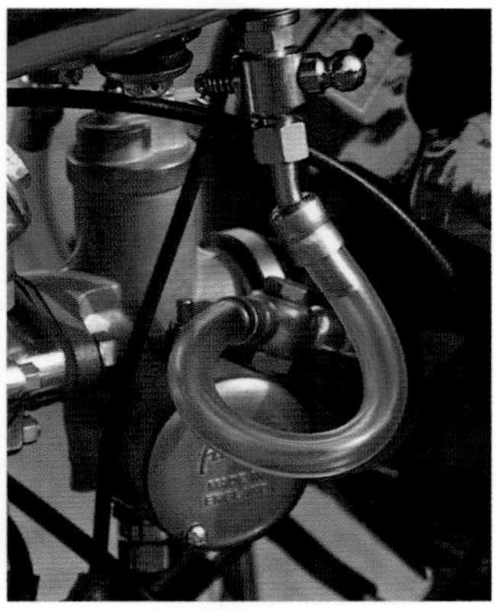

1957 T100. The dynamo gained a metal, not Bakelite, end cover. By the engine number at the base of the cylinder can just be seen the "wagon wheel" symbol, denoting camshafts with quietening ramps.

1957 T100. A single Amal Monobloc was standard, but the hot T100 ticket for 1957 was the optional kit featuring twin carbs on splayed inlet manifolds.

1957 T100. Sign of the times. The inspiration had been a Buick car grille.

1957 T100. The year's revised rear chainguard.

1957 T100. New 8in front brake for this year, still with air scoop and rear vent, but internally with new drum and hub plus modified back plate to suit revised, detachable fork ends. Front wheel's spokes became straight and butted.

1957 T100. The view for most Fifties road users of Triumph's Tiger 100.

1958 T100

1958

The main change for the T100 was unwelcome: the adoption of the patented "Slickshift" mechanism, intended to provide clutchless gearchanges.

Engine and Gearbox As 1958 5T (see page 46).

Frame and Suspension As 1958 5T (see page 47).

Cycle Parts

A new full-width 8in front brake featured a cast-iron finned hub, with two dished circular steel pressings riveted to the central internal hub flange, the inner bore diameters being induction-brazed to the machined central hub tube. Unlike the 5T/6T's 7in version, the chromed end cover was fluted with concentric rings. A circlip held this and the wheel bearing on the left side, while a lock-ring clamped the locating bearing on the right side. The front wheel's straight butted spokes changed to the same heavier 8/10G gauge as those of the rear wheel.

According to John Nelson, though there was no change in part number, the oil tank filler cap was moved inboard to avoid fouling the rider's leg while kickstarting.

The T100's exhaust pipes changed from the old 1¾in to 1½in diameter. The tear-drop silencers, while similar in appearance to the previous "absorption" ones, were now "straight through", for the T100 for this year only.

Other cycle part changes were as 1958 5T (see page 47).

Electrical Equipment See Optional Equipment.

Optional Equipment

The 1958 UK two-tone finish option (standard for US Export) was Black (tank top half) and Ivory (main mudguard colour, tank bottom half).

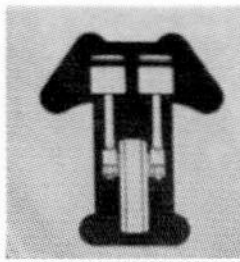

1959 T100

Some Export models, including all US Export T100s, had Lucas magnetos with auto-advance, not manual control.

A steering head lock was offered located to the right of the headstock lug, with a slot cut in the steering stem, and the whole detachable Niemen-type lock and key fitted in a tube in the head lug, with a thin metal dust cap to protect the cylinder when in use.

1959

This was the pre-unit T100's last year, as the pre-unit 650s hit peak form with the T120 Bonneville, and the cooking 500 mutated into an altogether less inspiring but lighter, heavily-panelled, iron-barrelled, unit construction model, the 5TA, and a 22-year run for the pre-unit 500 engine came to an end.

Engine and Gearbox

The T100 adopted a version of the one-piece forged crankshaft assembly introduced for the new 120, with its bolt-on central cast iron flywheel, with straight-sided crank cheeks and a 2¼in wide flywheel. The previous plug at each end of the crankpin changed to a single plug on the right end. The gearbox was fitted with a level plug.

Cycle Parts

Silencers reverted to "absorption" type with internal baffles.

Optional Equipment

For US Export models, rear wheel and tyre changed from 3.50 x 19 to 4.00 x 18 on a WM3 x 18 rim.

Also for US Export models, front mudguards became narrow sports-type, with a tubular centre stay plus front and rear stays, and with the number plate and chromed surround fitted.

The 1959 UK two-tone option (standard for US Export) was as for 1957.

6T THUNDERBIRD 650

The Thunderbird was not quite as historically significant as the Speed Twin, or as glamorous as the sporting Tigers and Bonnevilles. But it was well regarded from the start, and arguably the best all-rounder of the lot. Its debut had been spectacular enough - the successful record-breaking run late in 1949 by a trio of the new 650s at Montlhéry. It had been far from a foregone conclusion for the white-overalled riders, who rounded out their 500-miles-at-90mph with a flying lap of 100mph, and then rode the machines home to Coventry. The streamlined nacelle and the pointed-dart Thunderbird logo emphasised the 650 as the machine of the future, while its tractable nature and dry weight of just 370lb helped make it instantly popular.

1950 brochure cover with new 6T

1950

The 649cc, 34bhp 6T shared its cycle parts and much of its engine with the 1950 5T/T100. The single tapered front downtube cradle frame was the same, with the only rear suspension the optional Spring Wheel. In the bored and stroked engine (71 x 82mm, as against the 5T's 63 x 80mm), the 7.0:1 compression was the same as the 5T's (though there was an 8.5:1 option for the 6T). The bottom end was the same, with its bolted-up 3-piece crankshaft running on the same timing-side ball-race and the T100's drive-side single-lipped roller main bearings, and the white metal big ends on con rods were of the same big end width.

In the transmission, the single-strand primary chain and the same rear chain featured. The carburettor was the same Amal 276 but in a larger 1in, later 1⅙in size. Wheels and tyres were the same at 3.25 x 19 front and 3.50 x 19 rear, with the same 7in single leading shoe brakes. The negative earth electrics were the same too, with ignition by magneto, catalogued as the BTH, with automatic advance/retard, flange-mounted behind the cylinder, and for the rest, a Lucas E3L 6 volt dynamo ahead of it.

Engine and Gearbox

The 650's head and barrel were iron. The 6T's head differed from the 5T's in not being spigotted into the barrel and having a solid copper head gasket. Its finning was more generous. For details of the crankshaft manufacturing method introduced for that year, and related changes including the reintroduction of external oil drain pipes from valve wells in the head to the pushrod tubes, see 1950 5T (page 29).

A new gearbox had been introduced to coincide with the 6T's arrival; again for details see 1950 5T. The speedometer drive was taken horizontally from it; with the nacelle, the speedometers became standard equipment. The 6T's clutch featured an extra (fifth) corked driving plate, and (sixth) steel driven plate. The 6T's gearing was raised by the use of a 24-tooth engine sprocket against the 5T's 22-tooth.

Mid-year the Amal 276's carburettor size was increased from 1in to 1⅙in.

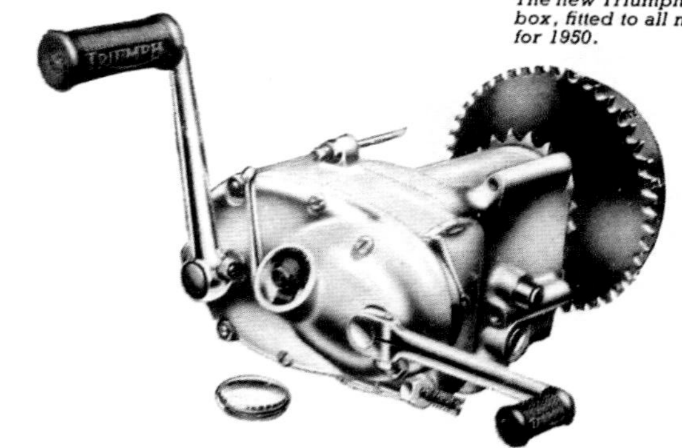

1950 6T engine, revised gearbox

Frame and Suspension See Optional Equipment for details of the Mk II Spring Wheel.

Cycle Parts

1950 featured all-painted petrol tanks, with the four-band tank embellishment and the 5-bar tank parcel grid now standard. The paint for the 6T was the uncharismatic blue-grey Thunder Blue, which like the 5T's Amaranth Red was applied throughout, including the frame; this was disliked by the Americans, who preferred a black frame for the greater ease with which chipped paint could be touched up. (Confusingly, this colour was sometimes catalogued as Polychromatic Blue, the following year's lighter, far pleasanter colour.) On the 6T's petrol tank a single push-pull tap was fitted on the left (near) side, incorporating a reserve setting. Initially the 6T's 4-gallon petrol tank, as well as its 6-pint oil tank, had quick-release hinged "butterfly" filler caps, but at eng. no. 13856N a bayonet-type petrol cap was fitted, while at eng. no.13959N (September 1950) a threaded aluminium cap went on the oil tank.

The mudguards with their raised central band were the same as the 5T's, including the chrome beading fixed around the front number plate. The saddle springs this year became barrel-shaped. For further cycle part details see 1950 5T (page 29).

Electrical Equipment

The regulator was a Lucas MCR 2L, and the horn a Lucas HF1441 Altette, inside the headlamp nacelle as with the 5T.

Optional Equipment

A new prop stand was offered.

8.5:1 compression pistons were available for US Export.

At eng. no. 7439N (April 1950) the Mk I Spring Wheel (see 1948 5T for details) was replaced by the Mk II following some spring breakages. The location of the moving parts changed, and the previous caged, angular-contact, large-diameter ball-race changed to conventional deep groove ball journal bearings with an integral oil seal. As before, the Spring Wheel could be fitted to the Triumph frame with no modification; it offered 2in of movement. It incorporated an 8in rear brake compared to the standard 7in; and it added an extra 15lb to the machine's 370lb dry weight. Externally the Mk II lacked the previous grease nipples, and featured more raised circumferential rings on its end plate.

A single-level Twinseat was offered for the first time.

The beautiful patina on this 1951 American Export Thunderbird might disqualify it from strict factory originality. It was not one of the small 1951 batch of bikes the factory sent out to America, and has clearly been resprayed more recently, but it features rare original cycle parts and detail, and its associations justify its inclusion. It was a very similar 6T from the year before that Marlon Brando rode in the seminal movie The Wild One. *The painted wheel centres and pin-striped mudguards might be absent, but with its authentic 1-inch "Flanders" bars this was how the Americans wanted them. (Brando's bike, which was standard Polychromatic Blue – but the movie was black and white – had even taller "Western" cowhorn bars, plus a custom saddle and pillion pad, and a drooping Crocker-style custom tail-light.)*

1951

The 6T's colour changed to the much more attractive lighter Polychromatic Blue.

Engine and Gearbox

Cam wheels with three keyways were adopted, as on that year's 5T and T100, to give more precise vernier adjustment to the cam timing for performance work. From eng. no. 915NA the 6T was fitted with stronger con rods. From eng.

no. 3918NA taper-faced piston rings were adopted. From eng. no. 10345NA (late June 1951) Stellite-tipped tappets were adopted to counter wear. The gearbox's filler cap changed from one with a knurled edge to one with a hexagon head.

The "Rev-o-lator" Chronometric speedometer, previously with "0" at the 1 o'clock position, was re-calibrated to put "0" at 7 o'clock, to make the 30-70mph section more readable.

Cycle parts

The petrol tank for this year only had two petrol taps, linked by braided pipe, with reserve on the left. The 1¾in exhaust pipes gained welded tags to marry with new angled brackets from the lower front engine plate. The front brake drum became made of a more rigid cast iron.

Electrical Equipment

Either the Lucas K2F magneto with automatic advance/retard was fitted, or the previous BTH instrument. A cone-shaped "shot-glass" Lucas 53216A tail-lamp was fitted, its tapered body giving a larger reflecting area, and providing room within for a brake light.

From the era when the new 650 6T was cutting-edge, this is a desirable model with its BTH magneto ignition and Amal 276, rather than 1952's SU, carburettor. The latter may have been economical, but some informed voices felt that the size Turner selected for it was too small, and it would not be fitted to American Export machines after 1954. At Meriden some said that the US spec machines "always looked better and rode worse", but it was horses for courses – those high bars might have billowed a rider out at speed, but they were certainly comfortable for endless freeway days in the saddle. Good for Ace Classics reimporting this evocative slice of America, which is where the T'bird had been primarily aimed at in the first place.

1951 6T. Barrel-shaped saddle springs had been adopted for 1950.

1951 6T. Extraordinary how a pair of handlebars can alter the whole mood of a machine.

1951 6T. Lucas 53216A tail-light looks tiny by modern standards, but was big enough to include a brake-light

1951 6T. Front number plates, not legally required Stateside, were either removed or were adapted by dealers for self-advertising, identifying a model, or as here, boasting – though the land speed record was not until 1956.

1951 6T. The one-piece mudguard adopted by twins from early 1948 looked sleek but had to be removed completely to work on the rear tyre.

1951 6T. Triumph 1-inch handlebars, uncluttered as Turner intended, with no advance/retard lever and no choke. Clear view of twistgrip's knurled friction "cruise control", and Triumph right-angle metal throttle cable guide, not appreciated by all for the way it could diminish fine throttle control.

1951 6T. The standard Lycett (or Terrys) saddle, with US bars, put the rider too close to the tank. US bikers favoured longer and more generous custom saddles.

1951 6T. Thunderbird logo is at home on the nacelle. Speedo with needle at 7 o'clock for zero was introduced that year.

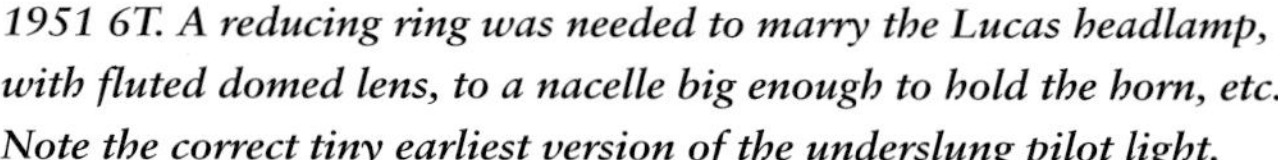

1951 6T. A reducing ring was needed to marry the Lucas headlamp, with fluted domed lens, to a nacelle big enough to hold the horn, etc. Note the correct tiny earliest version of the underslung pilot light.

1951 6T. Mk II Spring Wheel. The mounting for the optional pillion footrest also doubles as silencer support and rear stand spring holder – following Turner's favourite "minimum of metal for the maximum of work" principle.

1951 6T. Gearbox internals for the pre-unit twins had been strengthened in 1950 to cope with the 6T's power, and the 650's gearing was taller than the 500's. The clutch cable arm's rubber cover has gone missing.

1951 6T. Behind the cylinder sits a BTH KC2 magneto, in 1951 still the more numerous of the instruments supplied, and preferred by many riders to the Lucas K2F equivalent. On the 6T both featured automatic advance/retard.

1951 6T. Cast iron barrels, Amal 276, correct petrol taps and authentic early switch for brake-light, needed for 1951 as the new tail-light housing had room for one. The choke lever should be black painted, but America would have preferred chrome

1951 6T. The patent plate read simply "650 Twin" – the 6T was Triumph's only one at the time. Above the dynamo, the front pushrod tube on this well-used example is demonstrating a typical lack of oil-tightness.

1951 6T. The 6T cylinder head had no flange into the barrel, and was fitted with a solid copper head gasket. US Export models ran at the 8.5:1 compression ratio which high-octane gasoline allowed.

1951 6T. Four-bar tank embellishment and Triumph badge looked their best against gleaming black paint.

1951 6T. Feel the highway calling...

Thunderbird

Patent Nos. 475860, 474963, 482024, 469635.

The "Thunderbird" has achieved tremendous popularity all over the world in a very short space of time. Produced to meet the demand for a machine capable of maintaining the highest possible speeds over really long distances with complete reliability, it has done this and more. It has proved economical, easy to handle and is a firm favourite with sidecar men. This extra reserve of performance is offered in a machine of the same weight and dimensions as an average "500." The "Thunderbird" offers motor cycling at its thrilling best and will continue to add laurels to an already established reputation.

PAGE 4

O.H.V. vertical twin. Bore 71 mm., stroke 82 mm., 649 c.c. Dry sump lubrication. Air cleaner. Auto-advance magneto. Triumph telescopic forks. Triumph four-speed gearbox, with heavy duty five-plate clutch. Beautifully finished in a completely new polychromatic blue, lined gold. (For complete technical details see back pages.)

SPECIFICATION

1951 6T. Single-sided, single leading shoe 7in front brake was barely adequate for a 34bhp 100mph motorcycle. For 1951 it was given a Mehanite cast iron drum rather than the previous pressed steel one.

1951 6T. Rod operation for Spring Wheel's 8in rear brake.

1951 6T. Head-on view demonstrates the twin engine's remarkably slim profile.

1952 6T

1953 brochure front cover, 6T, showing underslung pilot light

1952

The main change for the 6T this year was the adoption of the SU carburettor, and the frame adaptation to suit. Fuel economy with the SU was excellent, at over 80mpg even in fast touring, but at least one contemporary tuner, Tyrell Smitt, considered the size of the instrument on the 6T to be too small. The electrics changed to positive earth. The Korean War nickel shortage affected the chrome-plated parts.

Engine and Gearbox

A single car-type SU MC2 vacuum carburettor was fitted, with a different induction manifold to suit. It featured a spring-loaded choke in the body of the instrument controlled by a lever on its bottom end. The only other motorcycle it was fitted to was the Ariel Square Four 4G MkII. For further engine and gearbox modifications, see 1952 5T (page 31).

Frame and Suspension As 1952 5T (see page 31).

Cycle parts As 1952 5T (see page 31).

Electrical Equipment As 1952 5T (see page 32).

1953

Engine and Gearbox

To conform with the 5T, which this year adopted alternator electrics, the 6T's engine shock absorber moved from the engine shaft to within the clutch assembly, now consisting of a four-paddle vane working in eight rubber blocks; though the former system was judged more efficient. A distance piece was fitted on the engine shaft to compensate for its removal.

From eng. no. 37630, new camshafts with quietening ramps were introduced, their presence indicated by a

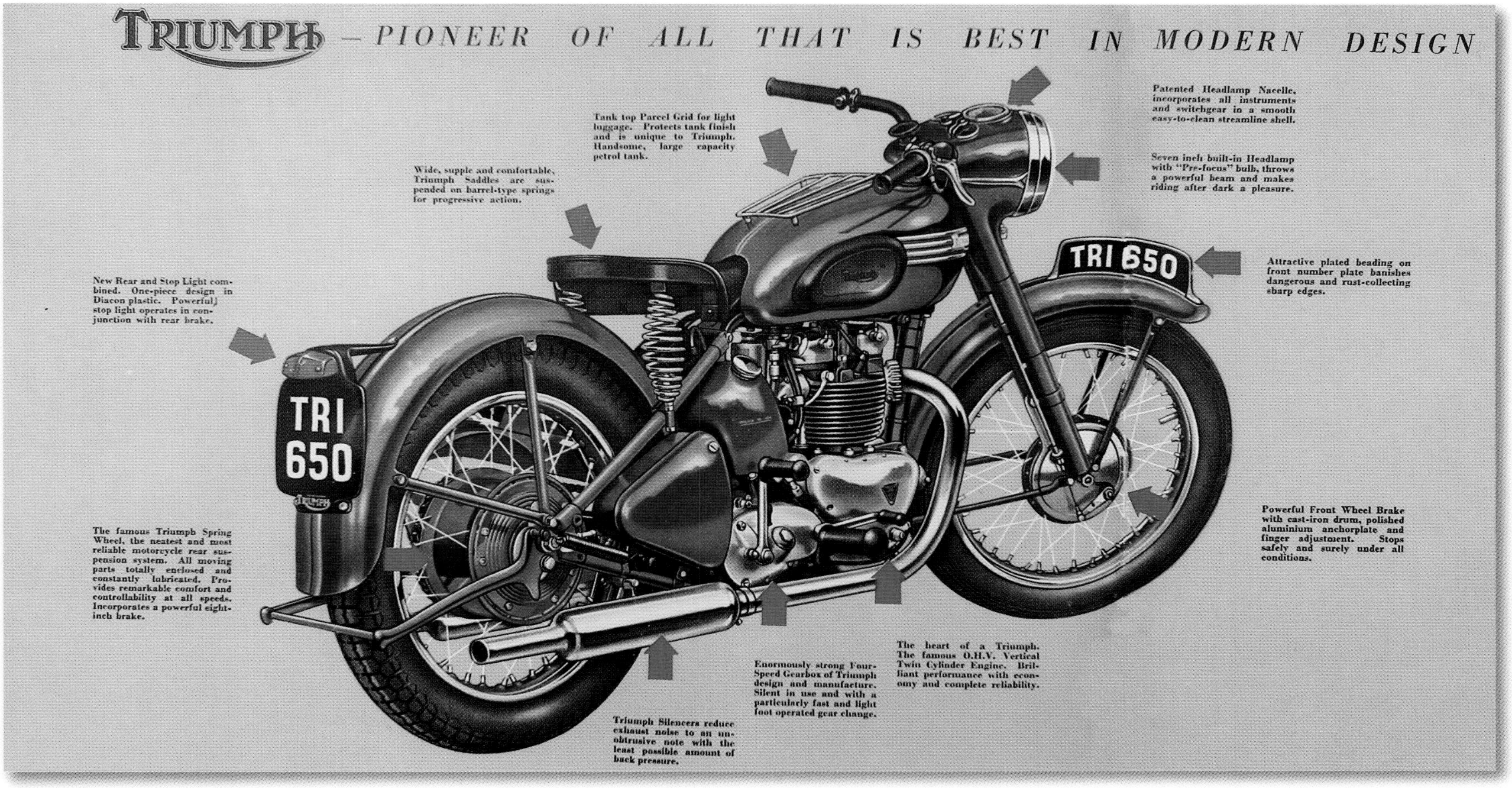

1953 6T anatomised

1953 brochure back cover

"spoked wheel" symbol stamped after the engine number. Valve timing with them fitted was unchanged, but tappet clearance altered to 0.010in.

From eng. no. 42654 (early May 1953) the alloy gear selection camplate was replaced by a steel one.

Frame and Suspension As 1953 5T (see page 36).

Cycle Parts

As 1953 5T (see page 36), excepting the change to the 5T's nearside exhaust pipe, and to its nacelle.

Electrical Equipment

A new rectangular Lucas Diacon 525 tail lamp was fitted, with stop-lamp operation via a switch fixed to a plate fastened on the left pillion footrest bolt.

Optional Equipment

For 1953 and 1954 only a US Export version of the 6T was The Blackbird, with an all-black finish, and gold-lined mudguard centres and wheel central strips.

1954 6T

1954

This year the 6T followed the 5T in adopting alternator electrics. Although only the new T110 sports 650, along with the T100, adopted the new swinging-arm frame that year, the 6T benefitted from the "big bearing" engine.

Engine and Gearbox

The "big bearing" stiffened-up crankshaft had increased shaft diameters and new flywheels. The crankshaft ran in the existing 1⅛in MS11 drive-side ball journal bearing, but this was now duplicated on the timing side, with the previous roller bearing there deleted, and a clamping washer between the bearing and the timing gear.

Externally the timing cover now featured a small crescent-shaped bulge. There was no longer provision for the dynamo drive on the cover or in the crankcase. The timing chest now housed the distributor drive shaft which projected horizontally into it. The primary chaincase also changed both its inner and outer covers, as within it the drive-side shaft was given a parallel section outboard of the engine sprocket splines, to carry the alternator rotor, which was retained by a stud. The stator was mounted on the inside of the new primary chaincase cover, behind an enlarged version of the previous "tear-drop" bulge, without the 5T's circular cover.

In the gearbox, the clutch cable adjuster lug was changed from vertical to a forward angle.

Frame and Suspension

Fork springs went from 19in to 20in length.

Cycle Parts

The 6T's nacelle was modified, this year fitting the Lucas PRS8 combined ignition/light switch, which went on the right, with the ammeter on the left.

On the petrol tank, a single push-pull tap with reserve facility was fitted, this time on the right, with a blanking plug on the left.

The left (near) side exhaust pipe, as on the 5T, was given a

1955 6T

kink to clear the chaincase bulge. The optional prop stand's footpiece was enlarged to go round it.

New "absorption-type" silencers with tapering tear-drop bodies were fitted, as on the T110/T100.

The previous rubber pad on the brake pedal was deleted.

Electrical Equipment

A Lucas RM14 3-wire alternator was fitted, with a new wiring harness and a Lucas 6 volt Q6 coil. A 4½in Sentercel rectifier was located under the seat, and at eng. no. 55494 (early July 1954) was replaced by a 2½in diameter one. A Lucas DKX2A distributor was mounted horizontally behind the cylinders in the old magneto position, driven by a pinion in the timing chest, and with the coil mounted directly above it. The Lucas PRS8 ignition/light switch included an emergency start position.

Optional Equipment

A heel-and-toe gear change was offered for the 6T.

The Twinseat which continued to be offered remained the old flat type, not the new two-level one found on the swinging-arm twins.

The prop-stand was lengthened as mentioned.

A valanced front mudguard, with stays formed in one and riveted to the guard, was offered.

The alternative close ratio gearbox's mainshaft and 3rd gear were modified.

Alternative higher-compression 7.5:1 pistons were offered.

1955

The 6T adopted the swinging-arm frame introduced the previous year for the T110/T100.

Engine and Gearbox

The crankshaft was fitted with a tubular sludge trap, pressed between the two crank webs. The gudgeon pin bore was reduced and tapered internally at each end.

New inner and outer primary chaincases were required to fit the swinging-arm frame and keep the machines' overall length down. The inner primary case now had the alternator stator bolted to it, rather than as previously to the outer chaincase. The primary chain's length was reduced from 80 to 79 pitches, while the rear chain increased from 92 to 101 pitches. The outer case now carried a cast-in "Thunderbird" logo and name, and a previous inspection cap was deleted.

The gearbox gained a new casing to suit the new frame, with fixed lugs top and bottom. The kickstart ratchet spring and sleeve changed, and an associated thrust washer was deleted.

Both engine and gearbox cover fixing screws changed from cheesehead to Philips-type crosshead.

Frame and Suspension As 1955 5T (see page 39).

Cycle Parts As 1955 5T (see page 39).

1956 6T

Electrical Equipment

As 1955 5T. In addition the 6T adopted a new Lucas distributor, with advance reduced from 15 to 12.5 degrees. The coil, previously mounted on top of the distributor, for this year was positioned under the seat.

Optional Equipment

A new prop-stand now common to all models was offered.

A QD rear wheel for the swinging-arm frame, which ran on special thin taper rollers, continued as an option.

For US Export models a 1¹⁄₁₆in Amal Monobloc carburettor was fitted.

1956

Engine and Gearbox

As on the whole range, the previous white-metal big end bearings were replaced by Vandervell steel-backed VP3 shell-type bearings, and con rods with a larger big-end eye were necessary to take them. The engine balance factor was adjusted accordingly, to retain the previous balance factor.

The inlet camshaft had its breather holes reduced to just one. The gearbox's previous phosphor bronze layshaft bushes were replaced with sintered bronze bushes. In the clutch the cork-insert driving plates were replaced by plain steel plates with bonded-on Neolangite, and the driven plates were also altered, becoming solid not pierced. The composition of the clutch shock-absorber's rubbers was changed.

Frame and Suspension As 1956 5T (see page 42).

Cycle Parts As 1956 5T(see page 43).

Electrical Equipment

As 1956 5T (see page 43), but in addition the 6T's coil returned from its 1955 mounting under the seat to its previous position mounted above the distributor.

Optional Equipment

The previous optional 7.5:1 pistons were changed in form.

This 1956 model represents the Thunderbird in its maturity, with swinging-arm frame and alternator electrics. It was the 6T's last year for all-over colour finishes, which unless they were black, the Americans at least disliked due to the difficulty of accurate matching when touching up chips. Colour matching here is a case in point, as on this typically fine model from the A.R.E. collection the 1956-only finish was described as Polychromatic Crystal Grey, and contemporary catalogues show it as more silvery than the shade seen here. However, the variations in original paint batches are well known (see Appendix A). A smoothie and a sidecar puller supreme, this vintage of 6T makes quite a contrast with the raw product just five years previously, as well as with its sporting T100 and T110 contemporaries. But for civilised everyday use it had few equals.

1956 6T. A neat package: mid-Fifties 6T was the Triumph for the discerning rider – and the sidecar man.

1956 6T. This was the last year for the 4-band tank styling strip, and it was still looking good.

1956 6T. Compact one-piece rear brake pedal assembly, SU carburettor and "Stream-styled" central unit. Alternator chaincase with Thunderbird logo, and engine plates where the dynamo used to be.

1956 6T. Among the pre-unit twins, the vacuum SU MC2 car-type carburettor was unique to "Captain Sensible" 6T.

1956 6T. This type of optional prop-stand introduced for 1955 was common to all models.

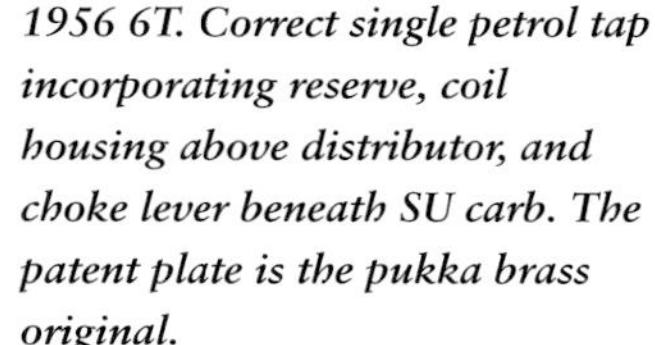

1956 6T. Correct single petrol tap incorporating reserve, coil housing above distributor, and choke lever beneath SU carb. The patent plate is the pukka brass original.

1956 6T. For this year the gearbox bushes became sintered bronze and the 6-plate clutch's plates were altered. The fastening screws on engine and gearbox should be Philips crosshead.

1956 6T. The correct position for the Oil Level transfer on the 5-pint tank, always lower down than you think.

1956 6T. Painted and lined wheel centres were optional for this last year. Front fork internals were modified to prevent bottoming out.

1956 6T. Lucas PRS8 combined ignition/light-switch had been in the 6T's nacelle since 1954. Beneath the nacelle, the '56 headstock lug was revised.

1956 6T. The unsupported swinging-arm was not so stressed by Thunderbird cruiser.

1956 6T. Detail without busy-ness; the trick the Triumph engine turned.

1956 6T. Right-angled throttle cable guide and knurled friction wheel for twistgrip, up close.

1956 6T. The Girling rear units had softer (100lb) springs for 1956.

1956 6T. This year brought the tank with central seam and 4-bar parcel grid for the 6T.

1956 6T. Sub-frame mounting for pillion footrest, brake light switch and silencer clip.

1957

The year of the "mouth organ" tank badges and of full width hub front brakes. On the left side of the petrol tank top, in line with the filler cap on the right, all machines from this year on carried "World Motor Cycle Speed Record Holder" transfers with the Thunderbird dart logo to commemorate Johnny Allen's 1956 feat on the Bonneville salt flats – even though the record was officially unrecognised. On the 6T's finish, only the tank and mudguards were now colour painted, with the rest black.

Engine and Gearbox

The 6T's cylinder head underwent a minor modification with an increase in the depth of material in the combustion chambers to combat the detonation that could be caused by the use of higher-compression pistons, which continued to be offered as an option.

Camshafts with single keyways rather than the 3-way ones were re-introduced.

To counter persistent oil leaks from the gearbox, new sleeve gears with bushes to suit were fitted, and the mainshaft high-gear sleeve bush extended through the primary chaincase oil retainer plate into the primary chaincase itself, to divert oil into there. The chaincase's oil retainer disc plate was now of larger bore to suit.

The kickstart cotter pin was modified.

On the clutch's vane-type shock-absorber there was another change as yet more oil-proof and resilient rubbers were used.

The SU MC2 carburettor remained unchanged but gained a new part no. (603).

Frame and Suspension As 1957 T100 (see page 46).

1957 brochure cover, 6T, with "mouth-organ" badge.

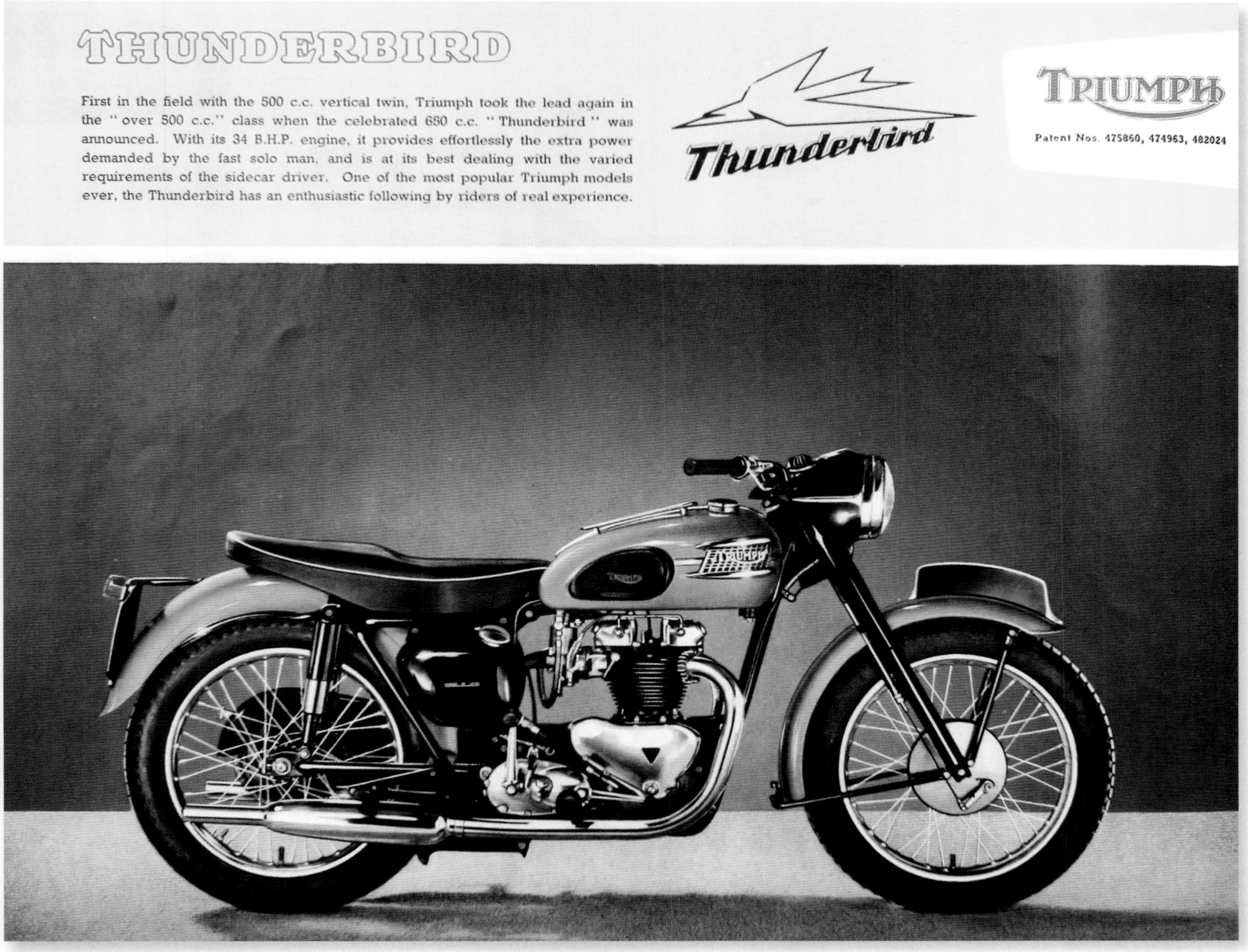
THUNDERBIRD
First in the field with the 500 c.c. vertical twin, Triumph took the lead again in the "over 500 c.c." class when the celebrated 650 c.c. "Thunderbird" was announced. With its 34 B.H.P. engine, it provides effortlessly the extra power demanded by the fast solo man, and is at its best dealing with the varied requirements of the sidecar driver. One of the most popular Triumph models ever, the Thunderbird has an enthusiastic following by riders of real experience.
Thunderbird
TRIUMPH
Patent Nos. 475860, 474963, 482024

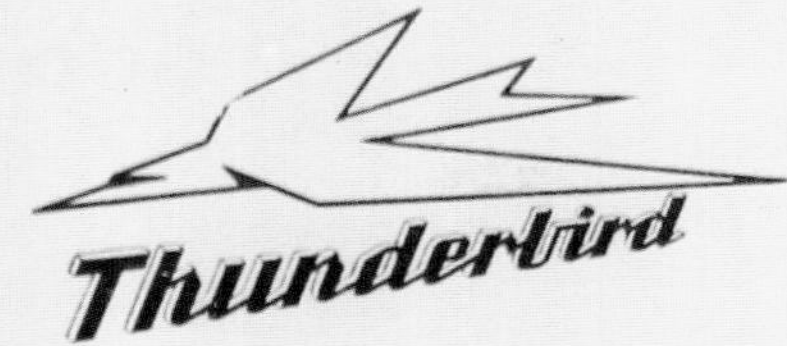

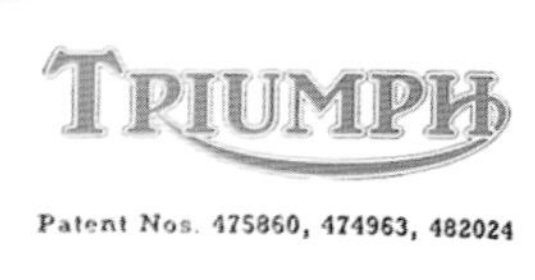

1957 6T

Cycle Parts

As 1957 5T (see page 46). In addition for the 6T a ribbed Dunlop front tyre was now fitted as standard, and from eng. no. 08374 the "Easy-Lift" centre stand developed for the Police became standard equipment.

Optional Equipment

A Twinseat central safety-strap, required by Californian legislation for US models there and sent out as a kit to be dealer-fitted, was offered.

On the QD rear wheel, the spokes became the same thicker 8/10G gauge as on the standard wheel.

The valanced front mudguard was no longer offered.

1958

This year saw the introduction in the gearbox of the Slickshift.

Engine and Gearbox As 1958 5T (see page 46).

Frame and Suspension As 1958 5T (see page 47).

Cycle Parts As 1958 5T (see page 47).

Optional Equipment

The optional heel and toe gear pedal was revised. Otherwise as 1958 5T (see page 47).

1959 6T

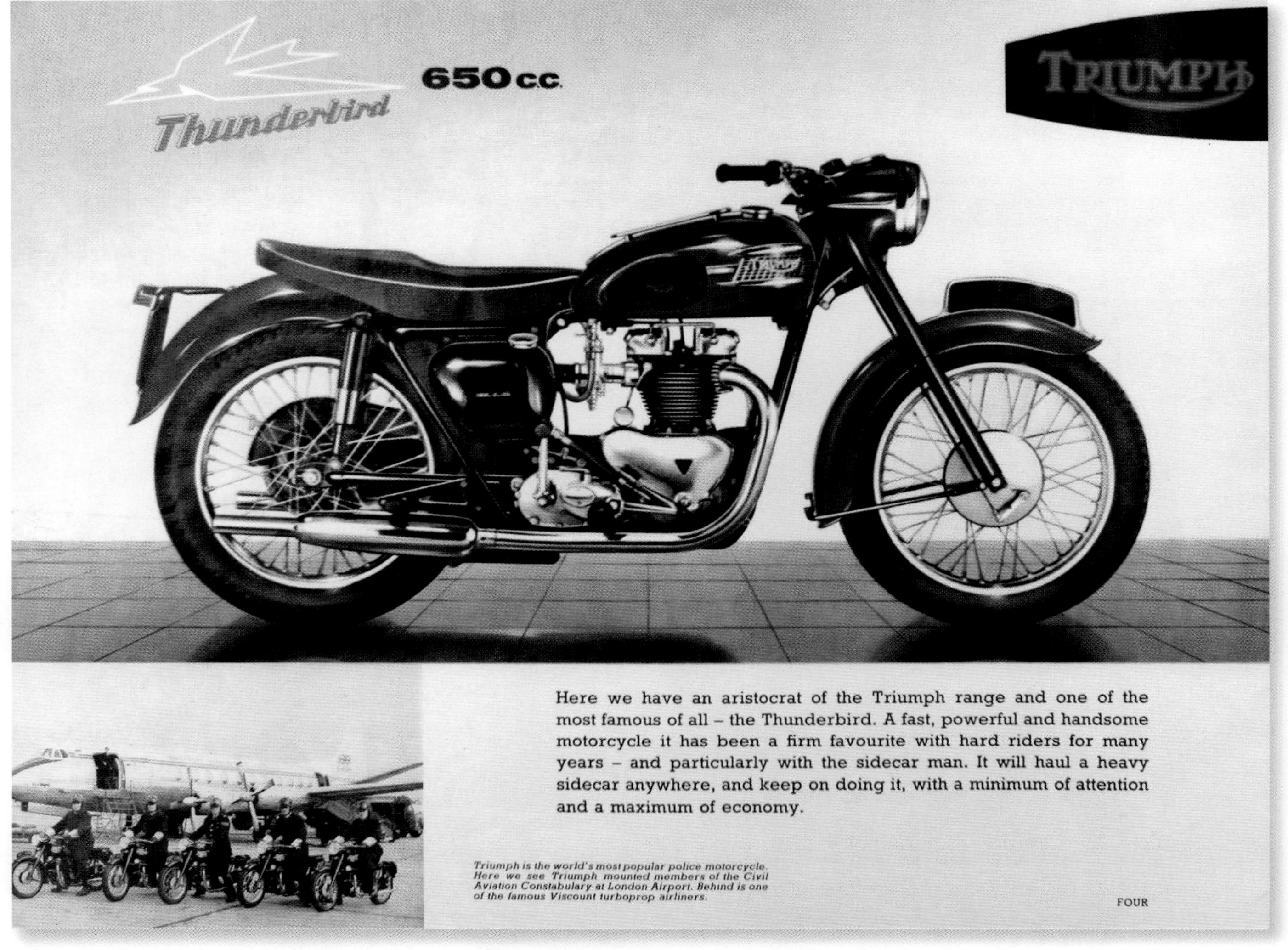

1959

As the T120 Bonneville arrived, the 6T gained the latter's stronger one-piece crankshaft, while in these more affluent times the economical SU carburettor was dropped in favour of an Amal Monobloc. The 650 machines, 6T included, were now known as the B-range (the smaller unit construction machines were the C-range, and the Tiger Cubs the A-range).

Engine and Gearbox

The crankshaft was forged in one piece, with 1⅝in journals and the shell-type big end bearings, and it ran on the same main bearings. The crank cheeks became straight-sided. A central cast iron flywheel was fed over the outer crank cheek, pressed into place and axially located by three 7/16in radial bolts, which passed through the outer periphery of the flywheel and screwed into the crankshaft itself. In mid-season, after some instances of flywheel bolt failure in competition, the interference fit of flywheel to crankshaft was increased by 0.0025in, and new bolts were fitted.

The 6T's compression remained at 7.0:1.

In the gearbox, an oil level indicator removable threaded plug was built into the inner cover. A boss was added just behind the layshaft bush housing of the gearbox inner cover. From eng. no. 023941 (early February 1959) induction hardening was introducing for the periphery of the gear control camplate, and from eng. no. 024029 also for the clutch sprocket centre bore.

The clutch used a different grade of Neolangite friction material on the driving plates.

The SU carburettor was dropped in favour of a 1 1/16in Amal Monobloc, on a suitable manifold from the T110/TR6.

Cycle Parts

The front brake cam lever angle was altered to improve leverage, its modified lever identifiable by a stamped "X".

The silencer internals reverted to the baffled "absorption" type.

1960 6T

A previous clip holding the plug leads to the inlet manifold was deleted.

Electrical Equipment
The Lucas alternator changed to the circular higher-output RM15.

1960
The 6T, like the other 650s, adopted the new duplex front downtube frame. Along with the T110 it was brought into line with the C-range unit machines and fitted with "bathtub" rear panelling and a flared "fireman's helmet" front mudguard, while the 6T also got 18in wheels. (The thinking behind the enclosures is explained in the Introduction.) In practice they complicated servicing and rear wheel removal, limited luggage carrying, and in addition were deeply unpopular in America, while some considered these "skirts" represented a loss of machismo.

Engine and Gearbox
From eng. no. D1564 (end of December 1959), the oil pump's brass body was replaced with an aluminium casting.

The oil pressure indicator button was modified to incorporate a synthetic rubber O-ring seal in the end cap for the indicator rod, to counter oil leaks there.

The primary chain adjuster draw-bolt was redesigned to provide a clutch cable abutment at the rear of the gearbox clamping stud, to suit the panelling.

The rubber cap on the gearbox's external clutch lever was reintroduced.

Within the panelling, a new box-shaped air filter was adopted.

Frame and Suspension
For details of the new frame, see 1960 T120 (page 171). At eng. no. D1563 the frame was modified with an added lower tank rail. Some of these rails also may have been retro-fitted to earlier duplex frame machines as part of a factory frame kit.

For the 6T (and T110) there was a different version from the T120/TR6's of the new tubular loops welded to the bolt-on rear frame, with the previous combined silencer/pillion footrest support plates there now deleted.

For the 6T/T110 there was also a different type of fork crown from the T120/TR6's. The 6T/T110 continued with the U-bolt bar clamp type, but with a revised clamp nut. All 650s had a single new bottom fork crown, along with a new steering damper knob and damper plate which located to the frame without a bolt.

The 6T/T110 fork legs were modified to accept the unit 3TA's nacelle, and for the 6T, its new 18in wheels. Internally the forks were redesigned along 3TA lines to reduce spring friction, with a greater volume of damping oil and, it was claimed, two-way damping. There were new internal tubular spring guides, top and bottom yokes, and fork springs of 18⅑₁₆in length. The forks had a steeper steering head angle, altered from 64.5 degrees to 67 degrees, which reduced the wheelbase to 54½in.

Cycle Parts

The deeply valanced, lipped front mudguard was exactly the same as the 3TA's. It featured just an integral central stay, and a rear stay which could still double up as a front wheel stand.

The "bath-tub" panels for the 6T/T110 consisted of two 22g steel pressings with ribbed edges, with a rubber beading between their junction at the rear. They carried on each side bolted-on metal "Thunderbird" or "Tiger 110" badges in cursive "toothpaste" script. The "bath-tubs" were similar to the 3TA/5TA's, but half an inch longer and with different fixing points. The previous unit models' panelling, joined by means of bolted-together flanges at their rear, had attempted to conceal the bolts, but for greater accessibility the flanges were now turned outwards, and the rear number plate was modified to suit. Beneath the panels a plain, black-painted pressing comprised the rear mudguard, and on top of them there was a new Twinseat. This was still two-level and in black Vynide with white piping, but now hinged on the left (rather than bolted in place), and held closed by a plunger with a chromed knob; again this was similar to the 3TA/5TA's, but slightly longer. When raised, it revealed the kit of tools in a rubber tray with shaped cut-outs for them, as well as the regulator, coil, battery, and the chromed bayonet-type filler cap, now set to the rear of its top face, for the new oil tank. For the 6T/T110, this 5-pint tank was slimmer than the version for the T120/TR6, and with different mountings. Feed and return pipes were both positioned after the rear mounting lug, and the anti-froth tower now moved to the rear, still projecting up outside the frame rail.

The petrol tank was all new, now with three rubber-faced fixing points, the front two on lugs protruding from the new frame's front downtubes, and the third one at the rear in front of the fixing bolt. The tank was held down by a central rubber-lined chromed strap. This strap proved fracture-prone and was to be modified five times by 1962. The 4-bar chromed parcel grid was fitted, and the "mouth-organ" badge and chrome strips were adapted for the new tank.

The nacelle was from the 3TA, featuring different bottom quarters, fork sleeves, and a shortened top compared with previously. The instrument layout was the same, with no kill-button between the ammeter and lights/ignition switch, and the black enamelled steering damper closest to the rider; but a different 125 mph Smiths speedometer, SC3304/19, was fitted due to the change of gearing.

The 6T's silencers were redesigned internally with a mute in the tail, more effective than that for the T110/T120. The silencer clip stays were modified, and there were new exhaust pipe brackets.

The "Easy-Lift" centre stand was given a new spring and connecting link.

The 6T's wheels and tyres were now 18in, the front a WM2-18 rim carrying a 3.25 x 18 ribbed Dunlop tyre, with the chromed hub plate reverting to its plainer concentric ribbed style of 1957. The rear wheel was WM2-18 with a 3.50 x18 Dunlop Universal tyre. The rear wheel sprocket was reduced from 46 to 43 teeth, raising the gearing, with the rear chain down a pitch at 99 pitches.

Electrical Equipment

The stop-light switch became a new D-shaped one, operated by a small lever contacting the rear brake pedal. The 6 volt ignition coil was moved to beneath the seat. The 6T's distributor became a Lucas Type 18D2.

Optional Equipment

A new side-stand to suit the new frame was offered. The original QD rear wheel's integral sprocket was reduced to the same 43 teeth as the standard wheel.

1961

This year the 6T was fitted with the other 650s' alloy cylinder head. It also (finally) adopted the larger 8in front brake. The T'bird looked well in two-tone black and silver. The dry weight was catalogued this year at 371lb, quite a drop from 1957's 395lb.

Engine and Gearbox

For the 6T, the T110's alloy single-carb cylinder head was adopted, this year featuring cast-in vertical buttresses added to each of its sides, tying the fins to reduce resonance. The alloy head also featured larger inlet valves, and at eng. no. D11193 new pairs of shorter valve springs were adopted. For 1961 a flat was machined on the large diameter of the exhaust valve cast iron seat insert, narrowing it to 1$^{11}/_{32}$in. This was to allow a greater thickness of aluminium there,

1960 6T

and it was hoped would help deal with the persistent cracking to which the head, with its 8 holding-down studs, had been prone.

The new head caused the 6T's compression to rise to 7.5:1, though output was still catalogued as 34bhp at 6300rpm. The head was used at first in conjunction with the T110's sporting E3325 camshafts, which carried no "spoked wheel" after the engine number. But at eng. no. D11193 (late December 1960) these were changed to the milder E3420 "Dowson" cams, requiring altered tappet settings. (The Police "Saint" version employed a mix of the Dowson exhaust cam and the T120's E3134 inlet cam, as part of the recipe for both flexible docility and strong acceleration.) The 6T also adopted the other 650's Stellite-tipped composite pushrods in place of the previous alloy ones with pressed-on ends.

From eng. no. D14438 (late June 1961) the one-piece crankshaft was fitted with a new flywheel of 2 11/32in diameter. Marque expert Harry Woolridge believes that this and the other changes resulted in the 6T's output rising to 37bhp at 6700rpm.

For all the 650s a 21-tooth engine sprocket rather than the previous 22-tooth one was fitted, lowering overall gearing, and reducing the rear chain pitches again to 98. In the gearbox itself, Torrington needle roller bearings replaced the previous bronze bushes at either end of the layshaft, with layshaft end float controlled by a bronze thrust washer fitting over the needle roller bearings, and with the gearbox shell and inner cover modified to suit. Gearbox adjusting screws were now fitted on both sides of the top clamp, rather than on the right side only. The clutch plates featured Langite facings improved for a second time to help counter stiction.

1962 6T

Frame and Suspension

The frame's steering head angle was altered a little, changing from 67 to 65 degrees, a compromise to suit both US off-road competition and road riding. In a change already adopted in mid-1960 season, the frame now featured a lower tank rail to stiffen the head lug area.

Cycle Parts

The 6T adopted the other 650s' full width hub single leading shoe 8in front brake. For this model year the brake was modified, as was the 7in rear brake, with the shoes being made fully floating, and friction strips re-sited at the trailing edge of the shoes. The front and rear shoes were now the same, and common to all models.

A folding kickstart was now standard.

To suit the altered gearing, the Smiths Chronometric 125mph speedometer was modified again, becoming the SC3304/24.

Electrical Equipment

With the alloy head, a long-reach (¾in) spark plug, Champion N5, was now specified for the 6T.

1962

This was the 6T Thunderbird's last year as a pre-unit, though the change when it came was perhaps less conspicuous than with other models, as the 6T had already lost its magneto back in 1954. A siamesed exhaust was fitted for that year only, presumably to try and suit the dwindling but still numerous ranks of UK sidecar pilots. Internally, there were heavier flywheels – an example of how the American tail would increasingly wag the Meriden dog.

Engine and Gearbox

A wider and heavier flywheel was fitted to all the 650s. Aimed at improving the engine's already good low-down grunt for US off-road and dirt-track competition, a first

Techniques of manufacture are constantly changing and to maintain the high standard of quality and accuracy which has been synonymous with the Triumph name for more than sixty years, the Triumph engineering staff conducts a ceaseless campaign to improve and perfect its methods. Illustrated here are some familiar components in course of manufacture on machines which work to incredibly close limits to ensure the superb quality and high finish which is a Triumph tradition.

1. Cylinder barrels of the twin cylinder engines have a controlled surface finish after this final machining process.
2. It takes exactly seven seconds by electronic means to harden the surface of the crank[illegible] bearing journal. A [illegible] nique devel[illegible]ively by Triu[illegible]
3. [illegible] drilling bolt holes on a "C" range crankcase. Initial boring and counterboring of the eight bolt holes are carried out independently.
4. A crank turning lathe for roughing and finishing bob weight journals. The two operations are carried out automatically, enabling one operator to control a number of machines.
5. Four boring operations are done simultaneously on four "Tiger Cub" crankcases. This involves initial roughing out and final boring of the main gearbox bearing and distributor housings to close tolerances.
6. The teeth of clutch chain wheels are formed by this gear cutter. Sixteen blanks are placed in position and the teeth are automatically shaped by a high speed cutting tool.

4 5 6

EXCELLENCE

1962 Meriden manufacturing.

version gave a balance factor of 71%. Then, according to marque expert the late Hughie Hancox, there was an interim version giving a 75% balance factor (Meriden's Experimental chief Frank Baker reportedly was obsessional about balance factors).

Then, at eng. no. D17043 (mid-January 1962), came a final version with a balance factor of 85%, which would continue for the 650s, including the T120, from then on. The new set-up featured pear-shaped cheeks for its previously straight-sided balance weights.

The 6T's outer primary chaincase was modified to give clearance for its new RM 19 alternator's larger diameter rotor.

In the 6T's gearbox, the Slickshift mechanism was deleted.

Frame and Suspension

The Girling rear suspension units were reduced in length from 12.9in to 12.4in, with the springs also reduced to 8in.

Cycle Parts

The 6T's seat became two-tone, with a grey lower trim strip, black sides, white piping and a grey top.

The siamesed exhaust system featured the left 1½in diameter pipe crossing just above the engine plate to join the right pipe. A single long "resonator" silencer was fitted.

The petrol tank now featured a pair of new-style taps with flat-plate levers, the one on the left offering a reserve supply.

Electrical Equipment

The Lucas RM 19 alternator featured a larger diameter rotor with straight, unrecessed sides. A Lucas 8H horn was fitted. From eng. no. D18419 (mid-March 1962) a new smaller Lucas rectifier was fitted.

Optional Equipment

For the 1962 season, US Export 6Ts abandoned the "bathtub" rear panelling altogether, though retaining the flared "fireman's helmet" front mudguard.

T110 TIGER 650

The 650 Tiger, or "Ton-Ten", has been outshone historically by the T120 Bonneville, but in its day it was a King of the Road. Its acceleration was searing, and speeds well over the 110mph indicated by its model number were achieved on more than one road test.

While test machines may have got special treatment, from the T110's beginning in 1954 until 1958 only one of the rare Vincent 1000cc twins or a tuned BSA Gold Star 500 single could hold a candle to it. Though not so durable, the Tiger 650 was lighter (at 395lb), more affordable, easier to start and – with its still-flexible and tractable engine – easier to live with than either of them. Fuel economy too remained good at around 70mpg overall. In those days even fewer cars, like Jaguar's XK120, could hope to keep up with a T110, so if you had the nerve, your Triumph really did rule the road.

The tuned 40bhp 650 engine was largely the fruit of the US importers' and mechanics' experiments with the 6T – higher lift E3325 camshafts, bigger valves, and the raised compression ratios initially made feasible by higher-octane US gasoline, all featured. It was the 1954 T110 which introduced the "big bearing" motor and the new swinging-arm frame, and while the high-speed handling provided by the latter was undeniably challenging, to some extent it could be learnt, and some riders relished the challenge.

The initial iron-head engine had a flaw but Meriden worked away, and with 1956's alloy "Delta" head the T110 became very much the machine from which the iconic Bonneville evolved. A streak of silver or Shell Blue against the drab background of post-war Britain, this was the archetypal Fifties Rocker's steed. Despite (or because of) the iron engine, and accounts of some harshness at lower speeds compared to the 6T (though not on the example I tried many years later), the 1954 was reckoned by some to be the best of the lot.

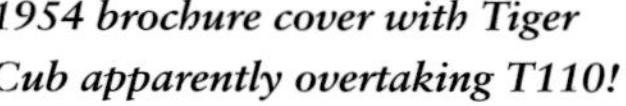
1954 brochure cover with Tiger Cub apparently overtaking T110!

1954

As with the 6T the engine featured the new "big-bearing" stiffened-up crankshaft with increased shaft diameters and new flywheels. Con rods with larger (1⅝in) diameter big end journals were fitted. The crankshaft ran in the existing drive-side 1⅛in MS11 ball journal bearing, but this was now duplicated on the timing side, with the previous roller bearing there deleted, and a clamping washer fitted between the bearing and the timing gear. The engine's balance factor increased from 64 to 70%. The "big bearing" motors were externally identifiable by a small crescent-shaped bulge on their timing case outer covers.

The T110, however, retained the previous 6T's Lucas E3L dynamo, and for ignition the Lucas K2F magneto with manual advance/retard and this year with its brushes in the rear of the points plate.

The T110's cylinder barrels and head were of iron, but its head, still secured by eight holding-down studs, was of a new design in shell-moulded iron, with modified ports and larger inlet valves. It came with the E3325 camshafts and followers based on the "Q" sports cam developed in America, and with 8.0:1 compression pistons, made possible in the UK now that

The Triumph "Tiger 110" offers the enthusiast everything he wants in a sports motorcycle. Up-to-the-minute in every detail of its specification, it combines superb suspension with an engine designed to produce the highest possible power output in a smooth and effortless manner.

SPECIFICATION

BRAKES. Powerful and smooth acting. New large diameter front brake with highly polished anchor plate. Cast iron drums.
WHEELS. Triumph design with dull plated spokes, Dunlop tyres and chromium plated rims. Fully valanced rear mudguard with side lifting handles. Q.D. rear wheel optional (extra).
ELECTRICAL EQUIPMENT. Powerful Lucas 7 in. built-in headlamp with combined reflector/front lens assembly, "pre-focus" bulb and adjustable rim. Separate parking light below. Lucas 6 volt 60 watt dynamo with full ball bearing armature, automatic voltage control and 12 a.h. battery. Wide angle rear/stop light. Gear driven magneto.

NACELLE. Triumph Patent 647670. Neat streamlined shell integral with top of forks, encloses headlamp, instruments and switch-gear. All instruments rubber mounted and internally illuminated.
SPEEDOMETER. Smith's 120 m.p.h. (or 180 k.p.h.) chronometric type with r.p.m. scale internal illumination and trip recorder.
OTHER DETAILS. Complete set of good quality tools and greasegun; new "Two-Level" Twinseat, latex foam covered with black waterproof Vynide; adjustable tension twist grip; tank top parcel grid.

For Technical Details see Back Cover.

New and massive crankshaft.

1954 T110

higher-octane petrol was becoming available. These pistons carried chrome-face second compression rings.

Oil circulation was increased by enlarging the pump's plunger diameters.

The T110's primary chaincases were revised. The primary chain itself, within a shorter chaincase, was shortened compared to the 6T's, to 70 pitches, as the gearbox was brought closer to the crankcase, all to keep down the overall length of the swinging-arm models. The inner primary case now carried a breather pipe forward of the footrest hanger rod; and the cast guard around the gearbox shaft was no longer a constant radius and semi-circular, but shaped a little. The shortened engine required new rear chain plates, and the lower chainguard previously found on the 6T was deleted, with the tyre inflator formerly mounted on the chainguard now fitted on hooks beneath the petrol tank. The gearbox shell too was modified to suit the frame. It also lost its gear indicator and gained a new pedal. Its clamping screw and adjusting screw were made more accessible. The T110 adopted a new cotter pin for the kickstart.

The T110's carburettor for this year only was a single 1⅛in Amal Type 29X, but with a TT-pattern float chamber. Its choke was controlled via a short cable by a lever mounted on the nearside rear frame top stay, beneath the Twinseat.

Frame and Suspension

For details of Triumph's new swinging-arm frame and suspension, see 1954 T100 (page 68).

Cycle Parts As 1954 T100 (see page 68).

Electrical Equipment As 1954 T100 (see page 68).

The 650 that took Triumph pre-unit twins to another level – and some say the ones like this one, from their first year, 1954, were the fastest of the lot, iron head and all. They certainly looked the part, with Shell Blue Sheen and Black finish, plus the elegant but fracture-prone 8in scalloped-edge front brake, featured for that year only. As a sportster, the "Ton-ten" retained magneto ignition and dynamo lights. Along with the T100, it introduced the "big bearing" engine and the swinging-arm frame. This excellent example from the A.R.E. collection, petrol taps aside, is very original.

Optional Equipment

A US Export 3 Imp. gallon/3.6 US gallon version of the petrol tank was available.

Alternative US Export 8.5:1 compression pistons were offered.

In the optional close-ratio gearbox, the mainshaft and 3rd gear were altered.

Valanced front mudguards, with the stays formed in one and riveted to the guard, were an option.

There was a new QD rear wheel for the new frame, with taper roller bearings within its hub. It carried a pressed steel anchor plate with a squared peg sliding location fitting onto the swinging-arm's left fork end.

1954 T110. "Looked like it was doing 100mph standing still" could have been coined for this 1954 machine.

1954 T110. The nacelle never looked better.

1954 T110. Nearside view of scalloped front brake and its drum side spoke flanges. Fractures across the flanges would limit it to this year only.

1954 T110. Nacelle layout for magneto models – lights-only switch, and central kill button.

1954 T110. The long advance/retard lever was rider-friendly. The handlebar grips are aftermarket items.

1954 T110. The works. The engine's cases were shortened to keep the overall length of the swinging-arm machine down. "Smoothstyled" central unit kept everything tidy. Note correctly black-painted frame-mounted choke lever.

1954 T110. The new swinging-arm rear end for T100 and T110, with new one-piece deeper valanced rear mudguard, revised rear chainguard, and Girling units which mid-season changed springs from 110lb to a notably stiffer 126lb.

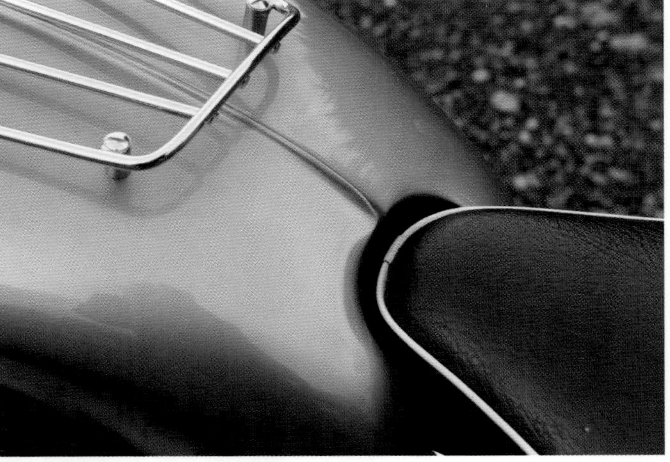

1954 T110. The new two-level Twinseat's nose married well with the rubber-mounted rear of the tank.

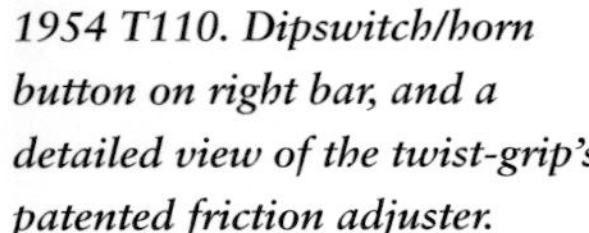

1954 T110. Dipswitch/horn button on right bar, and a detailed view of the twist-grip's patented friction adjuster.

1954 T110. Despite the tank's central seam, the trim strip and 4-bar parcel grid would not be introduced until 1956.

1954 T110. The Amal carb sits above a Lucas K2F magneto, and the rubber tube leads to a Vokes D-shaped air filter, now housed within the new central unit.

1954 T110. A one-off for the 1954 T110, this single 1⅛in Amal Type 29X featured a TT-pattern float chamber. The T110 still returned 70mpg

1954 T110. Despite the new swinging-arm rear, the front frame retained its trademark single tapered downtube, with dynamo behind it.

1954 T110. Star-shaped underside of steering damper. The tube parallel to the right fork leg guides the front brake cable.

1954 T110. The gearbox shell had been modified to suit the new swinging-arm frame, with a new top pivot fixing also. No more gear indicator, and a new gearchange pedal.

1954 T110. The iron-engined 650 with 8.0:1 compression and redesigned head put out 40bhp. Note the firm bracing for the carburettor's TT-type separate float chamber. Petrol taps are from later.

1954 T110. This model got its own name on the patent plate, to distinguish it from 6T's plain "650 Twin". A good clear view of the oil pressure tell-tale button.

1954 T110. Handsome polished alloy plate with air scoop and rear vent for new 8in single-sided front brake. The scalloped spoke flanges were for 1954 only. Note the good-looking painted and lined wheel centre.

1954 T110. The front brake's rear vent.

1954 T110. Tapering tear-drop silencers looked well. Lifting handles were a boon for this first model with a centre-stand. Tail-light is following year's Lucas 564, not the correct Lucas 525.

1954 T110. Pullback handlebars married well with the new two-level Twinseat to give excellent riding position.

1955 T110

1955

The T110's iron head had been found prone to overheating and developed a reputation for subsequent distortion and cracking. In a much-derided move Meriden now painted the head silver to give it the appearance of cooler-running alloy. Triumph expert John Nelson believed that the true problem lay not so much with distortion of the head itself, but in the fact that, because it did indeed fail to lose heat generated by the higher compression, head gaskets would blow and this could ultimately lead to holed pistons, especially on the 8.5:1 compression US Export models.

Engine and Gearbox

The T110's cylinder head was given a fifth cooling fin, located by the exhaust pipe clamp. The cylinder head, previously black, was now painted silver.

In the gearbox, due to gearchange locating problems, the 1938 camplate locating plunger was reintroduced. The kickstart quadrant was now made of nickel-steel chrome. The kickstarter's ratchet spring and sleeve were changed, and their associated thrust washer deleted.

The T110's single carburettor became the long-running Amal Type 376 Monobloc, in 1$\frac{1}{16}$in size. The choke was now operated by a spring-loaded plunger within the carburettor itself. The existing D-shaped Vokes air filter was modified slightly to accommodate that year's revised oil tank.

Frame and Suspension As 1955 T100 (see page 69).

Cycle Parts As 1955 T100 (see page 69).

Electrical Equipment As 1955 T100 (see page 70).

Optional Equipment

A new, more accessible prop-stand became available.

1956

The T110's overheating head problem was addressed with the adoption of the alloy "Delta" cylinder head, an improvement and a performance booster, though still sometimes prone to cracking between the holding-down bolts and the valve seats. A "Delta" head T110 was tested at an honest 109mph.

This year the T110 was joined by the dual-purpose TR6 Trophy 650, a mostly US-oriented model beyond the scope of this work, but one with which the T110 would often share mechanical components, and which would decisively influence the style of the T120.

Engine and Gearbox

The new die-cast light alloy cylinder head was known as the "Delta" due to its shape with the splayed exhaust ports, when seen from above. It featured cast-in air passages. It also eliminated the head's external oil pipes, by draining oil directly into the pushrod cover tubes. Valve inserts were of cast-in austenitic iron, and instead of each valve lying in a chamber in the head, both inlet valves were in one chamber and both exhaust valves in another. The pushrod tubes, now with thicker cover seals at their top end, and lacking bosses for the previous oil drain pipes, were seated on the underside of these chambers rather than in the rocker boxes. Each rocker box was redesigned, with an extra middle holding-down stud. Compression was raised to 8.5:1.

From eng. no. 75026 a revised cylinder head with a slightly different combustion chamber was fitted, in combination with new pistons with different valve cut-outs.

The con rods, previously with white metal big ends, now had Vandervell VP3 shell bearings, with the con rod eye enlarged to take them, and balance weights adjusted to maintain the 70% balance factor with the heavier rod assemblies.

In the gearbox, for all models, the layshaft bushes, previously phosphor bronze, were now of sintered bronze to aid lubrication. The composition of the clutch shock absorber rubbers was changed. Clutch plates were modified, with the driven plates becoming solid not pierced, and the drive plates now with bonded-on Neolangite, rather than cork, inserts (Neolangite was a cork material impregnated with Neoprene).

A heat-insulating fibre spacer was now fitted between the carburettor and the manifold, to help isolate the carb from the head's high temperature.

Frame and Suspension As 1956 5T(see page 42).

Cycle Parts As 1956 5T(see page 43).

Electrical Equipment

As 1956 5T (see page 43).

TIGER 110

The Triumph name has always been associated with performance, but in the 650 c.c. "Tiger 110" performance capabilities are available which exceed those of any standard production type motorcycle. Despite its high power output the engine is smooth-running, tractable and easy to start. It has an alloy cylinder head of advanced design, high compression pistons, special camshafts and a large bore carburetter. First class suspension, really powerful brakes and exceptional ease of control all combine to make the T110 a motorcycle of rare quality. The photograph illustrates the two-tone (Ivory/Blue) finish available as an optional extra on the T110 and T100.

Optional Equipment

The Lucas "Wader" magneto, with its vented cap, as well as the K2FC competition "red label" magneto, were offered as options.

1957

A year of restyling, with the "mouth-organ" tank badges introduced, and the T110's colour, like the T100's, changing to silver, though also with a two-tone option made possible by the new tank's design. Though outshone briefly that year by the T100's optional twin carbs, the sporting 650 was the majority choice, and this was another good T110 year.

Engine and Gearbox

Oil drainage from the valve pockets in the T110's "Delta" head was improved, while the compression ratio for the home and general export model was reduced back from 8.5:1 to 8.0:1.

The piston's chromed second ring was replaced by the previous tapered version.

For gearbox and clutch, see 1957 5T (page 45).

Frame and Suspension As 1957 5T (see page 46).

Cycle Parts

The T110's front brake remained single-sided and of 8in diameter, where those on the 5T and 6T became full width hub. The T110 however did gain a new drum and hub, as on the T100, with the drum cast iron and the anchor plate polished aluminium. It featured a chromed wire mesh-protected front air scoop plus a rear vent.

The back plate was also modified to take a new front wheel spindle, which had been revised to suit that year's split fork ends. As on the other twins, the front wheel spokes became straight and butted, while the spokes on the rear, to counter fractures, replaced their previous 9 gauge spokes with heavier 8/10G gauge at the hub end. The bottom brazed members of the front mudguard's middle stays gained brazed-on lugs, with the previous loose clip stays being deleted. The brake anchor plate mounting brackets also became induction-brazed. Stronger section silencer clip stays, plus added brackets and strengthened exhaust pipe brackets, now also featured. As for all roadster twins except the 5T, a Dunlop ribbed front tyre became standard.

Otherwise as 1957 5T (see page 46).

Optional Equipment

An "Easy-Lift" centre stand, developed for the Police, was offered.

The QD rear wheel still offered now featured the same heavy duty spokes as the standard wheel.

A two-tone finish, Ivory (tank top half, main mudguard colour) and Meriden Blue (tank bottom half) was an option for the UK (and a standard US Export finish).

The previous optional valanced mudguard was no longer available.

The safety strap on the Twinseat required by Californian legislation, which went out as a kit to be dealer-fitted, appeared to become an option.

1958

This was historically the T110's peak year. The point was made dramatically in the UK, by victory in the enthusiastically-followed Thruxton 500 production race battle. Although in former years the T110 had headed the 750 class, previously the overall winners had been smaller capacity BSA Gold Star 500 and even 350 singles. This year the T110 of Dan Shorey and a young Mike Hailwood won outright, after an epic struggle with Bob Macintyre on a big but less reliable 700 Royal Enfield twin. The next Triumph twin to win at Thruxton would be a T120 Bonneville in 1961.

What cemented the solid street cred gained by that 1958 victory was the fact that, for this year alone, the T110 was offered with an optional twin-carb version of the "Delta" head.

On the standard version, a revised alloy head to tackle the problem with cracking was fitted, which among other things meant that the combustion chamber was reduced in size. John Nelson noted that this "really was a pity as the engines, perhaps understandably, never seemed to run quite as well afterwards". But the T110 was still a flier, and this was very much the machine from whi/ch the T120 Bonneville directly evolved.

A step backwards was the adoption of the patented Slickshift mechanism in the gearbox to enable clutchless gearchanges, but as already noted, many riders would simply disconnect this unpopular device.

Engine and Gearbox

The alloy "Delta" cylinder head, in both standard single- or optional twin-carb form, was modified, with the combustion chamber reduced in size. There were reshaped piston crowns and smaller-diameter inlet and exhaust valves to suit. This provided more metal in the vulnerable-to-cracking area between the valve seats and the holding-down studs.

For gearbox changes and Slickshift details, see 1958 5T (page 46).

1958 was the T110's last peak year. Facing eclipse by the upcoming twin-carb T120, the T110 did not go gently into that long night – that year saw Shorey and Hailwood's Thruxton 500 victory. But there was a subtle tug of war going on here, between a sports bike with no baffles in its tear-drop silencers that year, plus an optional twin-carb kit, and Turner's styling – not just the nacelle, but the black-and-white optional two-tone colour scheme (too many echoes of the rozzers) and the deep pressings of the valanced mudguards adopted by the whole range, when the lads wanted alloy blades. The conflict would of course come to a head in 1959/60 with the urgent US-driven restyling of the T120. This model from Ace Classics represents a valuable historical record of a tipping point in time.

Frame and Suspension As 1958 5T (see page 47).

Cycle Parts

The T110 along with the T100 now adopted a full-width front hub, with the brake plate losing its air scoop and exit vent. For details and other cycle part changes, see 1958 T100 (page 86)

The T110 alone had its exhaust pipes modified with a slight bend to give a minimal upward tilt to the silencers.

Optional Equipment

The twin-carb cylinder head was similar to the one which had been offered for the T100 in 1957. The twin 1⅛in Amal Type 376 Monoblocs were mounted on splayed inlets via screwed-in steel adaptors, locked with large nuts, and with short bell-mouth intakes, no air filters being fitted. To help get the best from them and their T100 equivalent, Meriden offered a free Technical Information Bulletin (TIB), its second one, "TIB 2", which proved very popular.

The T110's 1958 UK two-tone colour option (standard for US Export), was Black (tank top half) and Ivory (tank bottom half, main mudguard colour), again as on the T100.

Otherwise as 1958 T100 (see page 86).

1958 T110. The full-width hub 8in front brake was new for the year, with decorative fluted backplate, but was not really up to the bike's performance. The wheel featured heavier-gauge spokes. Single mudguard stay came with new valanced guard.

1958 T110. The '57-on "mouth-organ" tank badges, with chrome trim at the front and gold dividing line at the rear, facilitated two-tone colour schemes.

1958 T110. Internally, the alloy cylinder head had been re-worked for 1958 to counter cracking, with a slight subsequent drop in responsiveness.

1958 T110. This year the exhaust pipes changed from the traditional 1¾in diameter to 1½in. The primary chaincase is fastened by the correct Philips head screws.

1958 T110. Gleaming demon. Correct Lucas headlamp in '58-modified nacelle, and chromed oval grille where the underslung pilot light had once been.

1958 T110. Pretty, and pretty loud – "tear-drop" silencers for T100/T110 lacked baffles that year. T110 exhausts were bent a little to give silencers a slight uptilt.

1958 T110. There were new holes in the nacelle for brake and clutch cables, but the other ones still went through big D-shaped grommets alongside the handlebars.

1958 T110. Correct '56-on 4-bar parcel grid and chrome trim. The waisted shapeliness of the Triumph tank was a big part of its appeal when compared to other marques.

1958 T110. This year the nacelle featured additional holes for front brake and clutch cables. Note how the tank's central decorative strip flattens out correctly to continue to the underside.

1958 T110. '56-on left-side mounting for horn/dipswitch, and usefully long advance/retard lever

1958 T110. New mudguard featured centre mounting bridge connecting to brazed-on bosses on fork legs.

1958 T110. This year saw the demise of the former steel tube guiding the front brake cable. Instead the cable stop moved to the bottom of the fork leg, with the cable adjuster previously located there now moved more conveniently to the handlebar end.

1958 T110. By now the 650 motor was producing a claimed 42bhp at 6500rpm.

1958 T110. The year's least welcome innovation was the "Slickshift" mechanism in the gearbox, identifiable by the new chromed inspection cover. Note also the revised configuration of the clutch operating arm.

1958 T110. Centre section transfers present and correct.

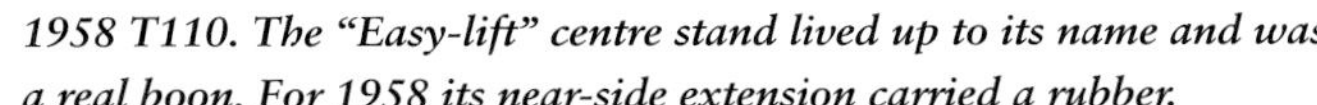

1958 T110. The "Easy-lift" centre stand lived up to its name and was a real boon. For 1958 its near-side extension carried a rubber.

1958 T110. This cylinder head with the vertical rib to counter ringing is from 1961-on. Lock-wiring the tank retaining bolts was a wise precaution against high-speed vibration.

1958 T110. The single 1⅛in Monobloc carburettor and the Lucas K2F magneto with manual advance/retard control. Correct petrol taps and pipes.

1958 T110. Picked-out colour of Triumph badge varied from model to model; this one was correct for 1958 T100/T110.

1959

The T110's glory days came to an abrupt end as it was leapfrogged by the twin-carb, super-sports T120 which had been developed from it. The T110 twin-carb option was summarily withdrawn. But the Tiger 110 did benefit from the uprating of the 650 engine with the new one-piece crankshaft, as well as from a strengthened transmission. This year for the last time it was close to being a single-carb Bonnie – though that description really belonged to the dual-purpose TR6 Trophy. As noted, from this year the 650s were referred to as the B-range, and within it the T110's status perceptibly shifted. A road test that year had a T110 pulling (commendably fast) a sports sidecar.

Engine and Gearbox

The T110, with the other 650s, adopted the one-piece forged EN16B crankshaft, developed in response to 650 power outputs which had risen from 34bhp on the original 6T to 48.8bhp on an experimental twin-carb machine early in 1958. So the previous 3-piece crankshaft was replaced by one manufactured from a single forging, with 1⅝in journals, and a ground central diameter which accepted the centrally mounted, 2¼in wide flywheel with its straight-sided cheeks. This flywheel was fed on over the timing side crank, and held in position by three 7⁄16in bolts which passed through the outer periphery of the flywheel into threaded holes in the crankshaft forging. The engine's balance factor was set back to 50%.

In mid-year, after some breakages in competition, the interference fit of the flywheel's three radial bolts was increased to 0.0025in when new bolts were fitted.

The T110's compression ratio remained at 8.0:1.

The T110's clutch used a different grade of Neolangite on its friction plates. A gearbox level oil plug was fitted, in addition to a boss just behind the layshaft housing of the gearbox

1959 "THREE MILES OF TRIUMPH" Brussels Rally

1960 T110

inner cover. From eng. no. 023941 (early February 1959) induction hardening was introduced for the periphery of the gearbox camplate, and from eng. no. 024029, also for the clutch sprocket centre bore.

Cycle Parts

The "tear-drop" silencers were replaced by the previous "straight-through" type, which were also used on the T120. At eng. no. 021941, they were replaced with the previous baffled type.

The angle of the front brake cam lever was altered to improve leverage, its modified lever identifiable by a stamped "X".

Electrical Equipment

During the model year, the Lucas K2F magneto changed from manually controlled to automatic advance/retard.

Mid-year. at eng. no. 024137, the previous Lucas RB107 regulator was replaced by the Lucas 37725H.

1960

The T110 gained the new duplex downtube frame and redesigned front forks. However the distinction between it and the T120 was now completely clear, as the latter emerged with slimmed-down, US-oriented cycle parts, while like the 6T, the T110 retained its nacelle and adopted the unit-twin style "Bath-tub" rear panelling and "fireman's helmet" front mudguard, flared and valanced, all in a Black and Ivory two-tone finish.

Like the T120, however, it also lost its dynamo in favour of an alternator, but did retain its magneto to the last. A sports tourer was what the T110 now aimed to be.

Engine and Gearbox

The adoption of a crankshaft-mounted alternator meant that the T110 now used a suitable version of the 6T's crank-shaft. It thus was also fitted with versions of the 6T's inner primary chaincase and its crankcases, though the T110's differed from those on the T120/TR6, while the outer timing case and primary chaincase for T110/T120/TR6 differed from the 6T's. It should be noted that only these alternator engines will fit readily in the 1960-62 duplex downtube frame.

From eng. no. D1564 (end of December 1959) the oil pump's brass body was replaced by an aluminium casting.

The oil pressure indicator button was modified to incorporate a seal, a synthetic rubber O-ring, in the end cap for the indicator rod.

The primary chain adjuster draw-bolt was redesigned to provide a clutch cable abutment now at the rear of the gearbox clamping studs, to suit the panelling.

Within the panelling, a new box-shaped air filter was adopted.

Frame and Suspension

For details of the new frame, see 1960 T120 (page 171). At eng. no. D1563 (end of December 1959) the frame was modified with an added lower tank rail to counter fractures at the headstock. The new rail made the engine more difficult to remove and to work on in situ. Examples of it may be found retro-fitted to earlier duplex downtube machines, as it was issued as a factory kit. For further T110 frame details, see 1960 6T (page 113).

Cycle Parts

As 1960 6T. Note however that unlike the 6T, which adopted 18in diameter wheels and tyres, the T110's for 1960 remained 3.25 x 19 front, 3.50 x 19 rear. Its silencers also remained the baffled type as on the T120, rather than the 6T's with their mute in the tail.

Electrical Equipment

An RM15 Lucas alternator was fitted. For ignition the magneto remained the Lucas K2F with automatic advance/retard as standard.

The stop-light switch became a new D-shaped one, operated by a small lever contacting the rear brake pedal.

Optional Equipment As 1960 6T (see page 114).

1961

The T110's last year, as the British market declined dramatically, the Americans did not care for panelling or the nacelle, and the Thunderbird filled the touring role, while in mid-season the TR6 SS took on the sports tourer mantle. But at least in terms of appearance, the one-time King of the Road went out in a blaze of glory, adopting a striking Kingfisher Blue and Silver finish.

Engine and Gearbox

The T110's alloy head, like all the 650s, had a vertical rib, tying the cylinder head fins, added to each side of it outboard of the plug positions, to help reduce ringing. This year within the head there was also a flat machined on the large diameter of the exhaust valve cast iron seat insert, narrowing it to $1\frac{11}{32}$in. This was to allow a greater thickness of aluminium, and was hoped would help deal with the problem of cracking, to which the head with its eight holding-down studs had still been prone.

For gearbox and gearing changes, see 1961 6T (page 114).

Due to gearing changes, the Smiths Chronometric speedometer became the SC3304/24.

Frame and Suspension As 1961 6T (see page 116).

1961 T110

For rarity value alone, this final-year T110 is worth inclusion, even if at the time it seemed a sad end for the one-time King of the Road. Of the pre-units, only the 6T and T110 went down the "bath-tub" route, the other models adopting unit construction engines before doing so. Possibly prescribing panels for the 1960/61 T110 had been a tactical move to head off Edward Turner imposing them on the T120! At least the T110 kept its magneto ignition, and in this final year regained a bit of the old spark with the Kingfisher Blue and Silver colour combination. This rare example belongs to Cliff Rushworth, the owner of Ace Classics. So many had their panels stripped off that this is a real rarity, and though a pain for owners to live with then, the model was as stylish in its way as everything else that Turner produced.

1961 brochure cover, T110

Cycle Parts

The brakes were modified with fully floating shoes; for details see 1961 6T (page 116).

A folding kickstart pedal became standard.

Electrical Equipment

The T110's RM15 alternator was given windings more suitable for use with a magneto, to reduce output and prevent the battery overcharging.

1961 T110. Final form of pre-unit nacelle, and chrome mudguard surround, made sense in terms of style. But not if you were young at the start of the Sixties and hungry for a Bonnie. There was a new tank for the 1960-on duplex downtube frame, with a stainless steel holding-down strap on rubber padding.

1961 T110. Petrol tank strap in fifth and final stainless steel form.

1961 T110. The Kingfisher Blue finish was achieved by painting over silver.

1961 T110. The nacelle had changed subtly for the panelled models, now being the one off the 3TA unit 350, with different bottom quarters, fork sleeves, and a shorter top than previously.

1961 T110. Duplex downtube frame with, out of sight below the petrol tank, the extra tank rail installed mid-1960 season to prevent fractures below the steering head. Head angle for 1961 had become a compromise 65 degrees.

1961 T110. A knob on the right-hand panel released the hinged seat, giving access to the oil tank and battery.

1961 T110. On 650s, the "bath-tub" rear flange was on the outside for easier dismantling, with rubber beading between the junction of the two halves. Note the modified rear number plate, and the legally required circular rear reflector.

1961 T110. New tubular loops welded to the rear frame, in a different version from the un-faired models, carried the rear footrests and silencer bracket.

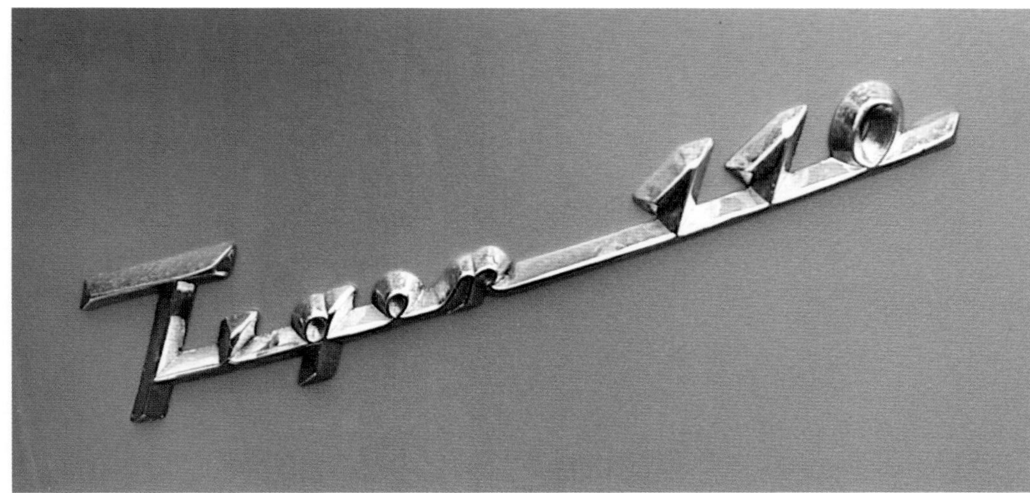

1961 T110. "Toothpaste" script let you know this was no puny C-range unit twin.

1961 T110. Undoing several screws fastening the panelling halves together would be fiddly; Norton used Dzus fasteners for quick-release panelling. Note the rear brake-light switch, operated mechanically by a shortened one-piece rear brake pedal casting.

1961 T110. Cross-pollination from the unit twins: the "fireman's helmet" mudguard came off the 3TA 350, and the internals of the revised-for-1960 front forks also followed 3TA practice.

1961 T110. Old-fashioned hip baths taken in front of coal fires were roughly this shape, inverted – hence "bath-tub". Wonder how often the new-shaped air filter in there got cleaned?

1961 T110. The primary chain adjuster draw-bolt, redesigned for 1960, doubled up as the clutch cable abutment, to suit the panelling.

1961 T110. Sports engine with smaller-bore exhausts, alloy head and automatic advance/retard magneto, contradicted the touring panelling.

1961 T110. Engine plates covering the previous dynamo position left the lower crankcase front vulnerable to spatter, even with that mudguard.

1961 T110. The Amal Monobloc on the single-carb manifold with heat insulating washer was easier to keep in tune than T120's twin instruments.

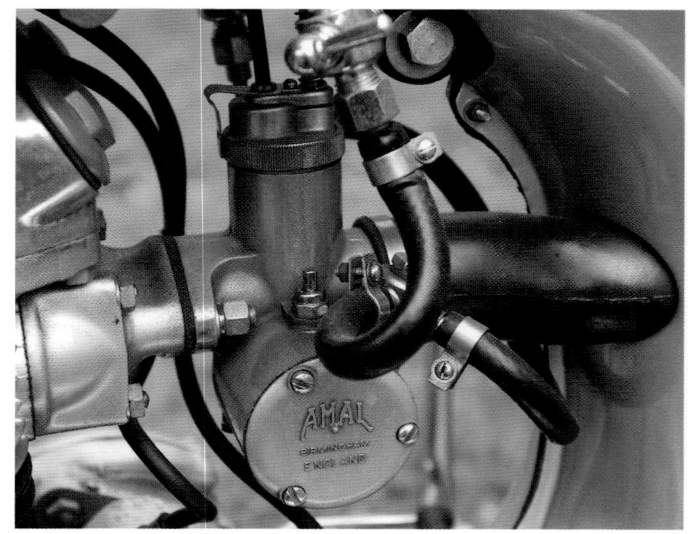

1961 T110. The faithful Lucas K2F magneto, now with automatic advance/retard, would be gone from Triumphs after 1962.

1961 T110. Note engine plates where the dynamo had been, replaced by an alternator in 1960. Also the built-in choke plunger on the Monobloc carb.

1961 T110. This year, inside the gearbox, Torrington needle roller bearings were fitted at either end of layshaft, with inner cover and shell modified to suit. The "Slick-shift" mechanism was still present, in its last year.

T120 BONNEVILLE 650

The T120 Bonneville represented the climax of the Triumph pre-unit twin story. The attention it attracted, then and subsequently, seems disproportionate for what was in fact something very little different from a twin-carb T110.

In fact, perhaps, but not in essence. An industry figure once described the pre-unit twins as "a triumph of development over design". The evolutionary nature of these models has been amply demonstrated in the preceding chapters, how they had been adapted ceaselessly to different demands and conditions (for instance, the initial post-war need in the UK to live with low-octane, rationed fuel and provide good petrol economy, giving way to the possibilities unlocked towards the end of the Fifties by higher-octane fuel and

1959 T120

increasing disposable incomes).

Almost as striking was what had not been changed. The limitations of Triumph handling had been present right from the start, with the 1939 Tiger 100, when Triumph's ex-racer and development man Freddie Clarke had modified an experimental machine's engine position, trail and steering head angle to successfully meet the problem, but Edward Turner absolutely would not countenance any major changes to his design. This was most probably due to a combination of Turner's insecurity about his lack of formal engineering training, and the egotism he developed to compensate, all amplified by recent personal tragedy after his beloved first wife had been killed in a car crash.

There was another insecurity in his background, the financial kind, derived from his having lived through the Depression. As a substantial shareholder in Triumph, he had a personal stake in maximising profits by avoiding expensive re-tooling wherever possible, an attitude later endorsed by Meriden's parent company after 1951, the BSA Group. Turner's continued unwillingness to modify his designs in the light of criticism had been most clearly demonstrated with his 1954-on swinging-arm frame. Known colloquially as "the whip-iron", its unsupported swinging-arm turned the seat tube into a torsion bar, a phenomenon that was actually visible at Production racing venues like Brands Hatch. Yet nothing substantial would be done to change that sometimes fatal feature until the 650s adopted unit construction for 1963, just before Turner stepped down.

The other major conflicting demand was between the needs of the UK market and the burgeoning US one. The story is well known that the T120 was only finally given the go-ahead in late August 1958, following a development programme on a twin-carb T110 that summer. The decision was announced at a meeting in Meriden's Experimental Shop, with the US West Coast bosses Bill Johnson and Wilbur Ceder, plus Dennis McCormack of the East Coast TriCor, also in attendance. There was the appearance of deliberation, but as John Nelson, who was present, has

The "Tangerine Dream" T120 has become famous for its back story, for the trouble it caused. Hastily offered at the last minute for the 1959 model year, it was very much a twin-carb T110 with an odd paint job. But the irresistible demand for the scorching performance from its 46bhp engine (this was in 1959, remember) was what led to the following year's quite radical redefinition in terms of stripped-down style and of a chassis intended to better handle the power. Since then the Tangerine one has become extremely sought after, and this example (registered 816 ACE) quite rightly lives at Ace Classics, in South-East London, since it is the model that started a legend.

1959 T120. US handlebars, 3-gallon tank and US-style decorated front number plate indicate a US Export model – appropriately, as this was a machine primarily demanded by, and aimed at, the States.

written, "one word from (the) Americans...and (the T120) was 'in'." Since May of that year US dealers had been selling T110s and TR6s with the splayed-port twin-carb head kit already fitted. They were certain that they could clean up with a dedicated twin carb-sportster.

Edward Turner was not so sure. There would be no spectacular launch for the Bonneville as there had been for the Thunderbird and even for the little Triumph Terrier single. The decision to proceed with the T120 had been taken too late for it to be included in either the UK or US sales brochures for 1959, and even on the hastily revised price list it was mistakenly included as a 500 twin, with the error then over-printed crudely with the words "ohv twin 650".

Turner's hesitation had stemmed from the fact that this was the definitive stretch of his original design, now twenty years old, away from the quiet and smooth-running machines originally envisaged. The new super-model was bound to run hotter, rougher and with more vibration – and consequently more warranty claims – let alone exposing the limitations of the handling.

And in some ways, Turner was right. Vibration would bedevil the T120's early carburation layout, and play havoc with Lucas electrical components built down to the price which the penny-pinching British motorcycle industry was prepared to pay. The T120's 1960-on alternators lacked proper voltage control and could boil batteries or even warp their plates. The second form duplex downtube frame's vibration would split battery cases, spilling acid on paint and chrome. Dip-switches and wiring harnesses were other victims/culprits, and the 1960-on quickly-detachable headlamp plug-and-socket could quickly detach itself and plunge the rider into dangerous darkness. The one vital bright spot was that the T120, like the TR6, being initially envisaged primarily as a competition machine, for which a magneto's adjustable spark was preferred, retained its reliable, self-contained ignition system.

The fractures of the initial 1960-on duplex downtube frame caused what American writer David Gaylin confirmed was "a flood of warranty claims". As described, Turner himself saw an American rider killed in competition when his frame broke below the headstock. When this was quickly remedied with an additional lower tank rail, frame fractures decreased but the level of vibration, for the machinery rather than for the rider, increased, and caused splitting fuel tanks to go with the existing rash of broken petrol tank straps and front mudguards.

Even in the area where Triumph normally shone, the styling of their machines, the first T120 in some terms famously got it wrong. First because it was offered in sports touring trim, with the valanced mudguards fitted to the T110 the previous year, the wide two-level Twinseat, the parcel grid and above all, the nacelle, whose day had passed for a generation on both sides of the Atlantic looking for racing styling cues. As writer Tim Remus put it, "the first Bonneville came to the beach party in a tuxedo, when everybody expected a T-shirt and jeans".

Neat as the nacelle was, there had always been practical objections to it, the way it made it difficult to work on the electrics, and the less-than-ideal routing for the control cables which it dictated. But the predominant problem with it now for the European fast boys was the way in which it prevented twinned speedo and rev counters being fitted, or fork gaiters which looked all wrong with it; while for Americans, it could not be removed for ventures off road. Since 1956 the dual-purpose TR6 Trophy 650 had been offered with a separate headlamp shell and an optional rev counter driven via an adapted timing cover. This was what they wanted.

The second famous style misjudgement came in the area where Triumph had led the industry and surpassed subsequent imitators like AMC and Norton – the T120's two-tone colour scheme. Turner selected Triumph's colours himself, and while his artistic flair was undeniable, nobody gets it right every time – witness the initial 1950 dull grey finish for the 6T Thunderbird. With the T120's Pearl Grey and Tangerine combination, perhaps he had looked sideways at another part of the BSA Group (for which he was currently serving as Head of the Automotive Division), namely Ariel. The latter launched their own sensation at the same 1958 Show as the Bonneville, the fully-enclosed Ariel Leader two-stroke 250 twin, with one of its colour options the fairly similar two-tone Cherokee Red and Battleship Grey.

The T120's Pearl Grey was in fact a pale blue shade and it was the predominant colour in the mix, on the tank top, the main part of the mudguards, and even the toolbox and oil tank, for some UK and all US models that year – early models in the UK went out with the T110/TR6-type black toolbox/oil tanks, but especially in America the others were grey to deliberately distinguish the T120 from those models. Pale coloured motorcycles had never had majority appeal, partly on practical grounds (showing up road dirt and oil), and partly cultural/aesthetic ones – they didn't look butch enough. It was an unpopular combination in the UK too, where in the latter part of the model year, months after America's restricted Spring selling season was over, an alternative with Royal Blue (described as Azure in the US) in place of the Tangerine, was offered for 1959 Home models only.

In the US, the original finish was near-disastrous – and this was a US-oriented machine, as Turner himself acknowledged publicly, with its Bonneville name chosen at least in part to emphasize that fact. There was a back-up of unsold Pearl Grey and Tangerine machines in the States, to the extent that a number had to be marketed the following year as 1960 models, despite their 1959 engine/frame numbers. According to Gaylin's *Triumph Motorcycle Restoration Guide*, they were models from late in the run, after the mid-year switchover from manual control advance/retard magnetos to ones with automatic control. The dislike of the original version was so pronounced that for 1960 only, the US importers redesignated the T120 as the TR7/A for the roadster and the TR7/B for the dual-purpose version then introduced (confusingly for us, as much later, from 1975 to 1983, "TR7" was how the single-carb versions of the T140 unit 750 Bonneville would be known). It was done to emphasise the difference between the originally styled and painted T120 and what followed.

Already in 1959 some US dealers, for an extra $100, had been converting the TR6/A with its sports headlight, rev counter, etc., by fitting a splayed head and extra carburettor. TriCor in the East legitimised the practice with a letter beginning, "If you feel that you will lose a sale of the T120 because of its nacelle forks..." With Edward Turner still at the helm, though, it could have been much worse: Triumph's export manager AJ Mathieu wrote to an American colleague, "Even

1959 T120

the T120 and TR6 were originally scheduled to appear in full skirts in the 1960 season. It was a veritable tooth-and-nail battle before that was reversed…"

Yet the Bonneville was a star, and the 1959 models had something about them as a whole that was indefinably satisfying. A seasoned rider once told me that although the '59 frame and much else looked identical to the T110, "somehow the Bonneville got it right," and that although his later 1961 model's ride with the duplex downtube frame had been more reassuring, overall he still preferred the first one.

And despite the lack of advance warning, the T120 did get off with a bang. In the UK, as a pre-election ploy, Harold Macmillan's Conservative government had released the squeeze on credit controls then in force, meaning lower rates on Hire Purchase, with the level of deposit left up to the finance companies, and no more 24-month time limit on repayment. HP was how the majority purchased new vehicles, "on the drip" or "the never-never" as it was known. The result for 1959, in combination with record-breaking warm weather from March to October, plus a 5% reduction in Purchase Tax, was that the sale of new two-wheelers would reach an all-time peak of 331,806 machines.

It was at that exact point in the curve of rising affluence when customers were using their increased wages and full employment to buy both cars, and motorcycles or scooters, as their primary transport. The year contained the seeds of its own destruction, in the shape of Honda's 1958 C100 step-through, and Issigonis's new-for-1959 Mini, which would quickly sound the death knell for three-wheelers and sidecars and spearhead the next shift, which was to cheap cars *instead of* two-wheelers; by 1969 there would be a car for every 1.5 British household.

That lay in the future, and in the current "you've never had it so good" atmosphere, the Mecca of British and indeed European motorcycling, the November 1958 Earls Court Show, did not disappoint. There had been no Show the previous year, and the 1958 ones in Frankfurt and Milan had been cancelled. Triumph rose to the occasion with a 100-foot long stand beneath 140 neon tubes (the design of the Show stand had been yet another thing Edward Turner had taken a personal hand in). The buzz word was of motorcycles and scooters converging, as with the Ariel Leader, and in that line Triumph displayed the new unit Speed Twin, fully panelled like its 3TA predecessor.

But for the cowboys, on the Triumph stand there was Hailwood and Shorey's Thruxton-winning T110; and there was the new "super-sportster" Bonneville. The UK's first motorway, a stretch of the Preston by-pass, opened shortly after, in December 1958, and there was talk of the T120 anticipating the coming motorway age. In fact almost the opposite would be true, as sustained high speeds would expose the parallel vertical twins' fundamental flaws – mixed going, with a quick blast on the by-pass, was more their forte. But on Triumph's stand at the Show a cutaway example of the new 46bhp engine was continuously thronged by a mass of enthusiasts.

1959 T120

Although Triumph had a very profitable decade ahead of it, largely in America, the economically friendly era in the UK would prove brief; the generous HP conditions were to be quickly reversed after Macmillan won the election in 1959, and by 1962 the home market sales figure had plummeted spectacularly to almost exactly half the '59 level. But Turner's luck had held, and his Bonneville got off to a flying start that established its legend for all time. The T120 may not have heralded the future, but as the apotheosis of the pre-unit twins and arguably the best all-round example of the type, it did, as Hughie Hancox once put it, encapsulate an era.

It was an era in which personal transport had become both a necessity, due to new-built spread-out housing estates and inadequate, expensive public transport, and affordable, thanks to full employment and reasonable wages. The late singer Adam Faith, who owned a pre-unit Bonneville in the late Fifties and frequented the Ace Café, once told me about the time when as a teenager he had ridden his first bike home from the big South London dealers Pride and Clarke. "That was the first moment of freedom," he said, "I ever felt as a person…it's easy to forget now what a huge thing it was to have your own transport. It was the working man's route to freedom, to liberty – the motorbike."

It was also an era which saw the emergence of an essentially American creation, the teenager. We may have exported to the States the magnetic sporting hardware, be it MG sports car or Triumph street scrambler, but spearheaded by Hollywood, American cultural imperialism dominated European popular culture. *The Wild One* may have been banned in the UK till the late 1960s, but there was *Rebel Without A Cause* with its black jackets and flick-knife rumbles. When working class teenagers and motorcycles met, as they did increasingly throughout the Fifties thanks to full wage packets, with the average age of motorcyclists dropping accordingly, the result was the Rocker, the coffee-bar cowboy, and the cult of the café racer. As with their favourite machines, the pre-unit Triumphs, for Rocker culture there was continuous feedback from the USA.

Blue jeans and a studded Lewis Leathers black lancer-front jacket, echoing the American Schott that Brando had worn, may not have been really practical for the British climate but they were the must-have items, along with white silk scarves which looked back at RAF fighter pilots and their need to keep their necks swivelling without chafing. The music on the jukebox might be Elvis, Buddy Holly and Gene Vincent, but it was soon joined by genuinely effective British covers and imitations, from Johnny Kidd to early (and surprisingly rockin') Cliff Richard. As with the Triumph Bonneville, in this culture something hybrid emerged.

Perhaps that even included the "Too Fast to Live/Too Young to Die" ethos, ("SUICIDE CLUB!" screamed the tabloid headline), not terribly British but a clear echo of transatlantic immature, romantic nihilism, as analysed by Leslie Fiedler's seminal *Love and Death in the American Novel*. Certainly teenage rebellion and juvenile delinquency got their templates from the Bronx and Westwood – with the same underlying motivation: youthful dissatisfaction with post-war conformity and respectability. The Rockers didn't want to go quietly into that soft suburban night, they wanted to rip it apart with the throaty roar of a Triumph on full song.

The Rocker cult, with the Bonneville at its heart, has stood the test of time. Its headquarters, London's Ace Café, re-opened in the late Nineties, and there are café racer clubs from Switzerland ("The Loud Mufflers") to LA. The most perfect retro-Rocker I ever saw was a young Japanese rider on the Isle of Man in 2007, on an equally perfect DBD34 Gold Star which he'd had flown over there. It lives.

The hardcore Rockers were utterly dedicated to the pursuit of speed, and surprisingly sophisticated. In his book *Café Racers*, Mike Clay, a former ton-up boy, wrote, "In the cafes there was never any serious argument about the Triumph frame, no matter what the magazine road testers tried to tell us. That single seat tube acted as a torsion-bar, and anyone in doubt had only to follow a Triumph through a few bends in the heat of a burn-up." But, as mentioned, they learned to live with it. Among the compensations were more available and better tuning parts and information for the Triumph than for its heavier BSA 500 and 650 pre-unit twin rivals, and a more affordable price than the better-handling but scarce Norton twin, which like AJS/Matchless would only expand from 600cc to the full 650, and adopt twin carbs, at the beginning of the Sixties; another instance of Triumph and the T120 leading the way.

Rockers were their own mechanics, and they firmly preferred the pre-unit format – for one thing, the pre-units' longer cases and separate gearbox were well suited for use in the larger Norton Featherbed frame, where if a unit construction engine was placed as far forward as it needed to be for good handling, chain length and tension became excessive, and the result didn't look right. They also found that the unit engines' progressively lighter flywheels lacked some of their predecessor's wonderful bottom end torque. And being mechanics, they understood the full implication of the T120 Bonneville's defining feature, its twin carburettors.

Superficially seeming a dubious benefit, twin carburettors made engines a bit thirstier than ones fitted with single instruments (the 1960 pre-unit T120 returned 52mpg overall on test) and, as was noted by the testers, needed adjustment, sometimes frequently, to be kept in balance. Their true advantage, however, was not just getting more mixture into the combustion chamber, but the way they allowed for wilder valve timing. With high-lift camshafts like the E3134 and appropriate "R" cam followers keeping the valves open longer, and a 3-keyway valve timing set-up allowing you to tune appropriately, the last ounce of power could be

1959 T120. Tank grid, nacelle and valanced mudguards were not wanted on board by our American cousins!

1959 T120. This was the first and last year for the T120 nacelle, which was essentially the same as the T110's. The "Bonneville 120" transfer should be forward, between steering damper and kill button, with the rectangular "Made in England" one on the nacelle lower edge, below the damper knob.

extracted from the top end.

The aim was to maximise the inlet gas charge time, but then prevent its loss from the combustion chamber by altering the exhaust timing overlap. This outside-of-the-envelope top end power was only really relevant to record-breaking and racing (though that could include street-racing), but the Bonneville's twin instruments, jutting out proudly and prominently from the splayed inlet ports, had another function – as they say today, implied performance! They were the ultimate go-faster badge. It was one more way in which the pre-unit Bonneville seized and encapsulated its era.

1959

The first model year T120s were a bit of a minefield regarding specification, as several features varied mid-year due to the factory reacting to the reception the newcomer received. There had been an apparent slight weight gain for the initial T120, which tipped the scales at 404lb, but this turned out to be the kerbside figure, and the Triumph twin remained the lightest of any of the British upright twins on offer –with its extra power more than compensating for any minimal extra weight.

1959 T120. The touring seat was another over-bulky item. Diminutive "Bonneville 120" transfer in black (initial ones were in gold) was a bit lost in Pearl Grey space!

1959 T120. Heart of the matter. The twin carb set-up in its first form, with the Amal 14/617's remote float bowl suspended from the seat tube and mounted on a rubber block. Larger screws on the Monoblocs' cover plates permitted factory lock-wiring. HT leads are correct black and yellow for K2FC competition magneto.

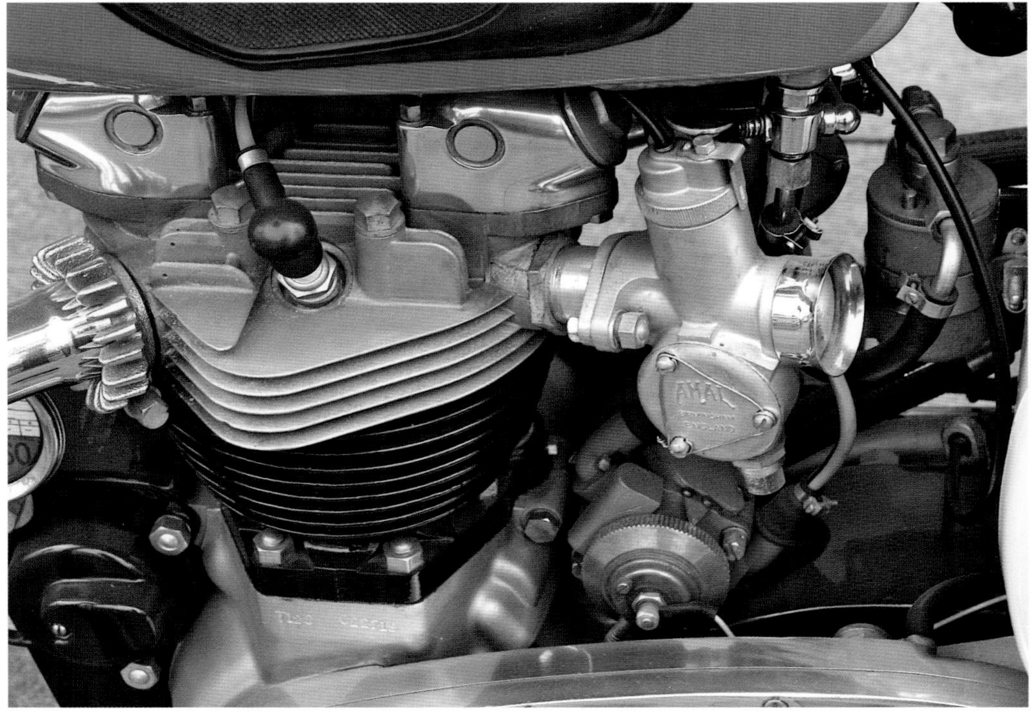

Engine and Gearbox

As David Gaylin and others have pointed out, the T120's defining cylinder head also demonstrated the way it had evolved from the T110, as on the first ones the inlet passages still contained the unmachined bosses of the parallel tracts previously used on the early optional twin-carb T110/TR6 heads. Also to be found by the oil drain well below the inlet rocker box was the cast-in, earlier "E3548" part number.

An external tell-tale for this evolutionary heritage from the earlier model was that some early T120s went out with their triangular riveted-on patent plates on the timing-side case headed "Tiger T110". Gaylin confirms that it was only a very few before Triumph, in the interests of simplicity, headed up the plates for all four 650 pre-units with simply "650 Twin", as previously found on the 6T, followed by the customary string of patent numbers for the big end design, the crankshaft, etc. Plates marked "Bonneville" should be approached with caution. The original patent plates were made of brass, which shows through when the paint over the numbers has worn away.

As with the previous conversions and optional models, the head featured flanged steel mounting stubs screwed into the threaded inlet ports, with the manifold and carburettors

1959 T120. The nacelle limited the degree of the US handlebars' rise. Unlike the 4-gallon tank's knee-pads which screwed directly into the tank, the 3-gallon's pads clipped over a frame.

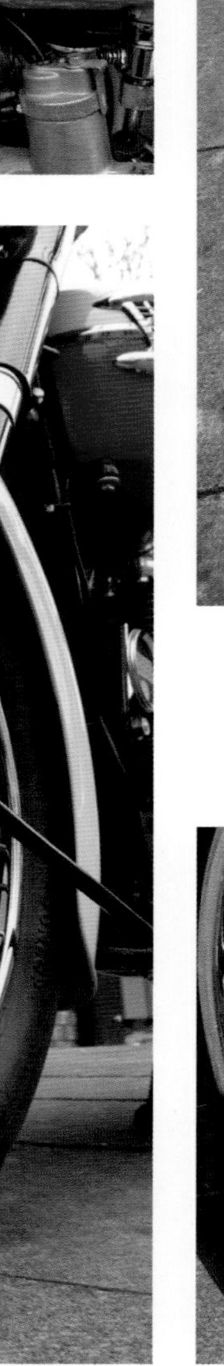

1959 T120. Earlier 1959 T120s retained the previous year T110's fluted front brake back-plate. Later ones went to the plainer type with two concentric rings.

1959 T120. All but the first few T120s had racing-type ball-end control levers. The full-width, cast iron hub 8in front brake was as introduced for the 1958 T110.

1959 T120. The smaller-bore 1½in diameter pipes in the splayed head were shared with the T110. The dynamo was in its last year. The smaller tank displayed a little more of the engine.

secured by large nuts. The splayed twin 1 1/16in Amal Type 376 Monoblocs were "chopped", i.e. with their float bowls removed, and with three special elongated screws for the covers where the bowls would have been. This facilitated the three screws being drilled and lock-wired together in a triangular pattern to secure the covers. This was standard racing practice appropriate for a machine initially envisaged as primarily for US competition, but also done in anticipation of the 46bhp engine's increased top end vibration.

Neither carburettor had an air filter, just bellmouths; nor was there a tickler button, as this was fitted to the remote float bowl; nor did they have a choke. Mounted at a slight downdraught angle, the carbs were a tight fit just ahead of the points on the petrol tank where the twin petrol taps with their tapered cylindrical metal levers emerged, and only the use of original specification components will prevent fouling in that area.

1959 T120. Carb and petrol tap were a tight fit, so the right taps were important.

The single remote float bowl employed was the Amal 14/617 from their racing GP instrument. It was fixed directly behind and in between the carburettors; the last time a similar arrangement had featured on a Triumph had been for the Forties' GP racer. The bowl was suspended from the seat tube, mounted on a solid, centrally-positioned rubber block, fastened at each end via ring clamps. The valanced edges of the T120's oil tank and battery box had to be modified around the opening to the now surplus-to-requirements air filter hole in the frame, to make room for the float bowl. In view of the subsequent problems associated with the use of the remote bowl, it is worth noting that for competition it could confer a real advantage. A 1961 *Motor Cycle* road test found that with it in place, available rpm rose from 6800 to 7500rpm (violating the experienced factory men's practical dictum for Triumph twins, "Never go more than seven"), and top speed from around 110 to 117mph.

However, in practice both hard braking and the T120's forte, hard acceleration, were found to cause surging in the float bowl and consequent misfiring. A partial remedy was introduced when, late in the season, a kit was offered to remedy this, consisting of a metal extension plate which attached to the rubber block and positioned the bowl 3in further forward, between the carburettor bodies themselves. But problems persisted, and many owners did what the factory would do early in 1960, namely replace the set-up with two 376/40 Monoblocs, each complete with float bowl.

The twin petrol taps supplied fuel via a siamesed banjo joint to feed the bowl, which in turn, through a joint on its bottom, fed petrol to the carburettors via a T-joint in the clipped-on black plastic tubing. Throttle control was via a one-into-two junction box, which permitted the continued use of the standard twistgrip with its friction adjuster.

Within the engine, there were altered and improved cast alloy pistons with thicker crowns and skirts, modified to clear the new crankshaft's bobweights at high rpm. The pistons gave a compression ratio of 8.5:1. It was found that the crowns of the Hepolite pistons could still collapse under the strains of US competition, so the crowns were thickened twice during the model year.

The crankshaft was the same strengthened one-piece forged EN 16B design as found in all that year's 650s, with its 1$\frac{5}{8}$in journals and central 2$\frac{1}{4}$in-wide cast iron flywheel threaded on over the outer crank cheek and secured centrally by three $\frac{7}{16}$in bolts; these passed down through the outer edge of the flywheel and located in threaded holes in the crankshaft itself. As mentioned elsewhere, the original bolts could give trouble at sustained high rpm, and mid-year, from eng. no. 027610, new specification bolts with an increase of the interference fit in the flywheel bore and the corresponding crankshaft spigot diameter by 0.0025in, were fitted. The engine's balance factor would later change from an initial 50% to an interim phase of 71%, before settling on the final long-running 85%.

1959 T120. Correct if not very neat routing of wiring to the familiar Lucas 564 tail-light. The central stripe, on full mudguard with lip, is squared off as it should be.

1959 T120. Early T120's silencers were unbaffled. 3.50 x 19 rear wheel and tyre were fitted until 1960. The '57-type rear chainguard was effective.

Externally the T120's outer cases were polished, and from eng. no. 022861 longer Philips-head screws were used to fasten the outer primary chaincase to the inner. The polished cases set off the T120's barrels, which were black-painted, to distinguish them from the silver-painted (*faux* alloy) barrels of the TR6.

The camshaft mix consisted of the racing E3134 for the inlet and the sports E3325 exhaust, transmitting lift via "R"-type cam followers and alloy pushrods to valves with diameters of 1$\frac{1}{2}$in (inlet) and 1$\frac{1}{32}$in (exhaust). The valves were controlled by double springs which had been strengthened at the very last minute after the author Barry Ryerson, one of the journalists who were given a preview of the model, had fudged a gearchange (had the Slickshift been involved?), sent the revs soaring and bent a valve. When Turner rode the machine in question it nearly set back the whole project, but then his engineer's instincts kicked in and he ordered the fitting of the stronger springs.

The gearbox may also have been altered thanks to that incident. For the T120 alone in that year, the Slickshift system for clutchless changes was disconnected, though the chromed oval cap which indicated its presence remained in place. It was done in the same way many owners had already resorted to, by the removal of the operating pin and roller.

The T120's box still contained the speedo drive, and shared the T110's ratios, with the latter's 24-tooth engine sprocket, 18-tooth gearbox sprocket, 43-tooth clutch sprocket and 46-tooth rear wheel one. As with the other 650 twins that year, an oil level plug was provided at the bottom of the gearbox in a cover. And also like them, at eng. no. 02311 an additional gearbox adjuster was fitted. After some early gearbox camplates had suffered distortion in US competition, at eng. no. 023941 induction hardening was used on the camplate's periphery. From eng. no. 024029, as a strengthening measure, the 4-spring clutch's sprocket centre also became hardened by that method. Finally, that year's change of Neolangite friction material on the 6-driving plate clutch's 5 driven plates was also specified. All the above measures were intended to help cope with the Bonneville's increased power.

1959 T120. A different view emphasises the jutting angle of the carbs on their splayed inlet mount.

1959 T120. Eye candy. Gleaming Bonnie's polished cases and prominent carbs had young men selling their souls on the never-never.

Frame and Suspension

The frame continued for this year exactly as the T110's single downtube cradle item, with 55¾in wheelbase and 64½-degree head angle. The Easy-lift centre stand was fitted as standard.

The rear suspension was by Girling units with 100lb springs.

The front forks too were unchanged, still only featuring one-way (rebound) damping.

Cycle Parts

Truly the devil was in the details for the first T120, for so many of those details failed to find favour with the young fast set on both sides of the Atlantic. They still loved the twin-carb super-sportster. despite the Tangerine/Pearl Grey finish of the petrol tank. The 4 Imp. gallon tank was standard for the UK, though the 3-gallon one, standard for US Export, was an option for all. The smaller tank came with a TR6-style chain retaining its petrol cap, and as before its knee rubbers

1959 T120. T120 barrels were black-painted to distinguish them from silver-painted TR6 ones.

1959 T120. Gearbox carried the 'Slickshift' inspection cover, but for T120 the device was disconnected.

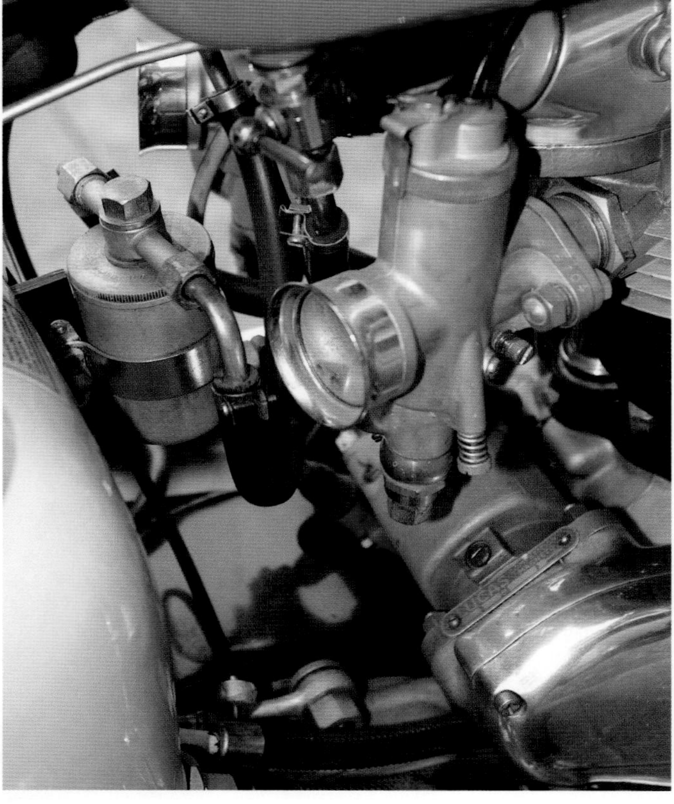

1959 T120. A clear view of the remote float chamber and carbs with bell-mouths, with correct black rubber tubing and petrol taps. Red label indicates K2FC competition mag – early 1959 US ones had manual advance/retard control, but this one has automatic control.

1959 T120. Some earlier UK toolboxes/oil tanks were black, but US ones were all Pearl Grey, to help distinguish T120 from T110.

1959 T120. Note slight down-draught angle on T120 carbs.

1959 T120. Excellent detailing – correct ¼-inch black-painted metal, not rubber, strap securing speedo cable; and valve clearance transfer on front cover above dynamo.

1959 T120. An 8-inch single leading shoe front brake, to stop a 117 mph motorcycle…

Still the 1959 model year, but what a difference a colour scheme makes! This late 1959 UK spec T120 benefitted from the revised paint job applied for Home and General Export machines later in the model year, anticipating the 1960 season, when it would be standard for all T120s. This gleaming example from Ace Classics is easy on the eye.

were pressed on to a bolted-on plate rather than screwed directly into the tank like the pads on the 4-gallon tank.

The fact that the parcel grid was still in place was not appreciated, though the "mouth-organ" tank badges, with the classic graphic of the traditional Triumph logo at their centre, still presented just the right degree of mid-Atlantic flash.

Doubly unappreciated was the nacelle, which, leaving styling apart, could not readily be removed for competition, and prevented twinned speedos and rev counters being fitted - at a ton-plus, you really did not want to take your eyes off the road to peer at the wavering rpm display on the "Rev-o-lator"! A rev counter could be fitted (see Optional Equipment), but it looked like an afterthought.

The nacelle also restricted the bends of the various handlebars on offer, which remained in Triumph's unique 1in diameter. The Home and General Export models continued with the T110's pullbacks, while the US Export ones, part no. H1010, were as high rise as the enclosure permitted. The control levers on these bars, except on a very few of the first ones which had the regular plain pressed steel levers (and which the 1959 Parts Book listed as standard), in practice were chromed ball-ended ones. In mid-season the Home/General Export T120 models went to straighter, more nondescript though still pull-back bars, while see Optional Equipment for details of a ⅞in diameter dropped bar which was offered.

The handlebars still wore the combined horn-button/dipper switch, fixed by a saddle clamp to the clutch lever pivot. For as long as models retained manual advance/retard control, the lever for that was mounted on the left too, but the T120's bars were unencumbered with an air lever due to the Bonneville having no choke facility. Traditional thin rubber grips were fitted, with the Triumph logo, facing in different directions, cleverly stamped above and below on each of them, so that any grip could be used on either end of the bar.

Initially the T120 carried the broader and heavier two-level T110 Twinseat, black with white piping. American feedback meant that during the model year this was soon changed to the lighter, narrow sports seat as found on the TR6, but confusingly this came in two finishes, either solid black with piping like the larger one or, in a styling move initiated by the 3TA, with a grey strip about ¾in wide around its bottom edge; both were fitted for the rest of the year.

Aside from the flange adjustment already mentioned, there was no change for the T120's one-piece oil tank/toolbox assembly. The oil tank had a capacity of 5 Imp. pints. For a time I believed the new T120 had reverted to the 8-pint tank, but John Nelson put me straight – that had been an option, and "not done by Meriden. TriCor and JoMo were a law unto themselves. Many things were marketed by JoMo's Pete Colman, but given Triumph part numbers". However, there was an issue over the oil tank/toolbox's colours. The first UK and General Export models went out with a black finish for the assembly, as on the T110/TR6, but for that very reason all the US Export models featured it in the blue-tinged Pearl Grey (or "Gray", as they called it), again to differentiate the new model.

Towards the end of the model year, the finish for the whole machine altered with the adoption of Royal Blue (or Azure in the States) in place of the previous Tangerine; the Pearl Grey stayed in place, but the two shades of blue worked well together. During the 1959 T120's time, with the back-up of

Late '59 T120. Thing of beauty. With this paint scheme, surely far fewer 1959 T120s would have remained unsold in the States, despite the touring style. Darker blue was "Azure" in the USA, "Royal Blue" in the UK.

Late '59 T120. US sports experience had discovered the power-boosting qualities of smaller bore exhausts. The T120 shared the T110's 1½in pipes (though the TR6's were even smaller at 1 5/16in). T120's polished cases set them off.

unsold "Tangerine Dreams" in the States, this blue finish was only found on Home and General Export models. It would become the standard scheme for the 1960 model year.

The mudguards were another bone of contention. The single deep pressings with their integral valances were not the light, sporting things that followers of the TR6 in particular had been hoping for. The front one also came with the shapely chrome-surround front number plate, which the Americans called "pedestrian slicers" and for which they had no legal requirement. Since it was there, US dealers often painted the plates with the logos of their shops, or as enthusiasts do now, with the model names, or with a cheerful leaping "Triumph" tiger. This front mudguard had proved prone to cracking around its middle mounting. As with the

Late '59 T120. On screw-in inlet stub, 1 1/16in chopped Monobloc with factory lock-wired cover

Late '59 T120. Very late 1959 models mounted the float chamber 3 inches further forward, but this one sports the original set-up. Proximity of taps to carbs could be fiddly.

Late '59 T120. Power pack. New 8.5:1 compression pistons, one-piece forged crankshaft, and E3134 inlet, E3325 exhaust camshafts, produced 46bhp and mind-blowing acceleration.

Late '59 T120. UK low bars and bigger tank suit the nacelle styling better.

Late '59 T120. Late form nacelle with grommeted hole for the clutch cable.

Late '59 T120. The nacelle in its last cutting-edge year. Note the persisting twistgrip friction device, made possible by a one-into-two throttle cable set-up. The long lever on the left bar indicates manual control advance/retard magneto, which lingered a little for the UK (and was always an option) after the US switched progressively to automatic as standard.

other 650s, at eng. no. 021941 the two short steel-strip centre stays attached to the mudguard stays, and previously riveted on to the mudguard centres, were now welded on.

The exhaust system was as on the T110, with the slightly uptilted pipes of 1½in diameter widening out just before the junction with the silencer. A narrower diameter had been found in the States to enhance the twin's power, and the TR6 fitted even skinnier pipes at 1⁵⁄₁₆in. The T120's silencers at first continued, like the previous year's T100/T110, to be "straight-through", but sanity, or at least the fear of upcoming Stateside noise legislation, prevailed, and at eng. no. 024337 they reverted to the T110's former baffled "absorption" type.

For UK models the 3.25 x 19 front, 3.50 x 19 rear wheels and tyres too were as on the T110, with the exception that where the other 650s changed the chromed front brake end plate with its radial flutes to a plainer one decorated with just two concentric rings, the T120 retained the flashier fluted one, until towards the end of the model year, when the concentrically-ringed one took over.

Electrical Equipment

Magneto ignition and dynamo lights were retained for the T120; for the US Export models, the magneto was the Lucas "red label" K2FC competition instrument, to begin with featuring manual advance/retard. It should be noted that the original HT leads from the K2FC were striped green and yellow. In mid-season magnetos for all T120s including the K2FC began to be supplied as standard in

Late '59 T120. The "Bonneville 120" transfer is where it should be. Yet what Bonneville riders wanted was not a Rev-o-lator speedo but a separate rev-counter.

versions with auto advance.

The main wiring harness, incidentally, was now fabric-covered. One change during the year for all 650s concerned the regulator, which altered from the previous Lucas RB107 to a more robust Type 37725H.

Optional Equipment

A Smiths rev counter was offered, as it had been since 1957 for the TR6A. The drive for it was taken from the exhaust camshaft pinion in the timing chest, and a special timing cover was necessary, with a small bulge from which the cable emerged at its top front, on which bulge the patent plate was relocated. Alternatively if the rev counter was only to be used when the dynamo had been removed for competition, drive for it came from a special unit taking the dynamo's place and located at the rear of the standard timing chest. In either case the instrument itself would be mounted asymmetrically on the left side of the handlebars.

Close-ratio and wide-ratio gear sets, suitable for on- and off-road competition, were available. If the latter was fitted, an 8-tooth pinion was supplied to replace the standard 10-tooth one in the gearbox-housed speedometer drive, so that the standard speedo could be retained.

The racing drop-handlebars with their special bend to fit the nacelle were of conventional ⅞in diameter, so they also needed adapter shims in the handlebar clamps, plus alternative rubber grips and control levers.

The K2FR racing magneto was an option, along with the K2F or K2FC, with either manual or auto advance/retard.

Late '59 T120. Heavier gauge rear wheel spokes had come for 1957 to counter breakages. The unbraced swinging-arm was pre-unit Triumphs' Achilles heel.

Late '59 T120. Girling units for 1959 housed soft-ish 100lb springs. The silencers housed straight-through internals.

Late '59 T120. The fluted front brake backplate, phased out towards the end of the model year, is still present here and suits the Bonnie's flamboyance.

Late '59 T120. A really attractive engine, now complemented by an appealing paint match.

Late '59 T120. Screw-on knee-grips, pullback bars, gold-lined mudguard stripes – it must have been hard for Edward Turner to realize that elegant style was passing.

Late '59 T120. Handlebar clutch cable adjustment, practical manual advance/retard lever, integral horn button/dipswitch – add ball-ended control levers and you'd have the whole set.

Late '59 T120. Later 1959 UK models went with the US-style coloured, not black-painted, toolbox/oil tank. The undersized black transfer was strictly from the following year – '59s were gold.

Late '59 T120. The twin carbs' open bell-mouths with no filters didn't suit Stateside off-roaders – or older traditional British riders, whose long "footing coats" got sucked into them!

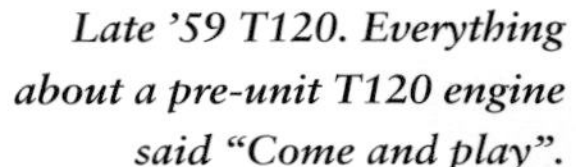

Late '59 T120. Everything about a pre-unit T120 engine said "Come and play".

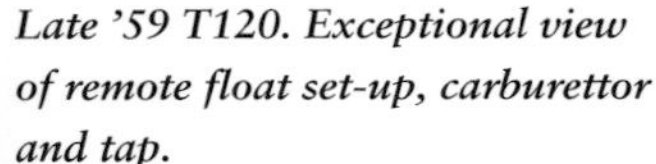

Late '59 T120. Exceptional view of remote float set-up, carburettor and tap.

Late '59 T120. The clutch operating arm had been modified in '58 to suit Slickshift, but retained its rubber end cover. T120's Slickshift was disconnected. Note exhaust pipes expanding at end to fit in silencer.

Late '59 T120. The carb's tickler lived on the float chamber. Note how the centre unit's segments were modified to accommodate the chamber's rubber mounting.

1960 T120

1960

The big change for the T120 mechanically was the adoption of the new duplex downtube frame, as well as the fitting of an alternator to replace the previous dynamo, and improved forks. In style terms, in this first year of the new liberated decade, the machine changed into the youth- and American-oriented sportster it had always seemed destined to be. Slimmer mudguards, smaller tank, new seat, separate chromed headlamp topped with (optional) twinned instruments, and gaitered forks, transformed it into a light, lithe beauty that sat like a coiled spring, its latent explosive acceleration (0-60 in 6.5 seconds) implicit in the jutting headlamp and in every forward-slanting line, topped by the swelling tank and black-case instruments like bunched shoulder muscles. Yet test after test confirmed that, thanks to the educated mix of camshafts, the Bonneville had lost none of the Triumph twin's characteristic tractable flexibility and rider-friendliness, being capable of speeds from 25 to 105mph in top gear, and with stomping mid-range power. Its exhaust note, assertive without aggression in town and out, was, like the rest of the bike, highly exhilarating. Despite the fractures in American competition, on the road the new frame was judged a real improvement.

As mentioned, for this year only, in the States the T120 was known as the TR7/A (the roadster), and as the TR7/B (for dual purpose/off-road ones).

Engine and Gearbox

The layout of the engine changed with the adoption of alternator electrics as well as with the new frame, so engine plates at the front, where the dynamo had been, differed, and a new timing side crankcase half lacked the mounting boss for the dynamo. The primary chaincase gained a tell-tale enlarged "horizontal tear-drop" bulge to accommodate the alternator, as on the 6T; while if the rev counter (optional for UK and

General Export models, standard for the "TR7/A", i.e. US T120R) was fitted, as it frequently was, the timing side outer case became the TR6's, with the patent plate on the bump housing the rev counter drive. The Smiths 120mph Chronometric speedo was revised and its face lost the "Rev-o-lator" feature.

In the gearbox, with American buyers fixated on a machine's standing quarter-mile time, the gearing was lowered for even punchier acceleration by reducing the teeth of the engine sprocket from 24 to 22, and those of the rear sprocket from 46 to 43. The rubber cap on the gearbox's external clutch lever was reintroduced.

The carburation set-up began with the remote float chamber retained, but now vertically suspended, just ahead of the carbs, from the engine head steady, by means of a threaded steel rod insulated by a rubber bush above the steady. But fuel surge problems persisted, and at eng. no. D5975 two complete Monobloc instruments, each with their own float chambers, were fitted, which took care of the problems at medium and high speeds. The tubing for this new set-up became pre-made transparent pipes. In mid-year the system was modified, with a balance tube fitted between the two inlet manifolds, intended to improve hesitation problems at tickover and low speed. It was also supplied as a kit, with two modified manifolds and a length of rubber tube, which was often retro-fitted.

Frame and Suspension

The all-new duplex downtube main frame was still of old-fashioned brazed-lug construction; this was in contrast to the similar chassis from Triumph's main rivals BSA, which was all-welded. The Triumph's still featured a bolted-on rear section, though that too was all-new, and it was of all-welded construction.

The twin tubes swept down to continue as the cradle underneath the engine/gearbox. The top rail, as previously, passed rearwards to form a right angle with the seat tube. But unlike the previous swinging-arm frame (and the BSA's) there was no lower tank rail triangulating with the top one, taking one end of a head-steady, and carrying lugs to support the petrol tank. Instead the latter function was provided at the front by two front petrol tank mounting brackets, brazed on part of the way down each of the downtubes, and fitted with rubber cups. The fact that they had to carry the weight of a tank full of fuel may well have contributed to the fractures below the headstock which began to occur during US desert and dirt racing. Meanwhile the lack of the rail did mean greater ease of assembly, with the head-steady coming in from the rear. The steady was now a single flat strip running from the bottom of the top frame tube to the inlet rocker boxes.

Although it made the frame safer, there was an unfortunate downside to fitting the lower tank rail to strengthen it. The former set-up had been notably smoother than the '59. The extra rail, however, amplified vibration for the machine if not for the rider. Sustained high speeds meant damaged electrical components, split tanks and mudguards, plus "bits-falling-off" syndrome from now on.

The rear petrol tank mounting, also involving a rubber cup, on the rear spine of the frame top tube, was part of an arrangement similar to that found on the Norton Wideline Featherbed frame. The similar-looking but all-new petrol tank was now without the raised top seam and its narrow chrome decorative strip, but with a broader chromed steel strap backed by a rubber strip beneath it. Rather than being bolted directly to the frame, the tank was held down by the strap, which was pinned to the frame at the rear, and tensioned via a yoke and draw-bolt arrangement at the front, with the bolt going down through the steering head casting and being tightened from below. Over-tightening could be a problem, leading to split tanks. Side wobbles were catered for by rubber blocks around the top frame tube, factory-supplied after eng. no. D104. Unfortunately, as mentioned, the straps themselves also proved fracture-prone and according to John Nelson would go through five modifications before ending in 1961 as stainless steel.

The new frame featured a quite notably steeper steering-head angle, going from 64.5 to 67 degrees, which shortened the T120's wheelbase from 55¼in to 54½in. The aim was to improve steering and to help end the high-speed weave.

As recounted, early in December 1959 Edward Turner saw a rider thrown and killed at the Triumph-dominated Big Bear Run when his frame fractured below the headstock. Turner instituted an immediate on-track development program at the UK's MIRA (Motor Industries' Research Association) facility, identified the problem and by the end of that month, at eng.

Desert Racing – Big Bear Run

This model was arguably the pinnacle of pre-unit Triumph twins, and looking at Barry Firth's stunning UK-spec T120, it's a hard proposition to dispute. In fact it's a machine from the latter half of the 1960 model year, but finished in the 1961 colours. The '60-on slimmer mudguards, separate chromed headlamp, twinned speedo/rev counter, new seat and gaitered forks, all built on the existing lightness and eager stance to transform the Bonnie into the bike, it now seems, that it was always meant to be. With that peerless 1961 two-tone finish, it certainly became a machine with one wheel in the (Sixties) future.

no. D1563, changed the frame's design to include the lower tank rail. This was also offered as a kit enabling the second rail to be retro-fitted, so duplex downtube machines with earlier numbers may well feature it.

The rear frame was bolted on as before to the top of the seat tube, but at the bottom the assembly was shortened, no longer reaching the front tubes and now fastened to a lug at the base of the seat tube. The mountings for the pillion footrests and silencers were no longer bolted on but were now a welded-on loop. At the top, stronger top tubes extended further back beyond the upper mountings for the Girling units, to support the rear end of the new back mudguard, so that the previous T110-style curved lifting handles/mudguard supports were deleted. It was a stronger, better performing assembly, but the swinging-arm was still unbraced.

New front engine plates were needed to secure the power plant to the two downtubes. The engine plate cover was a one-piece unit, with the bridging section at the top. According to David Gaylin, on machines other than the TR6/B and TR7/B (i.e. 1960 T120C), whose off-road kit included a bash-plate, without it the front of the crankcase was exposed to continuous splatter from the front wheel.

Another more familiar splatter, of oil from the end of the pressure relief tell-tale down by the rider's right boot, was addressed with a synthetic O-ring in the end cap for the indicator rod.

The frame's centre stand gained a new spring and connecting link, with the TR6/T120's link modified to differ from the T110/6T's.

In mid-year it was realised that the side stand was too short for the new frame and forks, and a longer one was fitted.

With the new frame came redesigned front forks for all the 650s. The springs were stiffer and the volume of damping oil in them was increased, with damping now claimed to be two-way. They strongly resembled the C-range unit twins' fork, though they still retained their detachable end-caps, and for the T120/TR6 had fork gaiters, in shiny black synthetic material rather than rubber. The fork sliders carried bosses which secured the brake backplate, as well as bosses which now moved down and onto the leg's centre line, mounting points for the mudguard's middle brace. For the T120/TR6, this brace became a C-type strip bridge, with tubular front and rear stays to suit. The T120/TR6 got their own top yoke, the former TR6 type with the handlebar clamps cast integrally and with detachable tops, the whole raised and pulled back slightly compared with previously. There was also a new steering damper, the lower plate for which located to the frame without a bolt.

Every road test agreed that though the suspension was on the harsh side, the new frame and forks were an improvement, with marginally heavier steering but still good to sling about, and lacking much of the previous insecure, "hinged-in-the-middle" feel. The riding position, especially with the flatter UK and General Export handlebars, had become more "jockey-like", but at Bonnie speeds a racing-type crouch that put more weight on the front wheel was no bad thing, except for really tall riders. One thing not mentioned in tests was the slightly limited ground clearance; full-tilt cornering could ground the undercarriage on left-handers.

Cycle Parts

The new but similar-looking petrol tank could be had as standard in either 3 or 4 Imp. gallon variants, both still with the parcel grid as a standard fitting. As described in the Engine section, these tanks lacked a top seam, and were retained by

1960 T120. As the steel blade rear mudguard lacks a lip, the lining stripe correctly continues on over the edge.

1960 T120. Twinned black instruments and jutting chromed headlamp conveyed T120 attitude – "Ride hard or stay home".

a bolted and tensioned steel strap. Their twinned petrol taps became the type with a flat, not circular, lever.

The battery box and the oil tank, this year painted Pearl Grey for all markets, were redesigned to fit the new frame, with new fixings, and the oil tank's froth tower was moved to the rear. The T120/TR6 tank was broader than the one for the panelled T110/6T's, and had its filler cap set further forward, with the feed and return pipes positioned at the front, not the rear like the "bath-tub" machines. The T120/TR6 toolbox gained an added mounting lug at the rear of its surface.

The T120 mudguards became as the TR6's, an alloy blade at the front and an unvalanced steel guard at the rear, with fixings as described in the Frame and Suspension sections. These guards did not have raised lips at their leading and trailing edges. The front number plate was now a plainer shape and without the chromed surround. Some were still going to the US, some not. The sizes of the T120's wheels and tyres in most cases became those of the TR6, 3.25 x 19 front and 4.00 x 18 rear, the latter on a WM3-18 rim; this was standard for US models and could be found in the UK, but some other markets continued this year with the former 3.50 x 19 rear. The T120's front brake backplate became the same plainer one with two concentric rings as the other 650s. The one-piece rear brake pedal was revised and became substantially shorter. According to Gaylin, the QD rear hub was fitted to "most American machines", with the standard one now having to be specially ordered there.

The T120's new chromed separate 7in headlamp shell was mounted on "ears" from the fork top shrouds, and carried the ammeter. They were all quickly-detachable, as on the TR6, and as well as sometimes plunging riders into unanticipated darkness, this was an unpopular feature because it dictated that the light switch be repositioned inaccessibly on a small mounting plate down on the right-hand side at the front of the Twinseat. With the nacelle gone, the horn too went under the seat, while the T120's engine kill button transferred to the right side of the handlebar close to the steering damper.

The Twinseats were all new and, though still low set and two-level, were better padded. This was the same seat as found on the panelled T110/6T, only bolted down, not hinged. The seat's cover was black vinyl with white piping and a black strip around the bottom.

The exhausts differed from previously as mentioned, and so did their brackets and the silencer clip stays.

Electrical Equipment

The T120/TR6 now had a Lucas RM15 alternator, with a rectifier, and with the ammeter in the headlamp shell, the light switch being under the seat nose as described.

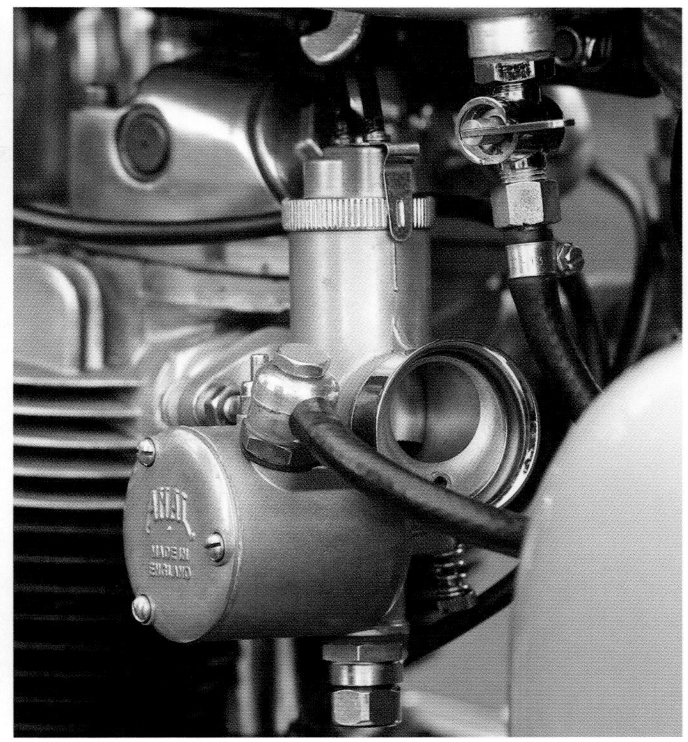

1960 T120. Float chambers would still have featured factory-fitted lock-wiring. Knee-rubbers on tank indicate that it is a 4-gallon.

1960 T120. As on other alternator models, the left-hand exhaust was kinked to clear the 6T-type chaincase.

1960 T120. The duplex downtube frame provided noticeably more reassuring handling. 6T-type chaincase contained alternator for lighting. "Made in England" transfer on frame tube would not arrive on Triumph twins until 1971.

1960 T120. The remote float set-up had been altered early in the 1960 year to two complete Monoblocs with integral float-bowls. According to the late Hughie Hancox, hoses on UK machines would have been transparent from then on.

The Lucas K2F and K2FC magnetos featured automatic advance/retard as standard. For machines fitted with optional manual advance/retard, the control lever was mounted on the left side of the handlebars.

Optional Equipment

A Smiths rev-counter, while standard for US Export T120 models, was an extra for Home and General Export ones. Where fitted, it and the speedometer were mounted on a single plate fastened to the top of the fork yoke. As mentioned, the geared drive was taken from the exhaust cam

1960 T120. "Absorption" tear-drop silencers had regained their baffles after 1959. Folding kickstart was now standard.

sprocket, with the cable exiting from the front of a modified timing side cover, and the bulge this created bearing the patent plate.

Magnetos with manual advance/retard control were optional.

The racing extras such as rear-set footrests were still available, but all altered to suit the new frame.

An 8 Imp. pint oil tank was offered in the USA.

Rubber grommets were available to plug the holes where either the parcel grid or the front number plate had been removed.

1960 T120. The right position for this transfer, opposite the petrol cap, now that the "Made in England'"rectangle had been displaced from the nacelle.

1960 T120. Without the nacelle, flatter but still graceful UK handlebars could be fitted, more suitable for high-speed road work. The choke lever is a practical later addition – Bonnies at this stage still had no choke.

1960 T120. The "mouth-organ" badge linked the new super-sportster to the fast roadsters of the Fifties. And Sky Blue loved Silver Sheen.

1960 T120. The final form of stainless steel strap holding down the tank. The front number-plate had lost its chrome surround in 1960 makeover.

1960 T120. Blade mudguard with revised brackets, and 8in single leading shoe front brake.

1960 T120. The rev counter, still optional for the UK, involved a modified timing case, with the patent plate re-sited on top of the bulge for the instrument's drive.

1960 T120. Detail of rev counter drive timing case. Not brass so not original patent plate.

1960 T120. Twinned black-face Chronometric instruments (rev counter was still optional for UK), including 1961's 140mph speedo. Steering damper would have been black-painted originally. Note correct centrally-mounted kill button.

1960 T120. Cylinder head lacks 1961's vertical rib, and engine number is from mid-1960.

1960 T120. The comfortable two-level dualseat adopted for 1960 was in common with panelled models, but bolted-on, not hinged. Black cover/white piping is correct for 1960/61.

1960 T120. Gaitered forks emphasized slimness while protecting fork seals.

1960 T120. Gleaming polished cases, and black barrels to distinguish T120 from TR6's silver-painted ones. Note awkwardly positioned underseat light-switch. The gearbox still carries the Slickshift inspection cover, though for the T120 the system had never been operational. Overall gearing was lowered for 1960 and 1961.

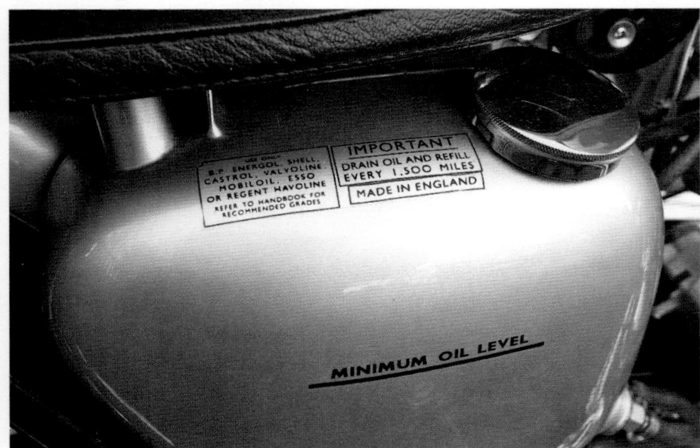

1960 T120. A few early '61 UK T120s had their oil tanks/toolboxes finished in black; their transfers would have been gold.

1960 T120. Beneath carburettor, auto-advance/retard Lucas K2F was one bright electrical feature. Note still-unbraced swinging-arm beneath oil tank

1961 T120R

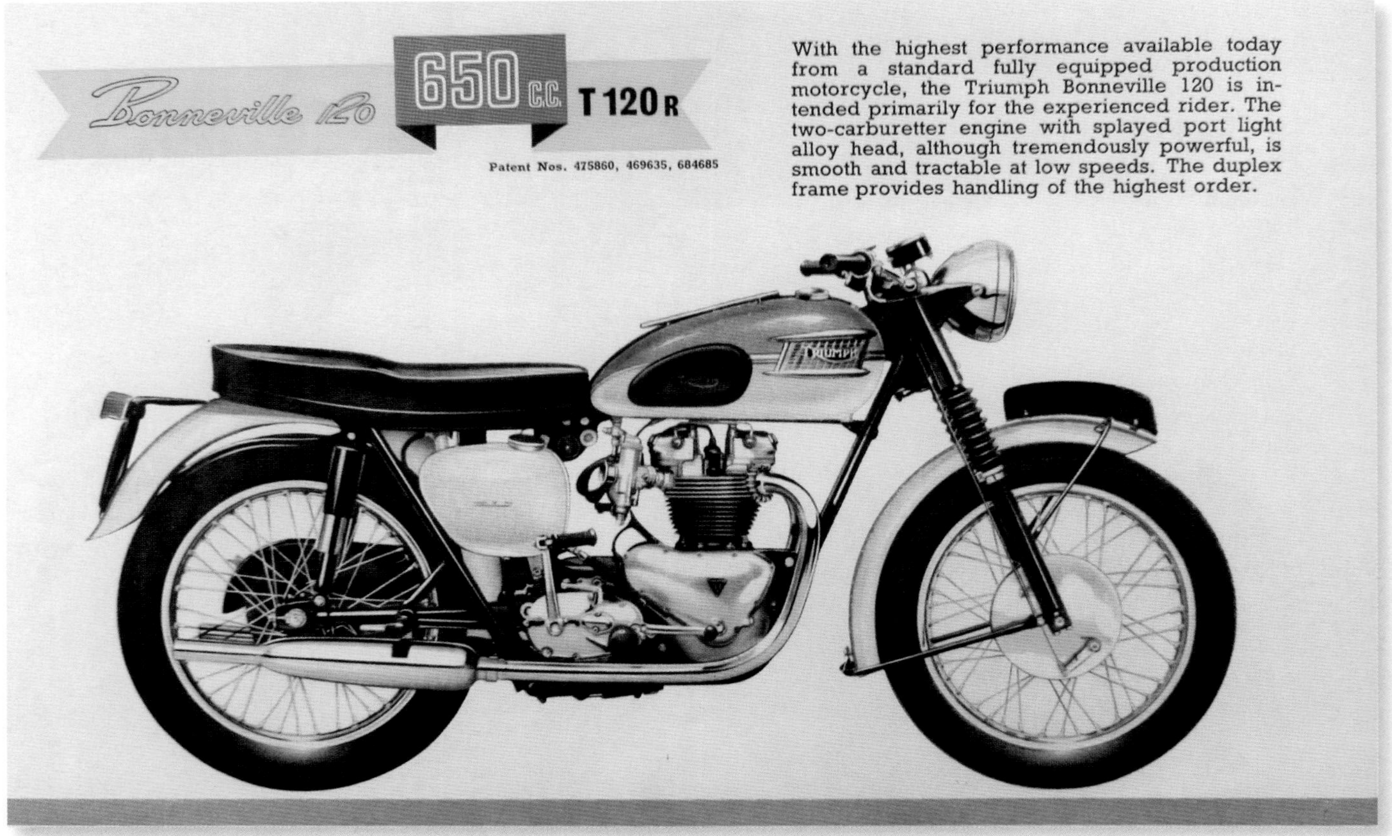

1961

This was one of the T120's peak years, not least because of the look of it. The finish went from the acceptable (Royal Blue and Pearl Grey) to the sublime (Sky Blue and Silver Sheen), with the oil tank/toolbox in the latter colour, though with a few UK exceptions in black. The blue colour on the tank's top and the mudguard's central stripe was sprayed over the silver base, giving it a brightened metallic look. The light, eager-looking T120 had come into its own.

A long overdue improvement was made to the brakes.

The smaller, less practical US-style tank became standard, and a few UK riders opted for the higher handlebars which complemented its looks.

It is worth noting here that American buyers were not all fashion victims besotted by the implied performance of stripped-down sporting touches. High and wide handlebars, which in the USA were the norm after 50 years of Harley Davidson and Indian, though they can balloon a rider out at speeds over 70, give better control if a machine is to be taken off road, as so many were in the States then. As to smaller petrol tanks, not many Americans rode long distances (the more practical 4-gallon tank was available if they wanted to), and unlike in the UK, 24-hour gas stations were plentiful.

Crucially the smaller tank also saved weight, and anyone who has ridden a motorcycle on tracks or in the desert knows that light weight is a prime consideration. Hence also the desire for lighter seats and skimpier mudguards. Freed from a ride-to-work function, most motorcycle use in North America took place in the summer riding season, and in sporting events which required good weather, so heavy wrap-around mudguards could be minimised, saving weight again.

There was therefore a rationale to the stripping down of the T120, though The Look was important in its own right. On this side of the Atlantic the pre-unit T120 was an instant icon, despite an almost feminine lightness and delicacy of line. Rockers thought they just looked the business, and with cheap spares, special parts such as ARE's alloy barrels and Morgo oil pumps, plus a wealth of tuning lore, they could go as well as they looked.

Engine and Gearbox

The T110's alloy head, like all the 650s, had a vertical rib, tying the cylinder head fins, added to each side of it outboard of the plug positions, to help reduce ringing. This year within the head there was also a flat machined on the large diameter of the exhaust valve's cast iron seat insert, narrowing it to 1$\frac{11}{32}$in. This was to allow a greater thickness of aluminium, and was hoped would help deal with the problem of cracking, to which the head with its eight holding-down studs had still been prone.

For all the 650s, a 21-tooth engine sprocket rather than the previous 22 was fitted, lowering overall gearing, and reducing the rear chain pitches again to 98. In the gearbox itself, Torrington needle roller bearings replaced the previous bronze bushes at either end of the layshaft, with layshaft end float controlled by a bronze thrust washer fitting over the needle roller bearings, and with the gearbox shell and inner cover modified to suit. Gearbox adjusting screws were now fitted on both sides of the top clamp, rather than on the right side only; the new inner one would prove inaccessible. The clutch plates featured Langite facings improved for a second time to help counter stiction.

The Smiths speedometer changed to a 140mph SC5301/26 instrument.

Very late on in the model year, at eng. no. D14438 (late June 1961), in an attempt to diminish vibration, the one-piece crankshaft was fitted with a new flywheel of 2¹¹⁄₃₂in width. This would lead to progressively altered engine balance factors, details of which will be found in the 1962 model year.

Frame and Suspension

The steering head angle became a little less steep, going from 67 degrees to 65 degrees, which was intended to be a compromise between the needs of road riding and off road, and certainly worked well on the road.

Cycle Parts

The most significant change involved the brakes. For this model year the single leading shoe 8in full-width hub front brake was modified, as was the 7in rear brake, with the shoes being made fully floating, and friction strips re-sited at the trailing edge of the shoes. The front and rear shoes were now the same, and common to all models.

A folding kickstart was now standard.

The petrol tanks, in both sizes, had their front ends strengthened at the nose to counter vibration, though the same part number was retained for them. And as mentioned, a fifth and final tank retaining strap, now in stainless steel, cured the previous chronic fracturing of the straps.

From eng. no. D9660 the toolbox was also remodelled with rubber-bushed anti-vibration mountings, with the same intention.

The rear wheel/tyre on most T120s was now the fatter 4.00 x 18 on a WM3-18 rim.

Electrical Equipment

The T120's RM15 alternator was given windings more suitable for use with a magneto, to reduce output and prevent the battery overcharging.

A new Lucas Type 22B brake light switch was fitted.

1962 brochure cover, T120

Optional Equipment

The Smiths rev-counter and its attendant timing side cover remained optional for UK and General Export markets.

1962

This was the last year for the pre-unit T120, and indeed for all its 650 cousins. By now the T120's catalogued weight was down to 390lb and it was well on the way to achieving iconic status, with its winning combination of tractability in traffic and thrilling acceleration away from it, to the accompaniment of a delicious throaty exhaust note. And they were about to radically change it all!

The biggest 1962 modification was internal, with altered engine balance factors via a new flywheel (as mentioned, fitted very late in the 1961 model year), culminating in a revised crankshaft with pear-shaped webs, giving a balance factor of 85%, which the T120 was to stay with thereafter. This went some way to achieving the desired effect of damping down the parallel twins' vibration, as well as improving dirt-digging torque and bite for the rear wheel off road, thought the heavier assembly did take a small edge off these engines' response to the throttle.

In the mid-1961 model year, the TR6 had been offered for the Home and General Export markets as the TR6SS, a road-

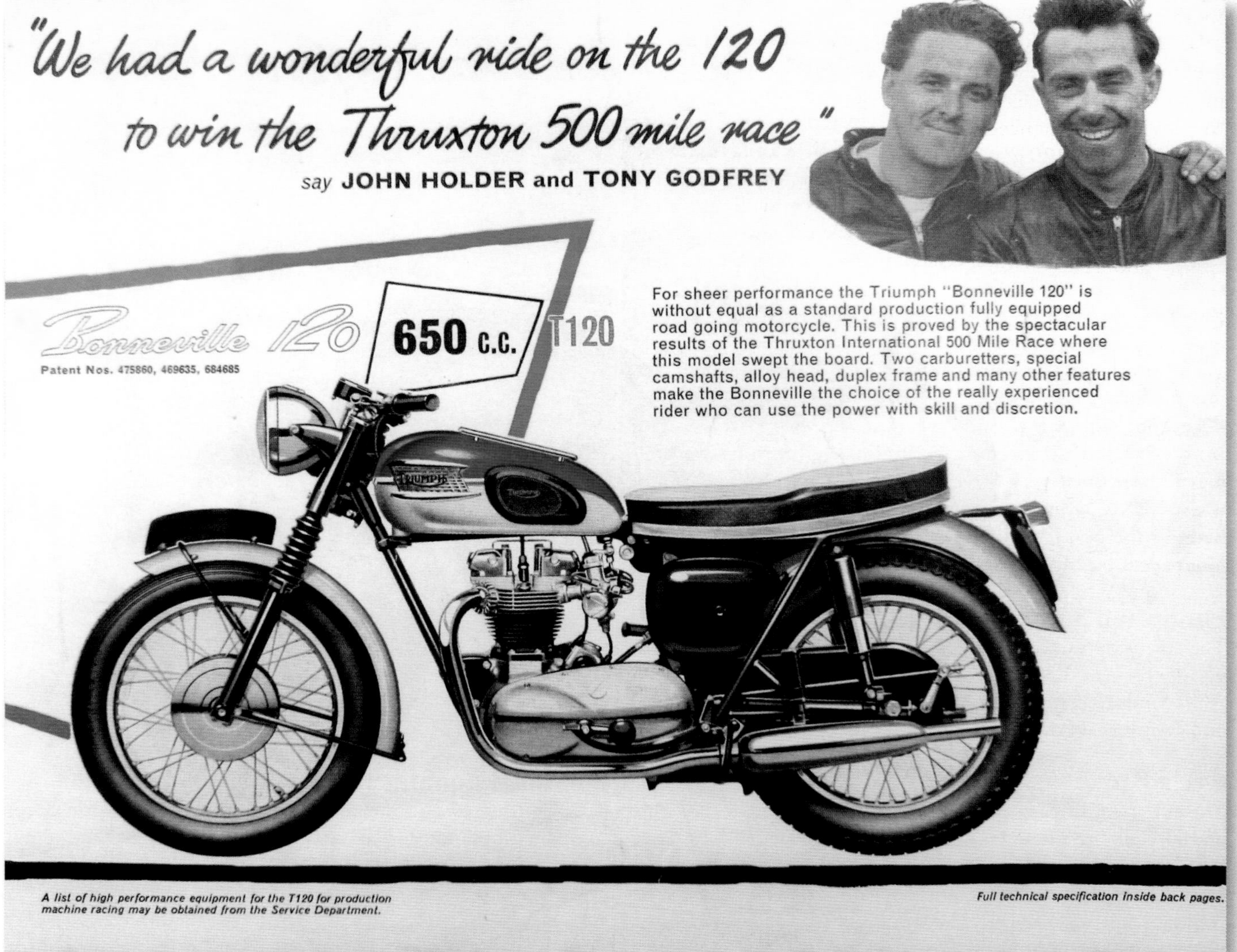

1962 T120 including Thruxton race winners John Holder and Tony Godfrey

oriented model which became to all intents and purposes a single-carb Bonneville. TheTR6 Trophy was never a big seller – for the 1961 year just 556 had been made – though its type, a single-carb off-road pre-unit 650 Triumph twin, certainly ruled the desert and dirt, but the majority of competition riders preferred to build up a machine to suit their own requirements and preferences, based on a secondhand model. But as we have seen, the TR6 had certainly influenced the look and ethos of the best-selling Bonneville.

The 1962 finish for the UK T120 model remained the excellent Sky Blue and Silver Sheen, but US Export models came in Flamboyant Flame (tank upper) and Silver. In mid-year the finish for the T120's oil tank/toolbox changed from silver to black. New look seats were fitted.

Engine and Gearbox

As mentioned, late in the 1961 season the T120 had been fitted with a new flywheel of $2\frac{11}{32}$in width. Then at the start of the 1962 model year, at eng. no. D15789, the balance factor was increased with a heavier flywheel to 71%. The late Hughie Hancox stated that there was then an interim version, giving 75%. Finally, at eng. no. D17043 (mid-January 1962), came the ultimate form, a long-running balance factor of 85% being achieved by a still wider flywheel, with the previously straight-sided balance weights being altered to pear-shaped side cheeks. All this improved low-down grunt in the dirt, at some expense to throttle response. Roadrace tuners and sprinters in the UK would often lighten the flywheel advantageously, as the factory would do to great effect for 1966.

The three-keyway camshaft drive pinions, at that time optional on the pre-units, returned as standard.

The gearing was raised a little in 3rd gear, while for the T120R it was raised slightly overall by the return to a 22-

tooth engine sprocket after 1960's 21-tooth.

The T120 carburettor feed tubes were modified by means of a connecting pipe between the twin float chambers. This meant that the engine could be run with one petrol tap closed, to provide an enhanced reserve facility, but at speed riders found that the T120 gave of its best with both taps open.

Frame and Suspension

The T120's already firm suspension got firmer, with 145lb springs adopted for the Girling rear units.

Cycle Parts

The most prominent change was to the Twinseat, which adopted C-series style with a grey top, white piping around the top edge, black sides, and a grey lower trim band.

The oil tank was redesigned with rubber anti-vibration mountings to counter fractures of its brackets.

Electrical Equipment

A new Lucas RM19 alternator was fitted, with its larger diameter rotor and straight sides, and not recessed as previously. For the T120 it retained the low-output stator to counter bulb failure and overcharging of the battery. In that line also, the Lucas rectifier was of a new type.

From eng. no. D18419 the QD headlamp was discontinued, though the light switch remained under the front of the seat. As well as a modified headlamp this meant the third change of wiring harness for the pre-unit T120 in its four-year lifespan!

The horn, also still mounted under the seat, was changed to a Lucas Type H8.

A new ammeter, intended to be less sensitive to surging voltage, was fitted to the T120R.

The previous Lucas type 22B rotary-style stop-light switch on some machines was replaced by a Wipac one.

THRUXTON 500 MILE RACE

Outright winner of this arduous International Race for standard production motorcycles was a Triumph "Bonneville" ridden by Tony Godfrey and John Holder. Above is a fine view of Holder at speed on the winning machine. Other "Bonnevilles" filled 2nd, 4th, 5th and 6th places in the multicylinder class.

TRIUMPH

TRIUMPH ENGINEERING COMPANY LIMITED · MERIDEN WORKS · ALLESLEY · COVENTRY · ENGLAND

Telegrams "Trusty Coventry" *Telephone Coventry 20221*

Printed in England *This catalogue published October, 1961* Ref. No. 696/61

GUARANTEE

In this Guarantee the word "machine" refers to the motor cycle, scooter, motor-cycle combination or sidecar, as the case may be, purchased by the Purchaser.

We will supply, free of charge, a new part in exchange for, or, if we consider repair sufficient, will repair free of charge any part proved within six months of the date of purchase of any new machine (three months overseas), or within three months of its renewal or repair in the case of a part already renewed or repaired, to be defective by reason of our faulty workmanship or materials. We do not undertake to bear the cost of fitting such new or repaired part or accessory. Any part considered to be defective must be sent to our Works, carriage paid, accompanied by the following information:—

(a) Name of purchaser and his address.
(b) Date of purchase of machine.
(c) Name of dealer from whom the purchase was made.
(d) Engine number and model.

This Guarantee shall not extend to defects or damage appearing after misuse, neglect, abnormal stress or strain, or the incorporation or affixing of unsuitable attachments or parts and in particular:—

(a) Hiring out.
(b) Racing and Competitions.
(c) Adaptation or alteration of any part or parts after leaving our Works.
(d) The attaching of a sidecar in a manner not approved by us or to an unsuitable motorcycle.

This Guarantee shall not extend to machines whose trade mark, name or manufacturing number has been altered or removed, or in which has been used any part not supplied or approved by us, or to tyres, saddles, chains, speedometers, revolution counters and electrical equipment or to parts supplied to the order of the Purchaser and different from our standard specification.

Our liability and that of our dealer who sells the machine shall be limited to that set out in this Guarantee, and no other claims including claims for consequential damage or injury to person or property, shall be admissible.

All other conditions and warranties statutory or otherwise and whether express or implied are hereby excluded and no guarantee other than that expressly herein contained applies to the machine to which this Guarantee relates or any accessory or part thereof.

We reserve the right to modify or deviate from the Published Specification without notice.

1962 T120 winning Thruxton 500 Production race, John Holder riding

APPENDIX A: COLOUR FINISHES

General Points on Finishes.

1. The following parts were painted gloss black on all pre-unit Triumph twins, with the exception of the 5T and the 1950-57 6T, where some were the colour of the machine.
Battery carrier
Rear stand return springs
Brake return springs
Front and rear number plates, the latter with "Triumph" transfer at their base
Pillion footrests
Horn
Instrument panel
Speedometer and tachometer bodies
Saddle frame
Rear light, body and mounting
Steering damper
The following were painted semi-matt black:
Speedometer angle drive
Voltage control box

2. All 5T models, and 6T models until 1958, had all their **cycle parts** (except those detailed in 1.), frame included, finished in the machine colour i.e. 5T, Amaranth Red; 6T, Thunder Blue/Polychromatic Blue/Crystal Grey. Otherwise, for other models and for 1958-62 6T, with the exception of petrol tank and mudguards, the frame, forks, nacelle, footrests, stays, brackets, etc., were finished in black unless otherwise stated.

3. Oil tanks/toolboxes could be either black or coloured, and sometimes both within the same model year (i.e. 1959 T120), which where possible will be specified.

4. Colour shades themselves varied from the start. Paint came to the factory from the suppliers in batches, which could and did differ from one another. As an example, Ace Classics' Cliff Rushworth accumulated half a dozen new old stock spare sets of Kingfisher Blue panelling for the 1961 T110 you will see in these pages; and no two were exactly the same shade.

5. Post-war **wheel spokes** were cadmium-plated, with one possible exception. Bob Innes, who co-owned Northwest Autos in London in the Fifties and Sixties, told me that the first T120s' spokes were chrome-plated, "and the rear wheels used to collapse. They went to normal spokes after that."

Striping

On wheels with painted and striped centres (Jim Lee, a VMCC expert who worked at Meriden, states that these were standard until 1954, and then continued to be available to special order until 1956), the pin-striping sandwiching the central colour was approximately ⅛in wide, and applied on the flat of the rim.

On the mudguards, the striping went on the sides of the guard's central raised band where present, and was again approximately ⅛in wide. If the mudguards were the type with a raised lip at their front and rear ends, the centre stripe stopped short of the edge and was squared off with the side-stripes' colour. But if there was no raised centre band and no lip, the centre stripe and pin-striping went on over the end of the guard.

On the petrol tanks, excepting 1938 5T, double striping on the pre-1950 5T and T100 consisted of a thin 3/32in outer line and a thicker 5/32in inner line, sandwiching a strip of chrome. With the '57-on "mouth-organ" tank badge fitted, there was a thicker (¼in but tapering to the rear) gold stripe dividing line at the rear where two-tone colour finishes were featured.

5T SPEED TWIN

1938-40. All painted parts including frame, forks, stands, etc., in Amaranth Red. Petrol tank chromed with red panels double-lined in gold from 1939-on with thin outer, thick inner lines. Wheel rims chromed, centre stripe red, gold-lined. Chromed headlamp shell.

1946-49. After early models with chromed shell, headlamp shell now red painted. Otherwise as 1938. Wheel rims occasionally silver-painted with gold-lined red centres, if chrome in short supply. Spring hub painted red. 1949, nacelle painted red.

1950-51. As 1946, but petrol tank painted all Amaranth Red with chrome styling bars, their background red, Triumph name-badge chrome against a raised red painted background.

1952. Most previously chromed parts now painted, due to nickel shortage. Handlebars red, wheels silver with gold-lined red centres. Kickstart, exhaust pipe finned clips, and clutch operating arm, now cadmium-plated.

1953-56. As 1950.

1957-58. New "mouth-organ" tank badge/chromed styling strip. Wheel rims all-chromed.

T100

1939-40. Chromed petrol tank with Silver Sheen panels double-lined in blue, thin outer, thicker inner lines. Mudguards in silver, with black centre stripe, lined with blue. Chromed wheel rims with silver centre stripe, blue-lined. Chromed headlamp shell. Other parts, including toolbox/oil-tank, black.

1946-49. As 1939, but headlamp shell painted black, and wheel rims occasionally silver-painted if chrome in short supply. Spring hub painted black. 1949, nacelle painted black.

1950-51. As 1946, but petrol tank painted all Silver Sheen, with chromed styling bars, their background black, and Triumph name-badge picked out in white, against a black background. Nacelle black.

1952. As 5T 1952, colour Silver Sheen not red, wheel centre stripe silver, blue-lined.

1953. As 1950, but wheel centre stripe now black with white lining.

1954-56. As 1950, but paint colour for petrol tank and mudguards Shell Blue. Mudguards have black centre stripe, white-lined. Wheels have Shell Blue centre stripe, black-lined until 1956, when they become plain chromed.

1957. As 1954, but paint colour for petrol tank and mudguards Crystal Grey. Petrol tank with "mouth-organ" badge and chrome styling strip, and Triumph name badge picked out in white on a black background. Mudguards with black centre stripe, white-lined. Alternative finish: petrol tank Ivory top half, Meriden Blue lower, with gold dividing line rearwards from back of kneegrip. Mudguards Ivory with light blue centre stripe, gold-lined.

1958. Standard finish as 1957, optional with petrol tank top black, Ivory lower, with gold rear dividing linee. Mudguards Ivory with black central stripe, gold-lined

1959. Standard finish as 1957. Alternative finish, petrol tank top Ivory, Black lower, with gold dividing line at rear. Mudguards as 1958.

6T

1950. All painted parts including frame, forks, nacelle, oil tank/toolbox, stands, choke lever, etc., in Thunderbird Blue. Petrol tank painted, with chrome styling bands against blue background, and the Triumph badge picked out in silver against a blue background. Wheels chrome-plated with blue centre stripe, gold-lined. Spring hub blue-painted. From eng. no. 10166N (mid-June 1950), a lighter shade of Thunderbird Blue specified.

1951. As 1950, but colour now Polychromatic Blue/Thunderbird Metallic. Alternative finish, eng. no. 11130NA, to eng. no. 11166NA, all Black, with gold lining for the mudguards' black centre strip, and for the wheel rims' black centre.

1952. As 5T 1952, colour Polychromatic Blue, wheel rims silver painted with gold-lined blue centres.

1953-54. As 1951, and alternative finish all-black as above, for US Export.

1955. As 1951.

1956. Colour now Polychromatic Crystal Grey. On petrol tank, styling bands have grey background, Triumph badge picked out in silver on a black background. Mudguards' grey centre stripe gold-lined. Wheel rims now plain chrome.

1957-58. Petrol tank and mudguards Bronze Gold, all other parts, including toolbox/oil-tank, now gloss black, except front hub in Eggshell Black. On petrol tank, "mouth-organ" badge has Triumph name in silver on a black background, with a black background behind the main badge. Mudguard centres black, white-lined. Alternative finish for US Export: petrol tank Aztec Red, mudguards red with black centre strip, gold-lined.

1959. Petrol tank, nacelle, mudguards and front fork Charcoal Grey. On "mouth-organ" badge, Triumph name picked out in white on black background, main badge background black. Mudguards centre strip black, white-lined.

1960. Colour Charcoal Grey, as above, but now also for rear "bath-tub" panelling, with inner mudguard black. On petrol tank, background to main badge becomes white. Front "fireman's helmet" mudguard grey, no striping.

1961-62. Petrol tank upper and nacelle black. Front fork upper black, fork legs painted silver. Petrol tank lower silver, divided from upper at rear by gold line. Front mudguard and rear panelling also silver.

T110

1954-59. As T100, including alternatives.

1960. Petrol tank upper black, and lower Ivory, divided from upper at the rear by gold line. Mudguards and all other parts, including rear panelling, black. Wheel rims chromed.

1961. Petrol tank upper Kingfisher Blue, and lower Silver, divided from upper at rear by gold line. Nacelle and fork upper blue, fork legs painted silver. Front mudguard and rear panelling silver. Other parts black.

T120

1959. Petrol tank upper Pearl Grey, and lower Tangerine, divided from upper at rear by gold line. Tank Triumph badge picked out in white, main badge background black. Mudguards Pearl Grey with Tangerine centre stripe, gold-lined. Toolbox/oil-tank, early UK, black, later UK and all US Export Pearl Grey. Nacelle, frame, forks, black. Alternative, late UK models, petrol tank top, mudguards, toolbox/oil-tank, Pearl Grey, with petrol tank lower Royal Blue/Azure, divided from upper at rear by gold line. Royal Blue/Azure also for mudguard centre stripe, gold-lined.

1960. As late alternative 1959. Headlamp shell chromed.

1961. Petrol tank upper Sky Blue, lower Silver Sheen, divided from upper at rear by gold line. Tank badge as 1959. Mudguards Silver Sheen, centre stripe Sky Blue, gold-lined. Toolbox/oil-tank Silver Sheen. Other parts black.

1962. For UK, as 1961, but toolbox/oil-tank black. For US, Flamboyant Flame in place of Sky Blue, second colour Silver Sheen. Early US Export machines had toolbox/oil-tank in Silver Sheen, but soon going to black as on UK models.

APPENDIX B: ENGINE AND FRAME NUMBERS

General

Triumph frames were built in batches with engines then assigned to them, so generally it is not possible to be specific about first and last engine/frame numbers of a particular model within a year. What is provided here are the start and finish numbers for all pre-unit twins within a particular model year.

The pre-war engine and frame details, together with records of numbers produced, were destroyed in the November 1940 Coventry blitz. However, some details of the system used are known. For 1938 and 1939, the year and model were shown as a prefix to a machine's engine number i.e. 8 (for 1938) – T - (for Speed Twin) –12345 (the number). Frame numbers, which at this stage did not correspond to the engine ones, carried the prefixes TH for the early 5T, and TF for the T100. Later pre-war 5Ts for 1940 adopted the T100 frame and thus the TF frame number prefix.

From 1940 to 1949, the engine number prefix became two numbers i.e. 40-5T-00000 would be a 1940 Speed Twin, although there were occasional errors/exceptions with post-war machines featuring single number prefixes. The date numbers were dropped at the end of 1949.

The frame numbers continued with the **TF** prefix for the rigid 5T/T100. When swinging-arm frames were introduced from 1954, they bore the prefix **S**.

Suffix letters over the years included:

W Pre-unit 5Ts for the Police
P Later Police models
A 1960-only US T120 roadsters
R 1961-on T120 roadsters

And not forgetting the "waggon wheel" symbol, denoting the presence of camshafts with silencing ramps.

Meriden workers building engines would stamp the motor's prefix (e.g. 6T or T100) on when the build was completed and before a number had been assigned, with a single stamp, so these details were even. Often the suffix (say, R, or W) was added later, with a different size stamp. The numbers themselves were often uneven, of different size, and stamped deep into the near (left) side of the top of the crankcase, below the cylinder barrels. Flawless, even engine numbers should be approached with caution! Much the same went for frame numbers, which were located on the near (left) side of the lower steering head.

Engine and frame numbers became the same from late in the 1951 model year, at no.16000N on 2 November 1950. The engine suffix NA was introduced just afterwards at 840NA on the 20 November 1950, and dropped in mid-1952. Towards the end of the 1956 model year, in early July 1956, to avoid engine/frame numbers going into 6 digits, the numbering sequence went back to 0101. The first '0' appears to have been retained from then on to prevent duplication of previous numbers. After the duplex downtube was introduced for the C-range for 1960, over a thousand pre-unit 650s seem to have been built before the 'D' prefix, signifying Duplex, was introduced at D101.

What is provided here are the start and finish numbers for pre-unit twins within a particular model year. For a few of the model years, the previously accepted start engine numbers differ from those kindly provided by the VMCC (Vintage Motor Cycle Club) who currently hold the Meriden records, and elsewhere from those recorded by authors Roy Bacon and Harry Woolridge. The latter, incidentally, in his excellent book *The Triumph Speed Twin and Thunderbird Bible* (Veloce, 2004), does provide model year start and finish numbers specifically for the 5T and 6T, for anyone particularly interested in those models. I have included these alternative figures in brackets.

Year	Engine no.	Frame no.
1946	From 72000	n/a
1947	79046	n/a
1948	88864 to 102235 (R.B. 88782) (H.W. 88227)	TF15001
1949	102236 – 113386 (R.B. 100762)	TF25000
1950	1001N – 16160N	TF33616, then
1951	101NA – 15808NA	frame number becomes same as engine number, at 16100N.
1952	15809NA – 25000NA then 25000 – 32302 (no suffix)	
1953	32303 – 44134	
1954 (VMCC: 44822)	44135 – 56699	
1955 (VMCC: 55495)	56700 – 70929	
1956 (VMCC: 70877)	70930 – 82799, then July 5 1956, back to 0101	
1957	0945 – 011115	
1958	011116 – 020075	
1959	020076 – 029633	
1960	029634 – 030424, then D101 – D7726	
1961	D7727 – D15788	
1962	D15789 – D20088	

Finally, a short selection of significant first and last numbers.

Last rigid 6T	No. 55593, July 9 1954
Last pre-unit 5T	No. 023705, Jan 6 1959
First T120	No. 020377, Sept 4 1958
Last single-downtube unpanelled pre-unit 6T	No. 029362, Sept 2 1959

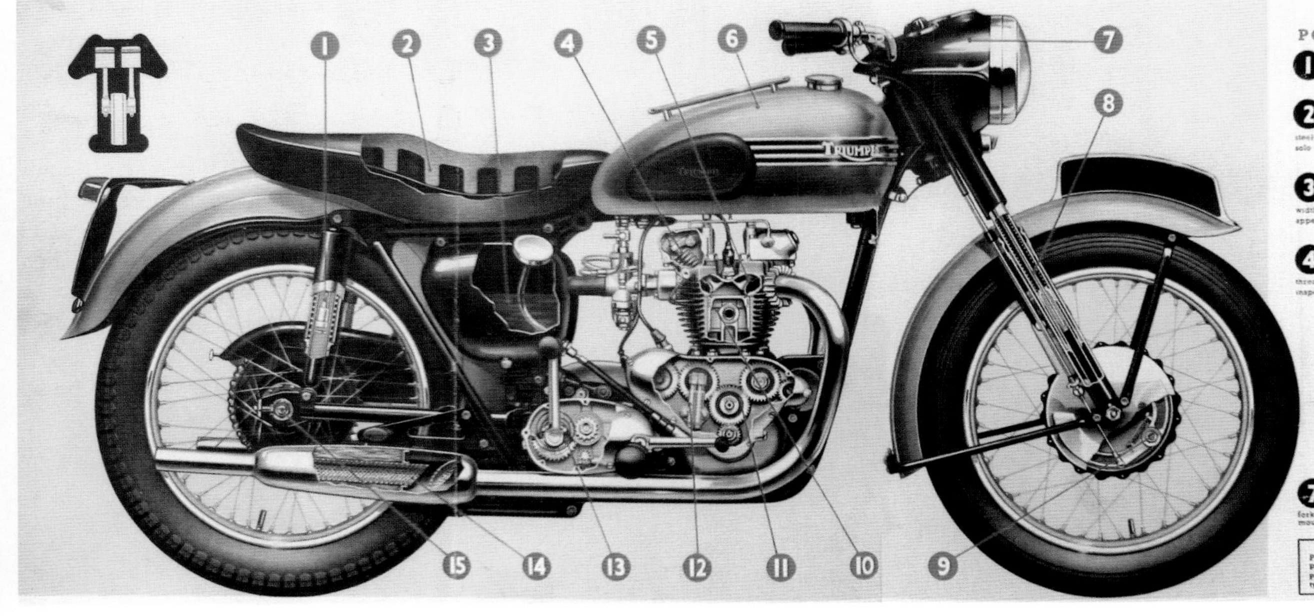

POPULAR FEATURES OF TRIUMPH DESIGN

1 Swinging Arm rear suspension with hydraulic damping readily adjustable for varying loads.

2 Triumph "Two Level" Twinseat. Soft latex foam covered with black waterproof Vynide. Specially shaped steel base rigidly mounted. The ideal seat solo or with passenger.

3 Combined unit exclusive to Triumph —incorporating oil tank, air cleaner, battery and tool box. Smooth full width exterior, easy to clean and neat in appearance.

4 Fully enclosed overhead valve gear lubricated under pressure. Alloy rocker boxes with accessible threaded valve covers for easy tappet inspection.

5 The famous Triumph hemi-spherical cylinder heads with large diameter inclined valves. Remarkable performance proves the outstanding efficiency of this design.

6 Shapely 4 gallon Petrol Tank with plated quick release filler. Useful tank top luggage grid. Chromium styling bands and rubber knee grips.

7 Triumph Nacelle (Patent No. 647620) encloses headlamp unit in neat streamlined shell integral with top of forks. All switchgear and instruments rubber mounted.

8 Triumph Telescopic Forks, long action with hydraulic damping. Ensure a comfortable ride and accurate steering at all speeds.

9 The Triumph Front Brake has always been renowned for its power, smoothness and safe operation. Large diameter cast iron drum with polished alloy anchor plate. Finger adjustment.

10 Alloy full skirted pistons with internal strengthening ribs. Two scraper and one oil control rings. "H" section connecting rods of RR56 alloy with massive plain big-end bearings.

11 Drives to the camshafts, magneto and dynamo are by a selectively assembled train of gearwheels. Accuracy in manufacture ensures silent operation and complete reliability.

12 The specially designed double plunger type oil pump driven from the inlet camshaft spindle delivers, under pressure, a constant supply of oil to the engine bearings and overhead valve gear, returning it subsequently to the oil tank.

13 The famous Triumph 4 speed Gearbox with positive foot operated gearchange. Multi-plate clutch with cork inserts operating in oil, sweet in action and light to handle. Polished alloy outer cover. Rubber pad type shock absorber in clutch.

14 Exclusive to Triumph, barrel shaped silencers heavily chromium plated. Particularly efficient in use, providing a very subdued but pleasing exhaust note.

15 The Triumph Q.D. Rear Wheel ends the bogey of difficult wheel removal. The wheel can be extracted by withdrawal of the spindle leaving the rear brake and chain untouched.

EXTRAS

PROP STAND. Retained by spring, out as a prop or folded back. For all models.
PILLION FOOTRESTS. For all models. Folding type, rubber covered.
TWIN CARBURETTERS. For Tiger 100 only.
QUICKLY DETACHABLE REAR WHEEL. For 5T, 6T, T100, T110, TRS.
TWINSEAT for "Terrier".

TRIUMPH